D0462327

My Favourite Restaurants

in Calgary & Banff
5th Edition

JOHN GILCHRIST

Edited by Catherine Caldwell

Escurial Incorporated

Calgary, Alberta

Copyright ©2003 John Gilchrist

All rights reserved. No part of this book may be reproduced, stored in a retrieval system, or transmitted in any form or by any means, electronic, mechanical, photocopying, recording or otherwise, without prior written permission of Escurial Incorporated.

Published by
Escurial Incorporated
9519 Assiniboine Road SE
Calgary, Alberta
Canada T2J 0Z5
Phone: (403) 255·7560
E-mail: escurial@telus.net

National Library of Canada Cataloguing in Publication Data

Gilchrist, John, 1953 –
My favourite restaurants in Calgary & Banff / John Gilchrist ;
edited by Catherine Caldwell. – 5th ed.

Includes index.
ISBN 0 – 9693106 – 4 – 1

1. Restaurants—Alberta—Calgary—Guidebooks. 2. Restaurants—Alberta—Banff—Guidebooks. 3. Calgary (Alta.)—Guidebooks. 4. Banff (Alta.)—Guidebooks. I. Caldwell, Catherine, 1956 – II. Title.

TX910.C2G54 2003   647.957123'38   C2003 – 911191 – 1

CREDITS:
Interior & Cover Design: Jeremy Drought, *Last Impression Publishing Service*, Calgary, Alberta
Cover Illustration: Kari Lehr, *Mosaic Artworks*, Calgary, Alberta
Printing: *Friesens Corporation*, Altona, Manitoba

Printed and bound in Canada

Table of Contents

Acknowledgements

EDITION number five. You'd think each one would get a little easier. Certainly improvements in technology have made the process more efficient, but each book is just as much work as the ones that came before. And there is no way I could do this all on my own. So I need to thank a few people.

My deepest thanks go to Catherine Caldwell, my wife and editor, who continues to wield her red pen over my writing, turning it into something readable. She provides sage and vital input and makes a darned fine espresso too. She tells me I use too many semi-colons and dashes—the result of so many years on the radio I suppose; without her, this book would not exist. I also want to thank the folks at the Education Resource Centre for Continuing Care who work with Catherine at her day job and graciously allowed her a leave to help publish this book.

Then there's the inimitable James Martin who has once again provided a scintillating Foreword. Here's how good he is. We had to cut the following from the Foreword for space: "I've cried at weddings (the cake just looked so...resplendent), wept at wakes (casseroles as far as the eye could see), sobbed at Tupperware parties (to paraphrase Col. Kurtz: The freshness! The freshness!)." Damn, even James's outtakes are better than my prime cuts.

And of course there's Richard White and the Calgary Downtown Association who have again joined in this project. Their participation is crucial and deeply appreciated.

Jeremy Drought of Last Impression Publishing Service has ably designed the book and made it easy on the eye. He knows more about kerning and picas than any human should, and I'm thankful for it.

And I can't forget all the restaurateurs, chefs, and servers who have created such a dynamic and appetizing food industry in Calgary and the Bow Corridor. Without them, I'm out of work.

Foreword

by James Martin

I eat food, like, daily. Heck, I grew up on the stuff.

One of my earliest, sharpest memories: padding downstairs one holiday morn (don't remember which) to find Grandma (or a caterer) hunched over the stove (toaster). Stirring and tasting, fussing and cussing. There were smells, and they were good. Was it Lunar New Year? Did we eat fondue? Beats me, but I had seconds.

Mine is a life measured out with coffee spoons, crepe pans, and 5-quart pre-seasoned Dutch ovens. I'm driven like a German shepherd with a snootful of fleeing perp, single-minded in the pursuit of filling me newingtons. I feverishly scan community newspapers and grocery-store bulletin boards for announcements (open house, union rally) featuring those four magical words: "Lunch will be served." I've borne witness to more Stampede pancake breakfasts than all the rodeo queens of the world combined. My idea of a good time often involves noodles.

Returning to my childhood tale: could it have been pork chops on Cinco de Mayo? Could've. Wasn't. I'll keep thinking.

Submitted for your approval, a list of things I will eat (abridged): Meals. Victuals and/or vittles. Anything served "on a stick," except a wasp nest. Humble pie à la mode. Feasts. Snacks. Grub. Not grubs. OK, maybe a few grubs. A little something to tide me over. Assorted foodstuffs. Your crusts (if you don't want 'em). Manna, be it from heaven or that little takeout joint down the street. Cheeses of Earth. I'm rethinking the wasp nest. Flora. Fauna. Dough.

Got it: home fries on Sadie Hawkins Day! Yes? Nope.

To be clear, I'm no gluttony apologist. (Altho it's by far my fave of the Seven Deadlies. Sloth will just hafta try harder to curry my favour.) Forsooth, it's quality over quantity for this chowhound—'cept in those rare instances when superhuman displays of mouth-over-mass will win me a prize, or land a pic of my mustard-ringed grin in tomorrow's paper.

And quality is very much the name of the game at hand. Only the best and brightest establishments win their way into Mr. Gilchrist's good books—and, by extension, into *this* book. Consider it your treasure map to the best eats in the land, your guide to where all the finest roots and berries are hidden, an escape from the doldrums of beans-on-toast six nights running.

Donair on Boxing Day? Prawns on Navajo Code Talker Day? Leftovers on Wednesday?

Awww, forget it. Verily and merrily, I leave the storytelling to the expert.

James Martin is the author of Calgary: The Unknown City.
Right this very instant, he's chewing.

v

Introduction

I can barely keep up these days. It's not that my faculties are failing. It's that the pace of change in the restaurant business keeps accelerating. Places open and close more rapidly, menus change seasonally or sometimes daily, and chefs move around frequently.

When I write a new book, especially the last few, I compress my research into a tight timeline (as in visiting sixty-two restaurants in forty days for this one!) so that I can roll with these changes and be as up to date as possible. There are entries for over 225 food establishments in these pages, 85 of which are new since the 4th edition. That means over one-third of the entries did not appear in the last edition just two years ago.

So, what is new in this, the 5th edition of *My Favourite Restaurants*? To start with, you'll see the arrival of Nepalese, Nuevo Latino, Laotian, Contemporary Indian, and not just one, but two, Persian eateries. You'll also see house-made Japanese noodles, more prix fixe menus, and the appearance of the $40 entree. And for the first time in any of my books, you'll see a restaurant starting with the letter Q.

Many of the reviews are updated from writing I've done about the Calgary-Banff area while working for CBC Radio One, the *Calgary Herald*, and *Avenue* magazine. None of the establishments have paid to be in here. This book is not about advertising—it is about what I feel are the best places for good food based on the twenty-three years I've spent searching it out. I've tried to achieve balance in terms of price range, food styles, geographic areas of Calgary, and out-of-town entries, but the main requirement for inclusion is quality.

I've divided the book into two major chunks: "Big Eats" and "Little Eats." Big Eats are full-page reviews of places I would typically visit for a full sit-down meal. Little Eats are shorter reviews, mainly of places that specialize in either certain food products like chocolates or bagels or coffee beans or in smaller, faster meals or snacks like smoothies or burgers or takeout sandwiches. To help guide you through the book, there are also indexes and a map of Calgary's downtown in the back pages.

Here are some other things you need to know:

• The "Big Eats" and "Little Eats" sections are each arranged alphabetically.

• All phone numbers begin with the area code 403, just in case you're calling long distance.

• The presence of the "Downtown That's the Spot" logo indicates that a restaurant or food outlet has a location in Calgary's downtown. Those locations are also noted on the map on page 166.

• Credit card abbreviations are as follows: **V** for VISA, **MC** for MasterCard, **AE** for American Express, **DC** for Diners Club, and **JCB** for Japan Credit Bureau.

• Cost categories are based on a dinner for two with appetizers, main courses, and desserts (or equivalents) and include tax but not drinks or gratuity: **$** means under $30, **$$** ranges from $30 to $60, and **$$$** pushes over $60.

• At the time of this writing, the provincial government is considering a new option for wine-drinking restaurant patrons. If passed, individuals will be allowed to bring pre-purchased wine to participating restaurants and to take home any unfinished bottle they brought or purchased on-site. Restaurants will be allowed to charge a corkage fee.

The Calgary-Banff area remains a great place to dine. There is diversity, value, and an overall level of quality that keeps increasing. Now, go eat something!

John Gilchrist
Calgary, Alberta

Aida's

Lebanese

2208 – 4 Street SW
Phone: 541 • 1189
Monday 11 am – 9 pm, Tuesday – Thursday 11 am – 10 pm
Friday & Saturday 11 am – 11 pm, Sunday 4 pm – 9 pm
Reservations recommended — Fully licensed — Non-smoking
V, MC, AE, DC, Debit — $ – $$

ALTHOUGH Aida's (pronounced eye-duhz) is on a busy stretch of 4th Street, it can be hard to find. Its street presence is minimal, but once you're inside, it is more open and airy than is initially obvious. Seating forty-four under a gold-painted tin ceiling, the L-shaped room bustles with activity and good food. The tables are close and the tone is relaxed. Aida draws an eclectic crowd for her Lebanese cuisine.

Aida herself oversees all the food. She's been in the business for years, having had Café Med just a few doors away back in the 1990s. And her food is very, very good. Lebanese cuisine is fresh and in tune with the public's desire for high-flavour, healthy ingredients and reasonable prices. Incorporating spices such as sumac (a dried, ground Middle Eastern berry that imparts a sour, almost lemony taste) and grains such as ferik (a lightly smoked wheat), Aida creates delicate, savoury flavours that meld dishes together.

The fattoush is a crunchy salad of romaine, cucumbers, tomatoes, radishes, and pita chips in a sumac and olive oil dressing. It is such a simple yet tasty dish, with a small portion costing only $4.50 and a large, only $5.75. The platters of things like lamb kebabs or falafel or shawarma include the fattoush or some tabbouleh (the parsley and bulgur salad) and a dip of either hummus or baba ghanouj (made with eggplant). These plates are also a great bargain. A salad, a dip, and a pile of falafel for $8.75 is outstanding value. As are strips of warm, marinated chicken with diced vegetables, tahini, salad, and dip for $9.25. The chicken is always tender, and the presentation is beautiful with all those fresh vegetables.

Vegetables and grains play as important a part in Lebanese cuisine as meats, making it a great cuisine for vegetarians. The lentil and spinach soup, for example, demonstrates more subtle flavours blended with skill and is a staple for us through the winter. Another dish we order on a regular basis is the mouhammara. This dip of roasted peppers, onions, walnuts, bread crumbs, and pomegranate juice continues to tantalize us with its depth and richness.

I like Aida's. The combination of food, service, atmosphere, and value has made it one of our favourite places since it opened in 2000. In fact, in one of my CBC Radio broadcasts, I chose it as the best new restaurant of that year.

Anpurna

Indian (Vegetarian Gujarati)

175B – 52 Street SE
Phone: 235•6028
Tuesday – Friday 11 am – 2:30 pm, 5 pm – 8:30 pm
Saturday & Sunday 11 am – 8:30 pm
Reservations recommended — Fully licensed — Non-smoking
V, Debit — $

I once named the Anpurna the most obscure restaurant in Calgary, noting that it was behind the Esso station on the corner of Memorial Drive and 52nd Street SE. Then they closed the gas station. But the location is only part of the Anpurna's uniqueness. Named after the Anpurna mountain range, it features the vegetarian cuisine of Gujarat, a western province of India. It is the only restaurant in the city that serves this cuisine.

The menu offers about thirty choices—all are totally non-meat, non-fish, and non-egg, though you will find dairy products used. There are chickpea and lentil dishes as well as samosas and rasmalai, but they are prepared just a little differently than in most Indian restaurants in town. For example, among the selection of samosas is a variation filled with bitter melon and green onion.

One of the most expensive items is the $5.25 masala dossa—that's their potato- and onion-filled crepe served with a lentil dhal and a coconut chutney. Hot from the grill, the huge, delicately crisp crepe crackles under your knife and fork to reveal the curried vegetables folded inside. It is a superb blend of flavours and textures. Order a few kachori, the round pastries made by rolling dough around a lentil-coconut mix, and you have one fine meal. Don't forget to top the kachori with a little fresh mint sauce.

For first-timers, ordering a thali is a great way to sample Gujarati cuisine. This is a combination plate offered weekdays at lunch and dinner for $6.95 and $9.95 respectively. It includes two vegetable curries that change every day, dhal, rice, roti, pickle, pappadam, and dessert. The curries I've had, one prepared with string beans and lima beans, the other with black-eyed peas, were both expertly cooked. The dhal comes in a unique form: the lentils appear sparingly in a thick soup rather than in a tasty pile. But tasty it still is. Both the carrot-mustard pickle and the fresh bread are excellent, and the rice pudding is rich and flavourful.

The Anpurna is a simple room that was once a fish and chip shop. It seats about forty in an unassuming environment. The tone is gentle and the people are pleasant. It is a family operation, so you get the friendly feeling of being invited into someone's home. But my mom never cooked like this.

eastindianrestaurant.tripod.com

Avenue Diner

Contemporary Diner

105 Stephen Avenue Walk SW
Phone: 263•2673
Monday – Friday 6:30 am – 5:30 pm, Saturday & Sunday 8 am – 3 pm
Reservations accepted Monday – Friday for over 6
Fully licensed — Patio — Non-smoking
V, MC, AE, DC, Debit — $

FOLLOWING the opening of the hyper-popular Diner Deluxe, owner-chef Dwayne Ennest didn't just kick back and enjoy the view of endless lineups out his door. Instead, he teamed up with Heather Brett to create Avenue Diner in the likeness of Diner Deluxe. The thinking was that if the concept worked on Edmonton Trail, then it might work downtown too.

They took over the space that most recently had been operated as Core Café, renovated it quite substantially, and opened in the summer of 2003. They created a wonderfully retro-contemporary diner, perfect for those with tight time and budgets.

This block of Stephen Avenue is one of Calgary's most interesting places to dine. It is also one of the most volatile, as places have come and gone quickly. But Avenue Diner has found a niche as a place that serves breakfast and lunch among a group of restaurants that focuses on lunch and dinner. Adding to its attraction is a menu that keeps almost everything under $10. (Two of the few items to surpass this mark are the short ribs with chipotle barbecue sauce for $13 and the AAA rib-eye for $14.) So the early morning and casual lunch crowds pack the place.

The renovation includes a full kitchen make-over in the back and the introduction of a lunch counter out front. Stools at the counter come in the form of old tractor seats welded to metal posts. In between the counter and the kitchen is a dining area where wooden chairs are pushed up against small tables. Surrounded by sandstone walls, it's a cozy environment for a quick meal. It's a very narrow space, but it has been used well, seating sixty-three in total

The new kitchen has allowed Avenue Diner to create an extensive menu that includes an all-day breakfast of the usual bacon and eggs plus warm organic barley with fresh vanilla bean and johnnycake with strawberry compote and rhubarb syrup. There are also omelettes, eggs Benedict in varying forms, and a range of waffles, pancakes, and French toast.

The lunch list is impressive: lamb shepherd's pie, duck confit with a sage and apple cider glaze, a buffalo burger with roasted peppers, and a halibut sandwich with Oka cheese and lemon-caper mayonnaise. This is diner cuisine gone way upscale and prepared with skill and value.

Note: Following the start-up phase, Ennest returned to the kitchen at Diner Deluxe, but remains a consulting chef for Avenue Diner.

Bamboo Palace

Laotian & Thai

314D – 10 Street NW
Phone: 670•0295
Tuesday – Sunday 11 am – 3 pm, 5 pm – 11 pm
Reservations accepted — Fully licensed — Non-smoking
V, MC, Debit — $ – $$

THE restaurant at this address has seen a number of operators since it was built in the mid-eighties. It's been Italian, Japanese, and Chinese to name a few, and in late 2002, it became Thai Me Up. An odd name, but the food was good, and big effort was taken with the look. The walls were textured tan, reminiscent of dried Asian grasses, there were bamboo highlights, and a major elephant theme trumpeted throughout.

Within months Thai Me Up disappeared, but was almost instantly replaced by the Bamboo Palace. Serving Thai and Laotian food, they took advantage of the leftover decor and went right to work.

The Bamboo Palace is owned and operated by the Sarasith family. They are originally from the Laotian side of the Mekong River in the area where the river defines the border between Laos and Thailand. Their familiarity with the food on both sides of the water has helped them create a menu that spans the two cultures. There are Thai favourites such as pad Thai noodles or masaman nua, beef in a yellow curry with coconut milk. And they expand on those offerings with the less familiar dishes of Laos, including some noodle soups and a dish of lab goong, minced and seasoned shrimp on greens.

The cooking of Laos is similar to that of both Thailand and Vietnam. Their Laotian bamboo rolls, for instance, are much like Vietnamese salad rolls. Instead of being served with a dipping sauce, though, the rice wrappers around the rolls are slit and the sauce is poured inside. The rolls are then topped with a crispy mix of fried lemon grass, dried shrimp, and other herbs. It's a great spin on what has become a common dish in these parts. The Bamboo Palace also prepares their pad Thai noodles differently by wrapping them in a thin omelette. Another good dish.

The Laotian lab gai instantly became one of Catherine's favourite Asian dishes. The chicken is minced and cooked and tossed with mint leaves, chilies, roasted rice, and tiny pieces of crisp chicken skin. Oh yeah, nice dish. The flavours are strong and lively, but meld together beautifully.

I'm also impressed with the friendly and knowledgeable service by one of the family members. Her suggestion to try the "Mango Mountain" dessert—an Everest of creamy coconut rice topped with fresh mango—was perfect. We climbed that mountain and liked what we saw. And what we tasted too.

Banffshire Club

Contemporary North American

The Fairmont Banff Springs, Banff
Phone: 762 · 1730
Tuesday – Saturday 6 pm – close
Reservations recommended — Fully licensed — Non-smoking
V, MC, AE, DC, JCB — $$$

For the second edition in a row, the Banffshire Club has the notoriety of being the most expensive meal in this book. So if dinner hovering around $200 per person is not what you're looking for, turn to the next page and Barpa Bill's. But if money is no concern, or if someone else is paying, read on.

The Banffshire Club is the most elegant and opulent of the many food outlets at The Fairmont Banff Springs, a hotel that can satisfy the desires of the most demanding visitor. The restaurant's setting is a rich replication of the Stuart era of Scotland, the service is the best of the best, and the menu is sublime. Dining at the Banffshire Club is an experience unto itself.

I've always felt they should send the menu to customers in advance. It is a serious read, a collection of unique ingredients prepared in intriguing ways. Sevruga caviar, argan oil, asparagus-oyster sauce, and radish confit are used simply as backdrops to complex concoctions. So a decision here requires diligent study and cogitation.

Or you can just go for the nine-course tasting menu and leave the cogitating to the staff. It's a bargain at $150 per person—a bargain considering that choosing two courses à la carte will be $100 anyway (and an additional $10 for each course beyond that). And if you're going to do the tasting menu, you might as well add on the six paired wines for another $75. They are skillfully matched by an excellent sommelier staff led by Anthony Chalmers, a master of wines.

Notwithstanding the above, on our visit for this book we eschewed the tasting menu and went à la carte: seared foie gras on brioche French toast; a Dungeness crab cake with sea urchin sauce; wild mushroom and duck confit salad; veal tenderloin with butter-poached lobster; rack of lamb with a black-trumpet mushroom rub; chocolate-banana bread pudding. Flavours that teased and tantalized. Textures that melted or crunched or danced on the tongue.

This is detailed dining that commands your attention. It does not hit you over the head or inundate your taste buds with excess. It's food that is conceived with great thought from chef Daniel Buss, one of the brightest lights on the Canadian culinary scene.

Complaints? Well, a small patch of the tablecloth was a touch wrinkled. Sorry, but that's the worst I can come up with. It just doesn't get any better than the Banffshire.

Barpa Bill's Souvlaki

Greek

223 Bear Street, Banff
Phone: 762•0377
Daily 11 am – 9 pm
Reservations not accepted — No alcoholic beverages — Non-smoking
Cash only — $

I can still taste lunch at Barpa Bill's. It's been almost twenty-four hours and I've brushed my teeth twice, but the bite of the Greek dressing stills resonates on my palate. And it's not just a lingering memory. I mean it's still there.

Barpa Bill's is like that. You can smell the grill and the garlic a block away, even if you're upwind. Inside the small space is an odourama of flamed Greek meats and lively sauces. It's as uncompromising as it gets. And that's how Bill's fans like it. Last time I was there, Bill told me about two Australian tourists who had shown up with directions from someone they had met in London. They had been told to try a souvlaki and the Greek salad. They weren't disappointed.

Bill's is located on Bear Street where it's been since it opened in 1997, next door to a new hardware store and just metres from some of Banff's fancier eateries. But it has expanded in recent times. There are now sixteen stools and a washroom. In addition, son Andreas has joined the business, and son Michael has decorated the walls with his wanderlust-inducing photos of Greece. The menu is still handwritten on an overhead chalkboard, but that just adds to the charm of the place.

And Bill's does not lack for business. The value and quality are outstanding, making it a favourite with the locals and a quick discovery for the hiking boot crowd. The sirloin steak with garlic toast (always the garlic) and fries is only $10. So is half a chicken with fries. And the Barpa Burger with tzatziki, onions, and tomatoes is a bargain at $5.50. Still high on the popularity list are the pork, chicken, or lamb souvlakia, the best I've had this side of Athens. Flame-broiled, wrapped in pita imported from Chicago, and liberally laced with greens and tzatziki sauce, they are just plain wonderful. Messy, sure, but an amazing blend of flavours and textures.

Bill's also carries a range of other eats, from calamari and dolmades to Greek salad and spanakopita, all of which rival or exceed most other Greek restaurants in the area. Barpa Bill's tzatziki sauce and his Greek dressing have gained such a cachet that they are available bottled at Keller's grocery store in Banff as well as at Bill's.

But Bill and Andreas like to keep it simple. There's no booze, no reservations, and no credit cards here. Just good Greek food.

Now, once more to the toothbrush.

www.barpabills.com

The Bavarian Inn

Bavarian & Austrian

75 White Avenue, Bragg Creek
Phone: 949·3611
Wednesday – Saturday 5 pm – close, Sunday 11:30 am – close
June – August: Also open Tuesday 5 pm – close
Reservations recommended — Fully licensed — Deck
Non-smoking dining room, smoking on deck
V, MC, Debit — $$ – $$$

THE BAVARIAN INN has the woody, spotless look of a Black Forest inn and a menu of Bavarian and Austrian dishes to match. It's divided into two sections, a dining room with booths and tables focused around a fireplace and a lounge with more casual seating. Outside there's a deck surrounded by big spruce trees. It's the kind of place where the beer steins are chilled and the welcome is warm whether you're in hiking boots or a jacket and tie.

And when spargel is in season, it is totally packed. Spargel is white asparagus grown under a straw cover so that the chlorophyll doesn't develop. During the May to June season, the folks at The Bavarian Inn fly it in regularly from Holland and Germany. Good white asparagus has a delicate, almost sparkly taste. I think much of the appeal is that it is one of the first spring vegetables to hit the plate, and it tastes so fresh and clean. And during the season, they do it justice at The Bavarian Inn with weekly menus of soups, salads, and main courses to satisfy their regulars' passion for the spears.

We started our spargel dinner with a plate of white asparagus in a sun-dried tomato vinaigrette and fresh spinach in a smoked-bacon and garlic dressing. The flavours offered a tart, forceful backdrop to the asparagus. We also had a bowl of puréed white-asparagus soup that was creamy and delightful. For the main course, I tried the white asparagus with Wiener schnitzel, steamed potatoes, and dollops of three different hollandaise sauces—tomato, tarragon, and regular. I liked it a lot. The schnitzel, a thin slice of breaded veal, was well prepared and leaned toward saltiness, but the sauces and the almost neutral quality of the asparagus worked well with it.

The salad was $10 and the schnitzel, which included the soup, was $25.50. On the regular menu, most main plates are in the $13 to $22 range. And always leave room for one of their desserts.

Service is provided by a team who are obviously proud of their food and familiar with the many regulars who come to The Bavarian Inn. They do an excellent job of bringing hot food and cold drinks promptly to their hungry fans.

The Bavarian Inn has a lot of good things going for it—good food, nice room, excellent service, and a lovely setting. And, of course, the spargel.

www.thebavarianinn.com

Belmont Diner

Diner

#1, 2008 – 33 Avenue SW
Phone: 242·6782
Daily 7 am – 3 pm
Reservations not accepted — No alcoholic beverages — Non-smoking
Cash only — $

THE BELMONT DINER is a small place in Marda Loop that seats a few dozen in a bright, south-facing space. There is a curved counter with red vinyl stools, four wooden booths, and a couple of tables. At one end there's a small open kitchen with a grill, and overhead there's a menu board.

The menu is short and direct. Basic breakfasts of ham and eggs with hash browns and toast. Buttermilk pancakes, huevos rancheros, and a breakfast burrito. Breakfast served all day. Then there's lunch. Burgers, a Monte Cristo, and a clubhouse, all with hash browns. Solid food.

While browsing the menu and twirling on a vinyl counter stool—which is not particularly comfortable with its light padding—it struck me that the Belmont looks a lot like the very popular Galaxie Diner. The vintage tables, booths, counter, and kitchen appear to have been set up in a mirror image of the Galaxie. When I noticed that the menu is pretty much identical as well, I began to think that someone had tried to copy the Galaxie's approach. And then there's the staff, a group of almost unnaturally pleasant young people who do a surprisingly good job of cooking and serving, just like at the Galaxie.

I mentioned the similarities between the two places to my server, and she told me that the same person owns them both. So it makes sense. The Belmont is not a rip-off; it's a clone.

The food itself almost replicates the original too. A pile of hash browns sizzles on the grill at all times, the eggs are served up quick and hot, and the vanilla milkshake is tasty. But I tried something I hadn't had at the Galaxie: the Belmont Bleu Burger, a house burger topped with a thick slab of melted blue cheese. Not just a cheese dressing—I saw the cook slice a slab off a hunk of blue cheese just a few metres away. Now it wasn't a great burger, but it wasn't bad either. The patty was a high-quality commercial variety, which is fine. It just wasn't as tasty as a homemade version.

The Belmont may not have the seat padding of the Galaxie, but it does have the same tang and tone. And when the lineup is long at one, you just might be able to sneak into the other.

www.belmontdiner.ca

The Belvedere

Global Contemporary

107 Stephen Avenue Walk SW
Phone: 265·9595
Monday – Friday 11:30 am – close, Saturday 5 pm – close
Reservations recommended — Fully licensed — Patio
Non-smoking dining room, smoking in lounge
V, MC, AE, DC — $$ – $$$

I'M often asked which restaurant is the best in the city. That's an almost impossible question. It depends on what a person is looking for. If I, however, was offered a meal out when someone else was paying, where would I most likely choose? The Belvedere.

Opened in 1999, The Belvedere quickly became one of the premier restaurants in the city under chef Alan Groom. He departed in 2002, but with chef Richard Desnoyers stepping into the kitchen, The Belvedere barely skipped a beat. Desnoyers is carrying on the tradition of rich, flavourful, creative food.

First, let's state the obvious. The Belvedere can be very expensive. A full lunch for two can run about $100, dinner about $150. That's with the tips and taxes but without getting carried away.

In the summer of 2003, though, the kitchen introduced two- and three-course lunches for $22 and $27 respectively and three-course dinners for $50. These are in addition to the à la carte menus and are great value: dinner might be sweetbreads with black truffles, wild boar loin with a brie and apple reduction, and peppered strawberries with Grand Marnier.

Regardless of price, The Belvedere delivers with style. Theirs is food that demands your attention. A slab of Brome Lake goose foie gras with Sauternes jelly is an explosion of fatty liver flavour smoothed by cubes of sweet, grapey jelly. It is a perfectly presented appetizer with abundant jelly for every mouthful of foie gras. That quality continues with an entree of duck done two different ways—the leg as confit, the breast roasted into a tender fillet with a Grand Marnier demi-glace. Simply superb with its spray of fresh, individual vegetables.

For dessert, The Belvedere makes one of the best crème brûlées we've ever had. Served in a broad, flat bowl, it is a quarter inch deep and eight inches across, allowing a large piece of crunchy crust with each bite. Now that's the way it should be.

The room suits the food with its subtly lit, dark wall panels under a big skylight, but the attached lounge does tend to spread any lingering smoke into the non-smoking dining area. Its scent disappears, however, when the kitchen starts cooking and the air is filled with more luscious flavours.

The service is amongst the best in the city, again commensurate with the quality of the food.

Ben Venuto

Italian with a Twist

118 Stephen Avenue Walk SW
Phone: 770·0600
Monday – Wednesday 11 am – 11 pm, Thursday – Saturday 11 am – close
Reservations accepted — Fully licensed — Patio — Non-smoking section
V, MC, AE, DC, Debit — $$ – $$$

ONE of the more recent additions to Stephen Avenue is Ben Venuto, an Italian restaurant in the Tribune Block. The owners have kept as much of the old look as possible, uncovering the sandstone walls and restoring the tin ceiling. It is another long, narrow space that is open from front to back, and it is highlighted by a long wood bar and dining booths. The mix of historic and contemporary brings a natural warmth to all the stone and wood.

The menu covers a range of Italian cuisine from tuna carpaccio to prawns seared in olive oil and garlic, veal Marsala, and rack of lamb. Prices are mid-range with dinner pastas in the teens and appetizers running roughly $8 to $14. The rack of lamb is the highest at just under $30. That is what passes for mid-range on this block of Stephen Avenue right now.

I tried the calamari appetizer with a tuna-caper mayonnaise at $9. The calamari was crisp, and the caper mayo provided a creamy balance. Catherine's Caesar salad was likewise well prepared with fresh romaine in a lively but not overpowering dressing. Some of the romaine leaves had been stylishly inserted into a dried piece of bread to add more texture and elevation to the plate. Pretty, but more impressive was the double-smoked bacon that topped the salad.

Our main courses were equally high quality. The linguine carbonara was rich and creamy with more of that bacon plus fresh tomatoes and herbs. And the veal scaloppini in a Gorgonzola and wild mushroom sauce was pungently rich. The pieces of veal were variable in tenderness, but their flavour was still good. Also good was the house-baked bread. We finished up by indulging in one of Ben Venuto's desserts, a pair of small pecan tarts served with chocolate ice cream. Perfect for sharing.

I do have to mention one odd thing about Ben Venuto. About three-quarters of the restaurant is earmarked as a smoking section, with a fairly small area in the back for non-smoking. We had to move from our non-smoking booth because cigarette smoke was being pushed directly into it. And of course non-smokers have to walk the full length of the smoking section to get to the semi-fresh-air area. Perhaps it's a bold move to accommodate the smoking crowd when so many other places are hewing to non-smoking, but personally I think it's unfortunate. It detracts unnecessarily from what is some pretty good food.

Big Rock Grill

Contemporary Grill

5555 – 76 Avenue SE
Phone: 236 • 1606
Monday – Friday 11:30 am – 2:30 pm
Reservations recommended — Fully licensed — Patio — Non-smoking
V, MC, AE, DC, Debit — $$

MANY wineries in the Okanagan and Niagara Peninsula have lovely restaurants attached to their facilities. Visitors love the winery tours, the bucolic settings, and the trendy wine country menus that round out the experience.

But in Alberta we don't have much of a wine industry; we have a beer industry. So when Ed McNally and the creative thinkers at Big Rock built a spiffy new brewery in 1996, they included a restaurant that was to be their own interpretation of the winery diner. The location was in a field off Glenmore Trail in an area where lunch out meant getting fries and a burger from a bus parked nearby. The idea of a 120-seat eatery with a big patio and a fireplace and a top-notch chef seemed, well, a little odd.

But Big Rock has always been known for odd, market-bucking ideas that somehow work: commissioned art on beer labels, no big marketing campaigns, beer without pasteurization. Those ideas have paid off in the past for Big Rock, and likewise, the Big Rock Grill has become a huge success. Now surrounded by other large buildings, the Grill has a built-in market that packs the place on a daily basis. Arriving without a reservation on most weekdays is risky business. And if it's sunny, you'd better get there early to procure one of the sought-after patio seats. Fully ensconced in greenery, it is an oasis in the Southeast.

The top-notch chef is Klaus Wöckinger, once the head chef at La Chaumière and former owner of Dante's (now La Tavola). Working with another Klaus, his son, Klaus senior has assembled a menu that satisfies the predominantly male lunch crowd and adds a depth of sophistication to the area.

Among the buffalo burgers and chicken wings (marinated in Grasshopper ale), you'll find salmon steak en papillote, penne forestière, and Wiener schnitzel. It's robust cuisine with an elegant touch, yet not overworked or pretentious. With the salmon being the most expensive item at $14, it's a menu that surprises first-timers.

The food is always well prepared and is served swiftly by attentive staff. Also adding to the pleasure is a long line of draft beer taps flowing with Big Rock, a huge cooler filled with more Big Rock in cans and bottles, and a gift shop featuring— that's right—Big Rock caps and shirts and other required paraphernalia. (You don't order a Miller Lite here.)

www.bigrockbeer.com

Bodega

Tapas & Spanish

Lower Level, 720 – 11 Avenue SW
Phone: 262 • 8966
Monday – Friday 11 am – 3 pm, Monday – Wednesday 5 pm – 10 pm
Thursday 5 pm – 10:30 pm, Friday & Saturday 5 pm – 11 pm
Reservations recommended — Fully licensed — Non-smoking
V, MC, AE, DC, JCB, Debit — $$ – $$$

I F we were strolling La Rambla in Barcelona and found a place like Bodega, we'd be talking about it for months. The cute room, the friendly staff, the great food, and the good value would make for a memorable meal while visiting an exciting city.

But Bodega is on a slightly less exciting stretch of 11th Avenue instead and sometimes gets forgotten in the headlong rush to the next trendy restaurant. Although its basement setting provides a sultry backdrop to the *bodega* (translated as "wine cellar") tone, it also means there is little street presence.

When Bodega opened in 1999, it was one of the hot places to go. It was part of that late last-millennium trend to tapas, the small portion style of dining. It brought a touch of the smoky, oily tang of Iberian cuisine to Calgary. The initial buzz is past, but Bodega has matured into a fine restaurant.

The kitchen turns out tapas with intensity and character. A round of Camembert is baked on a cedar plank and topped with a fig and sherry chutney. Baby squid are sautéed with smoked paprika and served with a tomatoey romesco sauce. Butter beans are elevated by a roasted garlic, tomato, and leek salsa. Shrimp are seared and served in a cast-iron pot with olive oil, garlic, chilies, and sea salt.

Each dish provides a visual treat. Grilled asparagus spears that have been bathed in white-truffle oil are fanned on a triangular plate. House-made sausage is arranged on a ceramic artist's palette.

The tapas are paced to match the mood of the diners, but are usually delivered in a sequence determined by the staff. With four of us sharing seven tapas (quite enough for our hungry group), the seafoods came out first, interspersed with vegetable dishes. The meatier dishes followed, and the roasted Camembert finished us off.

We did, however, have room for desserts: a warm banana, chocolate, and mascarpone strudel in phyllo and a chocolate tart with caramel and pecans. They both tasted as good as we had hoped. And with two bottles of wine, the bill for the four of us came to just over $140 before the tip.

Much of the credit for Bodega's maturity is due to the efforts of co-owner Jessica Battistessa, an indefatigable host who is always on the move with tapas, water, and sherry. She also has a talented partner in chef Paul Orr and a diligent staff to help bring the best of tapas cuisine to Calgary.

Bonterra

Rustic Italian Trattoria

1016 – 8 Street SW
Phone: 262 • 8480
Monday – Friday 11:30 am – close, Saturday & Sunday 5 pm – close
Reservations recommended — Fully licensed — Patio — Non-smoking
V, MC, AE, DC — $$ – $$$

BONTERRA has become a favourite of those who love Italian food but want a change from the checkered-tablecloth cuisine we have seen so much of over the years. A key member of Creative Restaurants (see also Catch and Wildwood), Bonterra features a menu that evokes the traditions of the Tuscan hills along with the more current trends found in Milan and Rome.

Bonterra is helped by one of the prettiest buildings in the city, the old high-ceilinged press room of the *Albertan* newspaper. It's been converted into a cozy Euro-style cavern with large glass and iron lamps that cast a golden glow over the table linens and big candles that illuminate the walls. With a cobblestone fireplace and an open kitchen, Bonterra has an elegant look, yet one that is not imposing.

Outside, considerable effort has gone into the construction of a partly enclosed patio that is well protected from both the elements and the traffic. With flowerpots overflowing and the smell of Tuscan food rolling out of the kitchen, there are few finer places to be on a warm evening.

One other key aspect to the overall ambience of Bonterra is the staff. The service enhances the professional tone of Bonterra; this is a well-trained crew. And the chefs are always amiable in their open kitchen.

The food, inside and out, is full bodied and rustic, yet light and fresh. A salad of oven-roasted prawns over greens and white beans in a tarragon vinaigrette creates a crisp balance of flavours and textures. A panzanella salad of Italian bread with three types of tomatoes in a balsamic reduction is tart and fruity, a bright start to a meal.

The salmon saltimbocca combines the best of Italian cuisine with delicate seafood. The saltimbocca (which means "to jump in the mouth") could easily overpower the fish, but the fennel salsa and toasted pine-nut brown butter complement it perfectly. It would be easy to lose the salmon under a landslide of excess, but Bonterra's balance works perfectly.

Bonterra always has a strong dessert list and excellent wines by the glass and bottle. They even have imported Italian water. Now whether you really want to spend $7.50 for a bottle of it is another matter. But generally Bonterra's prices are in tune with the market and have actually come down recently. That helps make them even more attractive.

www.creativeri.com

Bow Bulgogi House

Korean & Vietnamese

3515A – 17 Avenue SW
Phone: 686·6826
Monday – Saturday 11:30 am – 10 pm
Reservations recommended — Fully licensed — Non-smoking
V, MC, Debit — $ – $$

THE prettiest thing about the Bow Bulgogi House is the view across 17th Avenue to Ernest Manning High School. For those who know that view, that's not saying a lot.

But the crowd that packs into the Bow Bulgogi House is not there for the aesthetics. They are there for the bee-bim-bab, the bulgogi, and the various other fine Korean dishes on the menu. They cram into the small entryway, waiting patiently for a table or a takeout order as other diners are diving into their kimchi. The Bow Bulgogi House also serves a number of Vietnamese dishes, but far and away, the Korean items are the most popular.

The staff are in constant motion, delivering little bowls and sizzling platters. There doesn't seem to be enough of them to handle the crowd, but there's probably not room for more anyway. And surprisingly, everything gets done as it should. After seven years, they have it down to a science. They know how to methodically handle their thirty seats and serve takeout customers at the same time.

There doesn't seem to be enough room on the tables for all the food either. We ordered three dishes and ended up with at least eight serving plates of various kinds (I actually lost count). In addition to what we ordered, there were bowls of brined daikon radish, bean sprout salad, kimchi, and more covering the table.

The bulgogi, the popular Korean grilled meat dish, is served here as either beef, chicken, pork, short ribs, or squid. Soy-marinated, seared, and quickly presented on a sizzling hot plate, our chicken bulgogi exuded fumes that tantalized the taste buds and stimulated the appetite. I like a cuisine that considers scissors to be an indispensable piece of cutlery. The bulgogi meats are typically large but thin and are best dealt with by a quick snip of the scissors that they bring to the table.

Our favourite dish was the roasted tofu in a savoury sauce with sesame seeds and lots of green onions. The beef bee-bim-bab was a close second, but then we enjoy any dish where you mix up a red-pepper paste and a fried egg into some meat, vegetables, and rice. And we like the sound of all those B's when you order beef bee-bim-bab.

So we're happy snipping and mixing and eating Korean delights to our hearts' content. As are the rest of the Bulgogi's fans.

Boyd's

Seafood

5211 Macleod Trail S
Phone: 253·7575
Monday – Wednesday 11 am – 9 pm, Thursday – Saturday 11 am – 10 pm
Sunday noon – 9 pm
Reservations accepted — Fully licensed — Non-smoking
V, MC, Debit — $ – $$

WITH the explosion of sushi bars these days, it's easy to forget that some people still cook their fish before eating it. But a quick trip to Boyd's Seafood Restaurant is a good reminder of how seafood can be done when it's not served raw.

On any given weekday, Boyd's nautically themed restaurant is packed at lunch, all one hundred seats. Boyd's is most popular for its fish and chips, made with sole, haddock, cod, halibut, or pollock. I usually go for the cod with its slightly oily, flaky texture and its rich flavour. Boyd's does justice to the fish. It's always fresh—it would have to be since they go through so much of it. It's sliced in long strips and dipped in a medium-thick batter. They must change their oil frequently because the fish comes out a rich, golden brown and never tastes of the oil.

Same with the fries. They seem pretty serious about them too. They freshly cut the potatoes and explain on the menu that the texture will vary with the season. On a recent visit, I was served a plate loaded with little bits—very few full-sized fries. When I pointed this out to my server, she immediately brought me a fresh plate of full fries.

That service runs throughout Boyd's. They are cheerful and fast, and they know both their products and their customers, who range from seniors and construction workers to business lunchers and society mavens. No matter who we are, when that hankering for good fish and chips gets us, we want them done well. That's what Boyd's does.

They do other seafood too, from popcorn shrimp and lobster rolls to tiger shrimp stir-fries and seafood gumbos. It's not cheap – good seafood never is. A one-and-a-half-pound lobster or a pound of king crab legs are both in the $40 range, but again, they are fresh and well prepared. And in these days of constant price increases, Boyd's is one place that actually drops prices when costs drop. Nice.

My only complaint about Boyd's is that the menu is printed on an over-active background in a difficult-to-read script. It's the fussiest thing in the place, an odd juxtaposition to the general simplicity of their approach.

Boyd's doesn't try to be something they are not. They are first and always a seafood restaurant, and as long as the fish and chips remain a classic, Boyd's will be popular.

Brava Bistro

New World Mediterranean

723 – 17 Avenue SW
Phone: 228 • 1854
Monday – Saturday 11 am – 3 pm, Monday – Wednesday 5 pm – 11 pm
Thursday – Saturday 5 pm – close, Sunday 5 pm – 10 pm
Reservations recommended — Fully licensed — Patio — Non-smoking
V, MC, AE, DC — $$ – $$$

BRAVA BISTRO started life as Figbelly's, a gourmet deli where you could buy excellent prepared foods to take home. As it became popular, Figbelly's expanded by opening a café in an empty space next door. Over time the café became known as Brava Bistro and eventually consumed the deli.

Brava was one of the first local places to decorate in the taupe tones of the new millennium. Tables are wrapped in a horseshoe around a centralized wine bar that offers prime perches for those who like to see and be seen. And dress is comfortably casual, ranging from jackets and ties to jeans and T-shirts. The menu fits the broad definition of contemporary bistro with duck-confit ravioli, bison-sausage pizza, and rare ahi tuna, and it works well with the room and the neighbourhood.

Brava has had good chefs over the years, the most recent of which is Kevin Turner, a local boy who has returned to Calgary after years of experience in San Francisco. This guy can cook. The lobster gnocchi is a buttery blend of flavours rolled over house-made gnocchi, fresh baby carrots, peas, and chunks of delicate lobster. It's offered on the appetizer list for $15, but is substantial enough to be a main course. The artichoke salad features sliced, sautéed baby artichokes tossed with arugula and Parmesan in a lemon vinaigrette. Just delightful. And the crispy chicken with scallion mashed potatoes elevates a simple chicken dish to the sublime with a skilled balance of seasonings and that crispy coating. This is really good food. There's nothing precious about it. Every forkful has flavour.

Desserts are also outstanding and are contributed by pastry chef Dale Neisz. The warm gingerbread cake with butterscotch sauce and vanilla ice cream is a decadent finish to the meal. And a vertical lemon pie wrapped in phyllo rings is a treat for citrus lovers—you really have to try this one. The wine list is among the best in the city, prepared by another professional, Dewey Von Noordhof.

Service matches the food and wine, and if there are any criticisms, one is that their bread is weak. Served nicely on a wooden platter, it's fresh though it can be a bit doughy and not as flavourful as I would like.

And the room can get noisy. But that's because people are talking about how good the food is, so what can you do?

www.bravabistro.com

Buchanan's

Chophouse

738 – 3 Avenue SW
Phone: 261•4646
Monday – Friday 11 am – 10 pm, Saturday 5 pm – 10 pm, Bar open until 2 am
Reservations recommended — Fully licensed — Patio — Non-smoking
V, MC, AE, DC — $$ – $$$

I like restaurants that understand the meaning of medium-rare meat. So many cooks slide it past the warm-but-still-red centre into a pinkish medium. In fairness, this may be the result of having too many steaks sent back to the kitchen for more grilling.

But at Buchanan's there is no compromise. Medium rare is just that. And that commitment to quality flows into every corner of this downtown chophouse. From the popular burgers through to the lamb chops and the panko-crusted halibut fillets, consistent quality has been their trademark since day one.

That day was during the afterglow of the 1988 Winter Olympics when Carol and Michael Buchanan opened their chophouse on a deserted stretch of downtown real estate. They were among the first in Calgary to embrace the meaty chophouse style birthed in big East Coast American cities over a century ago. They were also among the first to consider the west end of downtown worthy of a good restaurant. A decade and a half later, they look like visionaries. The market has returned to meatier cuisines, and the west end has built up around them.

Many customers come just for the burger. On a good day, Buchanan's will go through more than one hundred pounds of extra-extra lean ground sirloin that has been formed into huge patties, charbroiled, and topped with everything from jalapeno jack cheese to roasted red onions. It remains the best dine-in burger in the city. Some chefs of meaty places won't do burgers; that's their loss.

You won't find many better steaks and chops either. The fillets and strip loins are aged twenty-eight days and are fork tender. Perked up with peppercorn crusts or brandy-morel butter, among other good things, the steaks come in various sizes from a smart four-ounce tenderloin ($22) to a twenty-ounce, bone-in, prime-rib chop ($34).

Non-red meat eaters needn't feel left out. Buchanan's makes excellent seafood and even a couple of pastas. And I'm always impressed by the salads; they are done with interesting ingredients such as poached pears or golden beets and with forceful dressings such as a peppered cider vinaigrette. The desserts are no slouches either, with a chocolate-whiskey cake and a white-chocolate and raspberry bread pudding on the list.

Buchanan's allows their lunchtime business clientele to be in and out in an hour and their evening diners to relax as they want. They are sincere about answering their customers' needs. Just remember that here, medium rare is medium rare.

Buddha's Veggie

Chinese (Vegetarian)

5802 Macleod Trail S
Phone: 252•8830
Wednesday – Monday 11 am – 9 pm
Reservations recommended — No alcoholic beverages — Non-smoking
V, MC, AE, Debit — $ – $$

BACK in 1998 an unusual restaurant opened in Southland Crossing. Called Buddha's Veggie, it offered Chinese cuisine made without meat or seafood. There were dozens of familiar sounding items on the menu, all the requisite dishes like lemon chicken, dumplings, and ginger beef. But no meat. Just soy protein and wheat gluten done up to look like chicken and beef and even squid and eel. The restaurant gained a loyal following with some vegetarians and even some carnivores who just liked the food.

By the spring of 2003, Buddha's Veggie was successful enough that they moved into their own building. Seating about seventy, the new facility is decorated in bamboo and other neutral tones. Plexiglas tabletops showcase colourful designs created from dried beans and lentils. It's disconcertingly close to Macleod Trail, but its increased street presence has garnered them many new customers.

The menu has retained largely the same list of unique items—stuffed veggie scallops in black-bean sauce, satay veggie beef, and curried veggie seafood. It's well prepared. I had a dish of kung pao chicken that was packed with baby corn, mushrooms, and peas in a biting chili sauce. And the black-pepper beef with Shanghai noodles featured a mountain of freshly cooked noodles with peppers in a sharp black-pepper sauce. But for me the weakest parts of the dishes were the actual meat replacements, the wheat-gluten chicken and the tofu beef. They just didn't replicate the real thing. I felt the dishes would have been stronger, taste-wise, without them.

Vegetarians run in two camps on this approach. There are those who like the idea that they can have some of the same dishes as non-vegetarians because of the meat replacements. Others feel they don't need a dish disguised as a meat preparation. For me, though I'm obviously not a vegetarian, it depends on the item. Although the two mentioned above were not helped by the veggie meats, the ginger beef here is a good version, superior to many that use real meat. And their pork dry ribs are excellent. They are just as crunchy and oily as a good pork version. (Non-meat does not necessarily mean low fat.) And there are many dishes on the menu that are made with just plain vegetables, with no veggie meats at all, like the spicy eggplant or the oyster mushrooms with broccoli.

So, judge for yourself. If you've never visited Buddha's Veggie, it is worth a trip, if only for the ginger beef.

Buffalo Mountain Lodge

Rocky Mountain Cuisine

Tunnel Mountain Road, Banff
Phone: 760·4484
Daily 7 am – 5:30 pm, 6 pm – 10 pm
Reservations recommended — Fully licensed — Patio
Non-smoking dining room, smoking in lounge & on patio
V, MC, AE, DC, Debit — $$ – $$$

THERE'S an odd juxtaposition to dining in the window-wrapped restaurant at Buffalo Mountain Lodge: as you are enjoying your elk sirloin, you can watch their brethren relax on the grounds outside. Sure, the plated elk is from the Canadian Rocky Mountain Ranch and the outdoor elk are National Park protected, but it seems we want it both ways in Banff. We want the game on the plate, and at the same time, we want it in the wild. And preferably without a lot of connection between the two. Buffalo Mountain offers the best of both of those worlds.

The dining room is gorgeous. It's dark green and heavily beamed with vaulted ceilings and a crackling fireplace in the lobby lounge. Most of the tables are parked by the huge windows. It's part way up Tunnel Mountain, so it's a tranquil departure from the bustle of Banff Avenue.

Buffalo Mountain serves meals throughout the day for guests and any other visitors who happen by. Breakfast rolls out with buffet and à la carte options such as brioche French toast at $10 and eggs Benedict at $12. Lunch features split pea and buffalo-ham soup, elk osso bucco, and honey-roasted chicken breast with organic greens. Dinner pulls out the stops with caribou medallions in a blueberry-port sauce for $34 and that elk sirloin for $33. For the gamey gourmand, the platter of smoked buffalo, venison ham, peppered duck breast, game pâté, and elk salami at $20 is a must. It's mountain-top pricing, but it's also one of the most unique menus and settings in Banff.

We usually end up at Buffalo Mountain for breakfast and are generally happy with the fare. The house-made jams are always a treat. But the crab cakes in the eggs Benedict provide a bland backdrop to the dish—you're better off sticking to the back-bacon option. And the French toast tends toward sponginess. We like ours crisper. But service is typically good, and at these prices, it should be.

Buffalo Mountain also operates the seasonal and rustic Cilantro Mountain Café in a former ski rental shop across the parking lot. That menu runs to pizzas and pastas with a Contemporary spin and a few loftier items such as elk chili with heirloom beans and lamb shank with polenta.

Buffalo Mountain and Cilantro also have two of the best and most unheard-of patios in Banff. Just watch out for marauding elk seeking revenge for their comrades.

www.crmr.com

Buzzards

Steaks & Burgers

140 – 10 Avenue SW
Phone: 263•7900
Sunday – Tuesday 11:30 am – 9:30 pm, Wednesday & Thursday 11:30 am – 10 pm
Friday & Saturday 11:30 am – 10:30 pm
Reservations recommended — Fully licensed — Patio — Non-smoking restaurant, smoking in pub
V, MC, AE, DC, Debit — $$

EVERY city needs a Buzzards, a little place across the tracks from downtown that is close enough to walk to at the end of the day, but far enough to take you away from any stresses of the day. It should have a sunny deck, locally brewed beer, friendly staff, and a menu that says something about the city. Buzzards has all that, making it a popular cookshack and waterin' hole for many regulars.

Buzzards has taken the history of Calgary to heart. It is coated in dusty prairie colours and is filled with branding irons, lamps, and other cowboy memorabilia, creating a tribute to the history of the Canadian West. The look extends to the deck with its corral feel.

To add to the image, Buzzards hosts a summer Testicle Festival where locals and tourists alike indulge in a slice of the Old West. Served with various sauces, prairie oysters are not to everyone's taste, but owner Stuart Allan still promises that you will have a ball.

Buzzards puts forth a meaty menu. There are steaks in numerous forms, from a steak sandwich for $11 to an eight-ounce sirloin for $16 to a bison sirloin for $23. You will also find beef, bison, and chicken burgers, fish and chips, and a big whack of salads, though many of those still have meat in them (but there are some versions for the vegetarian cowpokes who mosey in, and there's even a veggie burger).

I've always been impressed with the burgers, but here's a warning: they are big, sloppy things, not suitable for a serious lunch meeting with a client. Perhaps stick to the Thai shrimp and chicken stir-fry or the stuffed meatloaf for that. Regardless, you will not walk away hungry.

Beside Buzzards, and sharing the same deck and owner, is Bottlescrew Bill's, one of the oldest and best pubs in the city. They have an abundance of interesting beers, including Buzzard Breath Ale, the first custom-made beer produced by our local favourite, Big Rock Brewery. Buzzard Breath remains popular not only at Buzzards and Bottlescrew Bill's but in the export market as well.

Buzzards is not high-tone dining—it's closer to the bunkhouse than the ranch house. And I'd never claim that this food is highly complex or intricate. It's good, hearty, red-meat fare, great with a Big Rock or two, especially on the deck in the setting sun. That's one of the real tastes of Calgary.

www.cowboycuisine.com

Cafe Divine

Market-Fresh Cuisine

42 McRae Street, Okotoks
Phone: 938 • 0000
Monday – Saturday 11 am – 2:30 pm, Thursday – Saturday 5:30 pm – 9 pm
Reservations recommended — Fully licensed — Veranda & patio
Non-smoking restaurant & veranda, smoking on patio
V, MC, Debit — $$

OKOTOKS is one big, booming burg these days. Anyone who hasn't visited the charming town south of Calgary for a few years is in for a surprise. Housing developments are everywhere, and shops of all sorts have popped up. And in the middle of all the activity, some restaurants are doing great business.

One of these is Cafe Divine, a Victorian manor near the east end of downtown. But don't let its sweeping veranda and charming decor deceive you. The building is only a few years old and was built to house a restaurant. Inside it seats about forty-five, and outside the veranda and patio seat about the same. The interior has the wood and knick-knack tone of a tea house; tables are well spaced and sunlight spills in the windows.

The first impression is that this might be a nice place for a cup of tea and a sweet dessert. But Cafe Divine is so much more than that. It has a menu that ranges from falafel sandwiches and pan-seared salmon at lunch to buffalo short ribs and braised lamb shank at dinner. And these folks can cook.

Chef-owner Darren Nixon and co-chef Adrienne Penny focus on Contemporary cuisine that combines ingredients such as angel hair pasta, sun-dried tomatoes, and artichokes with skewered seafood. And tops pizza with capicollo, goat cheese, caramelized onions, and Mission figs. It's forceful, lively food that fills the plate, excites the palate, and satisfies any hunger walking through the door.

I had a bowl of fresh vegetable soup that perhaps had the best broth of any soup in this book, aside from that at Chez François. A few of the vegetables were overcooked, but the intense, natural flavour was superb. And the house-made burger with Gorgonzola, in a Vienna roll from the Black Diamond Bakery, was superb. Good ground sirloin, excellent cheese, and a great bun.

I didn't have room for dessert, but did take home a piece of their deep-dish apple-berry pie for later. It was a little soggy by then, but this signature dessert was well executed, with lots of fruit and decent pastry and without too much sugar. And it was a gigantic portion.

Cafe Divine also has some of the most cheerful and proficient service I've seen lately. The staff genuinely seem to enjoy their work. And they hustle. This is one busy place.

Just like the rest of Okotoks around them.

Café Metro

Montreal-Style Café

7400 Macleod Trail S
Phone: 255·6537
Sunday – Thursday 11 am – 9 pm, Friday & Saturday 11 am – 10 pm
Reservations accepted for 6 or more — Fully licensed — Non-smoking
V, MC, AE, Debit — $

OVER the past eight years, Café Metro has established itself as a refuge for ex-Montrealers who are longing for the salty, smoky taste of their favourite hometown smoked meat sandwich. The Macleod Trail café has built a reputation for good smoked meat sandwiches that are somewhere between those of Schwartz's and Ben's, two of Montreal's best delis.

To achieve the quality, Café Metro brings in briskets from Delstar in Montreal, and the meat is quite good. It's fairly coarse, with a reasonable amount of pepper, but it's not too fatty (though they'll do fatty if you ask). They layer six ounces of thickly sliced brisket hot from the steamer onto locally baked rye bread. You get a slather of French's mustard, a pickle, slaw, and a side choice such as fries or latkes for $8.95. If you are seriously hungry, you can drop an extra $2 for the nine-ounce "Big Mouth" version. Or you can try a bowl of smoked meat chowder, one of the richest soups I've ever tasted. The menu also includes chicken club sandwiches, Thai chicken wraps, and vegetarian quesadillas, among other things, but we tend to come here for the smoked meat. And the atmosphere.

The space has been created to look like an outdoor plaza in Montreal. That's no small effort considering it's just a large, high-ceilinged strip-mall bay. The concrete floor resembles a brick road, a fire hydrant and street lamps are planted on the floor, and the walls are painted with street scenes. The tables are well spaced, and a fireplace warms up one corner. It's a distinctive look that is charmingly out of place on Macleod Trail.

And Café Metro is a busy spot, especially at lunch. If you're not here by noon, you could be waiting a bit for a table. But things move quickly. The sandwiches are delivered by staff that are almost on the run, and they are consumed almost as quickly. There's nothing delicate about these sandwiches, including the way in which they're eaten.

For those of us who live in the south, Café Metro is a blessing. A quick, tasty lunch can be had for under $10, if you can stay away from the desserts. The maple sugar pie, New York-style cheesecake, and English gingerbread cake are all made in-house.

So you don't have to go all the way to Montreal for a decent smoked meat sandwich. A little jaunt down Macleod Trail should suffice.

Carver's

Steak House

2620 – 32 Avenue NE (Sheraton Cavalier)
Phone: 250•6327
Monday – Saturday 5:30 pm – 10:30 pm, Sunday 5 pm – 9 pm
Reservations recommended — Fully licensed — Non-smoking
V, MC, AE, DC, Debit — $$$

CONTEMPORARY steak houses are no longer the dark, overly upholstered rooms of yesteryear. They are bright and hip and dedicated to big service as well as to big beef. And one place that has adopted this approach is Carver's in the Sheraton Cavalier.

Over the past few years, Carver's has established itself as one of the best steak houses in the city with its sleek room, vested waiters, and pricey menu. Admittedly it is still a windowless room, but the decor is lighter and fresher than the true old-style steak houses. And it's all about beef here—thirteen of nineteen entrees are beef in various forms. A steak Diana is $38, a ten-ounce fillet is $40, and the surf and turf is $48. Not delicate prices, but then Carver's is aimed more at the business traveller (read expense account) than at the regular public.

Which is not to say that it is elitist. It has also gained standing with locals who just crave a good piece of beef. Carver's serves AAA Alberta beef well aged, well cut, and well cooked. Catherine declared her tenderloin to be the best beef she had ever eaten. She discouragingly added that it surpassed all my own backyard efforts. Just see if I cook for her again! But I have to agree. It was so good that it barely needed to be dunked into the demi-glace sauce they served on the side.

We also tried a Caesar salad prepared tableside, a bowl of lobster bisque (at a mouth-dropping $13), and some bruschetta. All were done well, and the bisque justified its price with a big whack of lobster in the bowl. For dessert, which we were barely able to consume after all that food, we had the peppered strawberry crepes, again prepared tableside. Excellent. And $19 for two. (Did I mention that Carver's is pricey?)

The service here is as outstanding as the food—professional and not the least bit pretentious. The staff are well trained and a pleasure to be around. Carver's also has an excellent wine list and more professional staff to assist in selecting the right wine for the cut and preparation of beef you are having. These people know their stuff.

It is impressive that the Sheraton committed to running a high-end steak house in their hotel. In doing so, they have created a landmark restaurant not only for the hotel strip in the Northeast, but for the whole city.

www.sheraton-calgary.com

DOWN **Spot** town
That's the

Catch

Seafood

100 Stephen Avenue Walk SE
Phone: 206•0000
Oyster bar: Monday – Friday 11:30 am – close, Saturday & Sunday 5 pm – close
Second level: Monday – Friday 11:30 am – 2 pm, 5 pm – 10 pm, Saturday 5 pm – 10 pm
Reservations recommended — Fully licensed — Patio — Non-smoking
V, MC, AE, DC, Debit — $$ – $$$

THE most anticipated and hyped restaurant opening of 2002 was that of Catch. Spending over five and a half million dollars on renovations will do that.

The result is nothing short of spectacular. The Creative Restaurants group converted an old sandstone Imperial bank into a four-level operation that includes three full kitchens and a great deal of creativity. The main kitchen is buried in the basement, the ground floor is a lively oyster bar, the second floor is a stylish Contemporary restaurant, and the top floor, which used to be the roof, has been glassed in to create a private-function room. Catch is a serious operation.

The two main dining sections are quite different in look, and although they have the same culinary roots, they are quite different in food tone too. The main-floor room is masculine, done in dark wood and blue tones. It's a roll-up-your-sleeves-and-suck-back-some-oysters kind of place. Or settle into a booth for some fish and chips or a shrimp and pancetta clubhouse. The food I've had here has been consistently good.

The second floor is brighter and airier, the perfect place for executive chef Michael Noble to show his creativity. Noble is a native Calgarian who returned from the West Coast to open Catch, and he is one good chef. As in, *Iron Chef* good. (He's the only Canadian to appear on that Japanese culinary show.) The menu up here is a mix of confit of tuna; sashimi of Digby scallops and house-smoked salmon; hazelnut-crusted halibut; and lobster beignet. There are even braised short ribs and maple-roasted chickens for the non-seafaring crowd.

On one visit to the second-floor restaurant, I started with some crab cakes in an Asian chutney. They were the best crab cakes I've ever had. Next, my shellfish risotto with saffron and chorizo was excellent—a deeply yellow dish of rice, sausage, and seafood with a perfect balance. And well served by an experienced staff member.

The second floor is pricey. Not unjustifiably so if everything works well. A friend told me he took his wife and a couple of friends there, spent $500, and felt it was worthwhile. A dinner for two upstairs doesn't have to be that high, but count on $150 for two.

Personally I'm happy to pay that if the quality and creativity remain high. This is no weak-kneed seafood joint. They've made a great start, and they're bound to become even better.

www.creativeri.com

Centini

Modern Italian

160 Stephen Avenue Walk SE
Phone: 269·1600
Monday – Thursday 11 am – 11 pm, Friday 11 am – midnight, Saturday 5 pm – midnight
Reservations recommended — Fully licensed — Patio — Non-smoking
V, MC, AE, DC, JCB, Debit — $$ – $$$

I N 2002, Fabio Centini opened Centini Restaurant and Lounge in the former Blonde location. (His first eponymous eatery in Calgary had languished in a poor location.) With the help of the Baboushkin Design Group, he gave the Blonde look a dye job—it had been stylish but too cold for many people. They splashed some roasted-tomato colour on the walls and re-covered the floors with a similar-toned carpet. More red appears in the chair upholstery. It's a pleasant, comfortable, and still stylish room.

There are two dining areas plus a private room in the back, and high seats surrounding the open kitchen allow for either a formal meal or a quick bowl of soup. These kitchen seats can be entertaining, especially when Fabio is cooking.

Dinner at Centini covers a range of pasta and meat and seafood, all done in an Italian style that is part classic, part contemporary. The seafood is particularly interesting. An in-house cured Atlantic salmon served with chili-infused oil and salad in a sun-dried tomato dressing is delicate but not the least understated. A trio of rare ahi tuna, a prawn, and a huge scallop over a bed of warm spinach and red-pepper confit is a rich blend of seafood and greens. Just delightful flavours. At $12 and $14 respectively, these appetizers are not cheap, but well within downtown price ranges. Good value for both the quality and the quantity.

Main courses at dinner run from veal scaloppine at $24 to ahi tuna loin at $30 to roasted venison chops at $40. But I am prone to stopping at the pasta list where there is gnocchi in a Gorgonzola sauce or wild mushroom fettuccine or a very good seafood linguine, each for $18. The linguine, with a pile of mussels, clams, prawns, and scallops, is lightly tinged with a tomato sauce that allows all the seafood flavours to come through.

One of the more popular items on the pasta list is a simple dish of crepes filled with chèvre and oyster mushrooms and then topped with a delicate tomato sauce. Lunch choices include this crepe dish too, along with items like a thin-crust pizza topped with salami and mushrooms and chicken in a sage and walnut sauce. Centini also carries a rich list of desserts including a Tuscan apple cake, profiteroles, a poached pear cheesecake, and a lemon tart. Good stuff.

And Centini offers free parking after 4 p.m. in the Telus Convention Centre. Now that's a deal.

www.centini.com

Chez François

French

1604 Bow Valley Trail (Green Gables Inn), Canmore
Phone: 678·6111
Daily 7 am – 2 pm, 5 pm – 10 pm
Reservations recommended — Fully licensed — Non-smoking
V, MC, AE, DC, Debit — $$ – $$$

I F there is a better soup maker in the Bow Valley than Jean-François Gouin, I don't know who it is. I can still taste the lobster bisque I had at his Chez François restaurant over a dozen years ago. In my mind, it defines how that dish should be prepared. And I was amazed at a consommé he brought to a function a few years ago. It wowed not only me (I had three helpings), but blew away most of the other chefs in attendance. The clarity of the broth and the sharpness of the flavours were superb. Gouin puts the time and effort into doing it right. That simple consommé took days of roasting and simmering and clarifying.

We often underestimate the skill of the soup maker. But to me it signifies the quintessential talent of any chef. Do they have the patience, the ability, the wherewithal to strip food down to its essence in a soup? Or do they hide it under thickeners and boost it with packaged mixes?

At Chez François, they do the real deal. Dropping in for lunch, I had a bowl of carrot-orange soup infused with cilantro. The flavours sang with richness and strength. Even the cilantro, an herb of which I am not particularly fond, added a subtlety to the dish I had not expected. Marvelous.

But enough of soup. A man cannot live on soup alone. Well, I probably could, but that's another story.

For the rest of my lunch, I had a Reuben sandwich made with good smoked meat, sauerkraut, and Gruyère in a less greasy version than I've had elsewhere. The remainder of the lunch menu includes salads, more sandwiches, pastas, and some bigger ticket items, along with more soup of course.

Chez François is also known to serve a superb eggs Benedict, making it a popular breakfast place for Calgarians heading west. Its location in the Green Gables Inn makes for a quick pit stop one hour from the city. And unless the tour buses really have the place packed, service is prompt.

But they don't stop at breakfast and lunch. In the evening Chez François moves upscale with a more classic French menu that includes pork tenderloin in a Roquefort sauce, braised duck in a Grand Marnier sauce, and escargots in puff pastry. They also offer a six-course table d'hôte menu for a reasonable $44 and a shorter, three-course version for $33.

Both come with soup.

Chili Club

Thai

#125, 555 – 11 Avenue SW
Phone: 237 • 8828
Monday – Friday 11:30 am – 2:30 pm
Sunday, Tuesday & Wednesday 5 pm – 9 pm
Thursday – Saturday 5 pm – 10 pm
Reservations recommended — Fully licensed — Non-smoking
V, MC, AE, DC, Debit — $$

THE corner of 5th Street and 11th Avenue SW is a busy intersection with vehicles in constant motion. On the southeast corner there is an awkward mini-mall that houses a Mac's and a couple of other businesses. In its most invisible spot sits the Chili Club Thai House. It's shielded by the large Singapore Sam's building so that, if you are approaching from the east, you don't see it until it's almost too late. And even if you know where to pull in, there's a good chance there will not be parking available in the crowded lot. So the Chili Club can be frustrating to get to.

But the result is worth the effort. The Chili Club is the oldest Thai concept in the city. This is its fourth location over the past dozen years, and it is as good as ever. (The Chili Club started on Centre Street N and had locations on 16th Avenue NW and 17th Avenue SW before slipping into hiatus for a while.)

The original chef who made the Chili Club popular is still in the kitchen, and he continues to crank out tasty and colourful food. The dishes are marked with chilies to indicate heat—no chilies means fresh and flavourful but without zip and the maximum three chilies means it's darned hot.

One of my enduring favourites is the vegetable dish called tom kati pak ruam, or "Evil Jungle Prince Mixed Vegetables." The name itself is enough to attract most folks, but the three-chili warning scares some away. Rightfully so. This dish is stinking hot. But it is also good—the peppers, baby corn, carrots, and other vegetables are crisp and bracing in the creamy hot sauce.

Comparatively, the two-chili kung pad mit ma mung, or cashew shrimp with chili and green onion, is a laid-back dish. Filled with shrimp and cashews in a savoury sauce, it is well balanced and crunchy fresh. And still spicy.

At lunch all the entrees come with rice (coconut or steamed) and spring rolls. That softens the price. Although the cost is not extreme, it is significant; the Evil Jungle Prince is $10, the shrimp $14. I have found the spring rolls unnecessarily oily, but otherwise fine for dipping in a sharp nam pla fish sauce.

The Chili Club is a small room seating about thirty-six in a deep sponged-red decor. Even the ceiling is red. It's a tone that suits the cuisine. And takes your eye off all that traffic outside.

Cilantro

California-Southwestern

338 – 17 Avenue SW
Phone: 229·1177
Monday – Friday 11 am – 11 pm, Saturday 5 pm – midnight, Sunday 5 pm – 10 pm
Reservations recommended — Fully licensed — Patio — Non-smoking
V, MC, AE, DC, Debit — $$ – $$$

THE move to Contemporary cuisine started in the eighties, not just in Calgary but across most of North America. With interest growing in fresher, tastier, healthier foods, "California-style" restaurants started popping up. In Calgary, one of the first was Cilantro.

Cilantro opened in a renovated tailor shop on what was then a more sedate stretch of 17th Avenue and instantly became the most popular restaurant in Calgary. Soon after, the owners fired up the first wood-burning pizza oven in town and expanded into the old house next door. A decade and a half later, Cilantro is still there and still thriving. It may not be as hard to get in as it once was, but when Cilantro is "on," it can provide a very satisfying experience.

We tend to plan our visits to Cilantro to coincide with warm weather. The greenery on the gorgeous patio has grown over the years, as has the height of the enclosing wall. The wall blocks out the 17th Avenue traffic, providing more comfort for al fresco dining.

Cilantro still adheres to the California creed of big salads, tasty sandwiches, and pizzas from that pizza oven. The oven has been refurbished a few times, but it works just fine. The pear, Gorgonzola, and pine-nut pizza has been on the menu since day one, and it continues to sell strongly. And with good reason. Another longstanding favourite is the black-pepper linguine with chicken, tomatoes, spinach, and sesame seeds, the legacy of Dany Lamote, Cilantro's first chef.

I typically find the sandwiches to be good choices. The elk burger, made from elk raised on their own ranch, is dense and gamey. The onion jam, cherry ketchup, and mustard aïoli provide strong flavour balances to the meat, and with a side of horseradish-cheddar scalloped potatoes, it's an intense and filling meal. For less intensity, there's the BLT with smoked Gouda on focaccia. You'll find bigger-ticket items on the menu too, such as sea bass with a tamale in a citrus-ancho sauce.

Desserts are usually good here. They change frequently and show creativity. A fallen chocolate soufflé is served with white-chocolate ice cream and peach-strawberry compote, and a sorbet is made with lavender, honey, and lemon. Plate presentation is always lovely.

Cilantro has survived because it has struck a balance between the familiar and the unusual. It's not too outrageous, yet the combinations are unique enough to appeal to food adventurers and are always worth a taste.

Clay Oven

Indian (Punjabi)

3132 – 26 Street NE (Interpacific Business Park)
Phone: 250•2161
Monday – Friday 11:30 am – 2 pm, Monday – Thursday 5 pm – 9 pm
Friday & Saturday 5 pm – 10 pm
Reservations recommended — Fully licensed — Non-smoking
V, MC, AE, DC, Debit — $ – $$

As far as out-of-the-way restaurants go, you can't get much more tucked away than the Clay Oven. It's squeezed into the far end of the Interpacific Business Park, which is hidden behind the big Husky truck stop on Barlow Trail. The business park itself houses an eclectic collection of food sites, from Thumbs Up Samosas and Chinook Edge's butcher shop to Cakeworks and a place that makes dim sum goodies for many Chinese restaurants.

Regardless of the location, the Clay Oven stands out as one of the best Indian restaurants in the city. Once parked and inside, you could be anywhere; the room has been stylishly decorated in an Indian theme, a buffet sits along one wall, and a bar consumes one end. It's not a large space and it is popular, so call ahead, especially for lunch.

The Clay Oven is considered by many Indian food fans—myself included—to have the best breads in the city. They are thick and dense and richly flavoured. Most Indian breads are good for scooping up the food; these are even tasty enough to eat on their own. There's a range of them, from simple chapati to onion-stuffed kulcha, and all are excellent.

The food you scoop up with them is pretty good too. We have found over the years that the vegetarian dishes are particularly well done. Certainly they do a fine butter chicken and a good lamb curry, but we especially enjoy their fresh-cheese paneer dishes. There is a mutter paneer, a shahi paneer, and even a shahi mutter paneer that combines the peas of the mutter along with the spicing of the shahi. They also do good things with a number of different kinds of lentils, and they make a fine aloo gobi of cauliflower, potatoes, peas, and ginger. And the khumb of mushrooms with potatoes is always a winner.

The lunch buffet is loaded with selection and, at $10, is a bargain. The food does not fall victim to the problem that afflicts some Indian buffets, that of a monotone flavour. The buffet is constantly replenished, and piles of that fine bread arrive frequently from the tandoor oven.

The Clay Oven is a family-run operation but still has a professional feel. Service is calm and purposeful. Expect it to take awhile unless you are there for the lunch buffet. Just relax and have another piece of bread.

The Conga Room

Nuevo Latino

109 Stephen Avenue Walk SW
Phone: 262•7248
Monday – Saturday 11 am – close
Reservations recommended, especially on weekends
Fully licensed — Patio — Non-smoking dining room, smoking in lounge
V, MC, AE, DC, Debit — $$

ONE of the freshest concepts to hit the global food scene lately is Nuevo Latino. It's a sultry cuisine that combines the food traditions of Central America and the Caribbean with international ingredients and the lighter cooking concepts of Contemporary preparations. Admittedly that's a mouthful, but a pretty tasty one.

The first place to introduce this cuisine to Calgary is The Conga Room on Stephen Avenue. Here you will find dishes made from seafood, plantain, mangos, and citrus combined with Jamaican spices, Cuban rice and beans, and Mexican chilies. Much of the high-fat food tradition of Central America has been replaced with grilled meats and fruit and chili flavours. So we see dishes such as plantain-crusted salmon in a guava glaze and adobo-marinated beef tenderloin with tequila-flamed prawns.

It's lovely food with tropical colours decorating the plates. The pollo supremo combines a chicken breast with brie and a prosciutto-style ham under a bright green citrus sauce. With a pile of coconut-flavoured rice and a spray of asparagus and grilled zucchini, it is both a gorgeous and a beautifully flavoured dish. So are appetizers of scallops in a mango-chipotle cream and a ceviche of fresh seafood marinated in rum and lime. This is crisp food that jumps with flavour. It is not especially hot, but is intensely flavoured with the fruits and the spices.

Dessert is not forgotten either. A chocolate crème caramel is a silky pudding richly flavoured by the chocolate. Lovely. The Conga Room also serves a great mojito, the current Latino drink that suits this food perfectly. A combination of crushed mint, lime, and white rum, the mojito is fresh and light and potent. Beware.

Aside from the food and drink, The Conga Room offers a warm tone in a friendly room. The former Latin Corner space has remained much the same but with a brighter paint job. It is long and fairly narrow, flowing from a lounge past a stage used for live music on weekends to a dining area in the back.

Owners Alex and Orlando Morante bring warmth and professionalism to their restaurant and set the tone for the staff. The Conga Room is meant to be fun but also to have a strong kitchen. Chef Erick Carrillo provides the skill in that area.

The Conga Room's food may be too different for some, but it is being embraced by those who are looking for exactly that—the new and the different.

www.thecongaroom.com

Copper Door
Casual Continental

726 – 9 Street, Canmore
Phone: 678 • 5233
Daily 5 pm – 10:30 pm
Reservations recommended — Fully licensed — Non-smoking
V, MC, Debit — $$ – $$$

FOR years the Peppermill was one of the most popular restaurants in Canmore. Tucked away on 9th Street just a block off Main Street, it was an alpine island surrounded by tall pines and filled with full-bodied Bavarian cooking. But in 2003 it changed hands and became the Copper Door.

I like that the Copper Door actually has a copper door—heavy and hand-tooled by local artist Tony Bloom at that. It's a perfect entry point for the eclectically decorated forty-seat interior. The walls are done in rich tomato and sage tones, and the look is turn-of-the-millennium garage sale. Two dining areas are divided by a bar that resembles a giant butcher block. It's a comfortable room, a little more upscale than the neighbouring Zona's.

There are inevitable comparisons with Zona's, the popular late-night bistro just a couple of doors away. And they are legitimate: Chris Dmytriw owns both places. He has positioned the Copper Door a touch higher than Zona's with a more elegant but casual Continental menu and an atmosphere that attracts a less rambunctious crowd. Zona's has a party-friendly feel to it while the Copper Door is for slightly more serious dining.

The summer 2003 menu included such main courses as roasted lamb leg with Parmesan-herb risotto ($19), wild salmon stuffed with sherried raisins and mushrooms ($19), and seafood bouillabaisse ($22). Appetizers included couscous salad, garlic prawns, and stuffed mushrooms. But watch for the menu to change quite substantially with the seasons.

A Caesar salad of crunchy romaine with roasted garlic and Asiago dressing was sharp and tangy. Excellent. And a bowl of mussels was proof to any non-believer that you can indeed find fine seafood dishes in the Rockies. These mussels were fresh and fat and not overcooked. Served in a white-wine sauce with tomatoes, garlic, and shallots, this dish had me asking for a soup spoon so as not to miss any of the broth.

Service at the Copper Door was smooth and tourist friendly. The server was able to keep up with my high water consumption from an unseasonably warm day. He also brought fresh-from-the-oven bread and a ceramic bowl of oil and vinegar. All in all, it was a pleasant meal.

The Copper Door has loads of potential to become another long-time Canmore resident, and it makes a fine contrast to its sister restaurant. It may take a little effort to find, but it is worth it.

www.copperdoor.com

Coyotes

Contemporary Southwestern

206 Caribou Street, Banff
Phone: 762 • 3963
Daily 7:30 am – 10 pm
Reservations recommended — Fully licensed — Non-smoking
V, MC, AE, DC, JCB, Debit — $$

WE most often end up at Coyotes for breakfast. Few other Banff eateries outside of the hotels offer breakfast, but that aside, Coyotes has a nice morning tone. The long lunch counter and the menu of buttermilk pancakes, honey-baked granola, and huevos rancheros are always attractive. The food is big and hearty and always served with a smile.

But occasionally we stop in for lunch or dinner, at least when there's a table available or we've thought to call ahead. Reservations are almost always necessary because Coyotes is one of those places that both locals and tourists frequent. It's a constant hum of activity, with closely placed tables filled with hikers and bikers and weekenders from Calgary.

Coyotes' dinner menu conjures up visions of the Southwest—meaning the Southwestern states of New Mexico and California, not the Southwestern neighbourhoods of Lakeview and Killarney. So you'll find enchiladas, blue corn, and chorizo, but you'll also see pesto, polenta, and penne. Coyotes is one of only two Southwestern restaurants in our area (the other is Mescalero), but it's not slavish to the style. It almost qualifies as Southwestern-Mediterranean-Californian.

We can get pasta in other places, so we order dishes such as the classic sweet potato and corn chowder garnished with red-chili sauce and sour cream. It's a blend of smoky flavours, as good a soup as any in Santa Fe. The Southwest sushi roll is a tortilla filled with smoked salmon and cilantro mayonnaise in a cross-cultural twist that brings the coast and the desert to the mountains. (It's pleasant, but as a sushi addict, give me raw fish or give me, well, a fishing rod.) Another starter, the orange-chipotle prawns, is a dynamite combination.

Main course selections fill the need for Southwestern purism. A blue-corn chicken enchilada ($17) is lacquered with a dark colorado sauce that turns the dish almost black. Stacked New Mexican-style, it's a forceful enchilada, not for the meek. Slightly less intense is the grilled chicken breast with citrus salsa ($18). Shellacked with Coyotes' own barbecue sauce, the chicken is tender and tasty and well balanced by the salsa.

They don't carry an extensive list of different tequilas, but they still make a pretty good margarita, an essential drink for a Southwestern restaurant. And always the pleasant service. It seems no matter how busy they are, they are consistently good to their customers. And that's a big part of Coyotes' continuing popularity.

Crazyweed Kitchen

Global Cuisine

626 Main Street, Canmore
Phone: 609·2530
Daily 11:30 am – 3:30 pm, 5:30 pm – 10:30 pm
Reservations not accepted — Fully licensed — Small patio
Non-smoking restaurant & patio
V, MC, AE, Debit — $ – $$

THERE is no more aptly named restaurant in this book than Crazyweed. The creation of Jan and Richard Hrabec, Crazyweed has become a culinary landmark not only in Canmore but in the entire area. The food is so good it can bring tears to your eyes, but eating here is no typical, traditional experience. It's a little off-kilter and, well, a bit crazy.

Part of that craziness is due to the fact that it keeps changing. It looks a little different every time we visit, which is fairly often considering it's in Canmore and we live in Calgary. Crazyweed started five years ago as a deli for takeout foods, with limited dining in at counters. The dining-in aspect has expanded over time, and now finally there are tables and table service.

And then there's the food. Jan Hrabec is the calm culinary genius of the couple. She can squeeze more flavour out of ingredients than any chef in our area. And I mean Any Chef In Our Area. This is the place where other chefs go to eat. Her lamb sandwich with eggplant relish has transported me to another plane of consciousness, her pizzas are the best we've had outside Italy, her salads, her desserts, and her salmon and potato pie are all beyond reproach. To be more succinct, if I were looking at a "last meal" situation, I'd ask for Jan to cook it.

And I might ask for Richard to serve it. Because he'd tell so many bizarre and fascinating stories, I might just forget why I was there. Richard provides the creative, crackling energy to Crazyweed. His ideas push the space to evolve, moving Crazyweed along at the front of Contemporary cuisine. And his personality fills the space; a meal at Crazyweed is not complete without a Richard experience.

But enough praise. It should now be abundantly obvious that Crazyweed is one of my absolute rave-faves in this book. And I know that I am far from alone. But is there a downside here? Sure: they don't take reservations, and with only twenty-four seats inside, you may have to wait a few minutes because the place is so darned busy.

Crazyweed may be a bit too unusual for those treading the tried and true. That's fine. It's not for the drive-through crowd. It's for those who want creativity and that slightly off-kilter attitude.

And it doesn't hurt to be a little crazy yourself.

Da Paolo

Italian

121 – 17 Avenue SE
Phone: 228•5556
Monday – Friday 11:30 am – 2 pm, Monday – Saturday 5 pm – close
Reservations recommended — Fully licensed — Non-smoking
V, MC, AE, DC — $$ – $$$

TEN years. It's hard to believe that it's been that long since Paolo De Minico and Claudio Carnali opened the first Da Paolo Ristorante. Back then they were already restaurant professionals with lengthy experience, Paolo's in the kitchen and Claudio's out front. They wanted their own place, though, a place where Paolo's food could be showcased and Claudio's service style could shine.

So they took a space on 17th Avenue and 4th Street SW, but when La Chaumière moved to its flashy new place down the street, the pair quickly scooped up the vacated location. They did some renovations, added a couple of windows, and have been doing a gangbuster business ever since.

Da Paolo presents the best of classic, traditional Italian cuisine. From a carpaccio topped with shaved Parmesan and caperberries through to the pastas and the veal saltimbocca, the food sings with the flavours of the old country. Paolo packs each plate with flavour—he's one of those chefs who have "the touch." His personal effervescence seems to flow into the food, giving it a depth and texture beyond the ingredients.

The pasta alla Paolo is a perfect example. House-made ravioli is filled with veal, ricotta, and herbs and served in a rosé sauce with mushrooms. It's a symphony of flavours, the kind of dish I'd want more of if I weren't so full after finishing it. The rest of the pasta list shows Paolo's creativity too, with dishes such as fettuccine with creamy scampi or pheasant- and porcini-stuffed ravioli in butter and sage sauce. For those who can't decide, there is the chef's choice of three pastas. I find the pastas so inviting, I rarely get to the veal or seafood dishes. Once upon a time, though, I did have a veal chop that was memorable. And that veal saltimbocca.

The food seems to instigate a liveliness in the room. An evening at Da Paolo can start fairly quietly. It is an elegant, upscale dining room after all. But it can quickly become boisterous as diners are energized by their meals and the elaborate wine list. It's not like you'll be hit by flying meatballs, but it's far from somber here.

Part of the energy is due to Claudio's approach to the room. He's calmly in control and has a strong staff to support him. It's classic service that suits the food.

So that is what ten years of experience looks like.

Daikichi

Japanese

111 Stephen Avenue Walk SW
Phone: 265·1398
Monday – Saturday 11 am – 9 pm
Reservations recommended, especially at lunch
Fully licensed — Patio — Non-smoking
V, MC, AE, DC, Debit — $ – $$

FROM the outside Daikichi doesn't look all that big. But inside it holds a large, bright kitchen, a row of tatami rooms, a bunch of tables, and two huge double-decker conveyor belts.

Each belt runs along a deck in front of about a dozen dining chairs, then turns a corner and heads back along the opposite side in front of more chairs. The belts are about four inches wide, broad enough to hold small plates. The bottom levels are used to transport plates of fresh sushi, and the top levels, warmed by heat lamps, are used to deliver hot food such as gyoza dumplings and tempura. There is basically non-stop food rolling around the room.

Like some other Japanese restaurants around town, the food served this way is priced by the plate. You take a plate off the belt, and the cost is calculated by its colour. At the end of the meal, the staff count up your plates and you pay the bill. But during lunch, they frequently have an all-you-can-eat sushi and hot food offer for $15. That's a stunning price for sushi fans. I can eat $15 worth of sushi just as an appetizer.

So I plunked myself down at one of the conveyor belts and started picking off plates as part of that lunch special. On the lower level, the tekka rolls came out first, a nice variety of spicy tuna, salmon, and crab meat. Then the nigiri sushi—the usual salmon, snapper, and shrimp—appeared. There were some tuna and smoked eel versions as well as a few scallop-mayonnaise ones, but these premium sorts weren't as common as the cheaper cuts. Still, all the other sushi fans gathered around the belt seemed to be getting enough of their favourites.

And then there was the hot belt. The fried stuff was a little heavy, but the tempura and gyoza dumplings were still okay. To ensure freshness, the staff hand-delivered some of the hot trays, such as the chicken teriyaki and the yakitori, in a dim sum sort of approach. It was a continuous food assault.

Generally, it was good food. The sushi was not the most exact I've seen, and there was little in the art of presentation, but it was fresh. And I noticed some power lunchers came and went in twenty minutes.

So not only can it be cheap to eat at Daikichi, it can be one of the quickest sit-down meals in downtown.

Deer Lodge

Rocky Mountain Cuisine

109 Lake Louise Drive, Lake Louise
Phone: 522•3747
Dining room: Daily 7 am – 11 am, 6 pm – 10 pm; Lounge: Daily 7 am – 11 pm
Closed mid-October – mid-November
Reservations recommended — Fully licensed — Patio
Non-smoking dining room & lounges, smoking on patio
V, MC, AE, DC — $$ – $$$

A H, the view from the bucolic dining room at Deer Lodge. The mountains, the burbling stream, the chipmunks frolicking on the patio, the traffic jam of RV's trudging up the incline to the Lake Louise parking lot. 'Tis paradise. Seriously, the view is gorgeous, and the interior of Deer Lodge ain't half bad either. It's appropriately woody, following the historic mountain-lodge theme. The floors are wood, the tables and walls are wood, the ceiling…you get the idea. I mention it because the soundscape of Deer Lodge is predominantly that of creaking wood. But this is no musty, falling-apart mountain hovel. It's well appointed, much like the other Canadian Rocky Mountain Resorts (Buffalo Mountain Lodge and Emerald Lake Lodge, plus Calgary restaurants Cilantro and The Ranche). So there's a sense of style, a commitment to the history of the facility, and a contemporary tone that shakes out any cobwebs.

Deer Lodge offers a variety of dining options ranging from breakfast and dinner in the sixty-five-seat dining room to snacks on the patio and all-day dining in the lounge. Dinner can be a full tilt Rocky Mountain affair with caribou medallions in a raspberry and black-pepper sauce at $35 or buffalo strip loin in a rose-petal glaze at $33. Breakfast continues the theme with a mixed grill of eggs, elk-cranberry sausage, bacon, back bacon, potatoes, and toast at $11 (there'd better be some serious hiking after that) and beef tenderloin with a poached egg, Béarnaise sauce, and bacon rösti at $16 (break out the pitons Ma—we're goin' mountain climbing).

On my most recent visit, I tried one of the company's new products, buffalo pastrami (Canadian Rocky Mountain Resorts has their own game ranch where they raise elk, deer, and buffalo, and they use the meats on their menus). Layered with Oka cheese and roasted red onion on grilled sourdough bread, it made a great sandwich. All the elements worked together perfectly, especially the onion. If you're a pastrami fan, this buffalo version is a must. Sided with a creamy bowl of roasted corn bisque with chunks of potato and wild salmon, it was one of the best lunches I've had in the mountains. It was robust enough to match the surroundings but not so over-the-top as to make me want to nap the afternoon away.

So, nice view, good food, pleasant service too. Maybe next time I'll even stroll the extra few hundred yards to the lake.

www.crmr.com

Des Alpes

Swiss-French

702 – 10 Street, Canmore
Phone: 678 • 6878
Tuesday – Sunday 5 pm – 10 pm
Reservations recommended — Fully licensed — Veranda for drinks only
Non-smoking restaurant, smoking on veranda
V, MC, AE, Debit — $$ – $$$

TWO-inch-thick tabletops are the first indication that dinner at Des Alpes is serious business. Built from slabs of tree trunks embedded in epoxy, the tables are as solid as the Alps after which the restaurant is named. And about as solid as the food served on them.

Des Alpes is the restaurant of Marianne and Xaver Schurtenberger, two Swiss expatriates and veterans of the Canmore dining scene. They have been active in the food business here for almost two decades, having opened the original Boccalino in the early 1980s. They've operated Des Alpes since 1989 in a lovely thirty-five-seat log building a block off Main Street, and it has always been one of the finest places in town.

The prices have barely changed over the years, and with the arrival of some pretty high prices in Calgary, it seems quite affordable. To be sure, it's not cheap—a curried shrimp dish is $24, a lamb loin in a mint cream is $28, and a beef tenderloin with Béarnaise sauce is $32. But the chicken émincé is a bargain at $16.

It's a huge platter of sliced chicken breast sautéed with mushrooms and onions, finished in a cream sauce, and served with a spray of green beans, an artichoke heart, carrots, and broccoli and a huge pile of spaetzle (or rice or potato if you prefer). It took Catherine forty-five minutes to eat her way through it, and she loved every bite. My veal émincé, a similar preparation at $24, was equally excellent.

The Caesar salad is another example of one of their rich, tasty dishes. With chopped lettuce that actually fits onto the fork and a thorough but not excessive coating of a creamy dressing, it is a definitive Caesar.

Then there are the desserts, including perfectly baked meringues with whipped cream and fruit or chocolate sauce. I could barely pull Catherine away from the table after this. She wanted to move in with the Schurtenbergers.

Sometimes it's the small things that impress the most. They deliver a pepper mill to the table to use at your leisure—no hovering as you decide whether or not a dish needs extra seasoning. And since the beginning, they have baked some of the best bread in the Bow Valley. It's dense and flavourful. It doesn't even need butter, but they bring it anyway.

So Des Alpes remains a Canmore classic. They just don't get any better.

www.telusplanet.net/public/desalpes

Diner Deluxe

Contemporary Diner

804 Edmonton Trail NE
Phone: 276·5499
Monday 7:30 am – 3 pm, Tuesday – Friday 7:30 am – 9:30 pm
Saturday 8 am – 3 pm, 5 pm – 9:30 pm, Sunday 8 am – 3 pm
Reservations accepted Monday – Friday for over 6
Fully licensed — Patio — Non-smoking
V, MC, AE, DC, Debit — $

DINER DELUXE opened in December 2001. Now December is not traditionally a good month to open a restaurant, but Diner Deluxe has been packing them in ever since. It seems to have the perfect mix of location, food concept, value, and service, things that make a restaurant popular.

It is great looking too. It's a retro diner that has been done way better than any other I've seen. The room is a wash of diner pastels highlighted by a raised roof and windows that allow sunlight to stream in. A collection of vintage lamps shines over the restored tables and chairs in the evening, and a diner counter zigzags into the room. It's not just a long lunch counter, it's a comfortable dining zone.

The food is a new-millennium upgrade on the diner concept. The meat loaf is made with veal and served with Dijon-mashed potatoes, and the roasted peach pancakes come with a lemon-lavender butter. There are more flavours, better textures, and higher quality ingredients than you'll find in most old-style diners.

The biggest decision at Diner Deluxe is whether to have breakfast—which is served all day—or to indulge in the lunch and dinner items. They do a good eggs Benedict, a rich maple-fried oatmeal with lemon curd and cream, and a fine French toast with Gouda and bacon. Not exactly delicate stuff, but very tasty.

After 11 a.m. they bring out the hearty beef and barley soup (made with house-roasted beef bones), the bacon-cheddar burgers, the grilled pork chops with creamed barley, and the AAA Angus sirloin steaks. Not only are these good meals, but they don't cost an arm and a leg. Almost everything on the menu is under $10.

There are few downsides to Diner Deluxe. On weekend mornings there are big lineups, and the food does not come out at traditional diner speed. It can't—it takes longer to prepare this style. But the wait is worth it, if just to stare at the decor and enjoy the ambience of the place, which includes pleasant service. It can also be a bit tricky to find the first time. It's on the east side of Edmonton Trail just as you crest the hill as you drive north from the Bow.

Diner Deluxe has been so successful that the owners have recently renovated the space next door into a bakery. So now we can take all that diner goodness home.

Divine Ambrosia

Italian Fusion

4824 – 16 Street SW
Phone: 214·3616
Sunday – Thursday 5 pm – 10 pm, Friday & Saturday 5 pm – 11 pm
Reservations recommended — Fully licensed — Patio — Non-smoking
V, MC, AE, DC, Debit — $$ – $$$

IT took a long time for me to get to Divine Ambrosia. That's partly because it's only open for dinner and partly because Altadore always seems to hide its culinary gems—remember the late Le Flamboyant, Calgary's best obscure restaurant for years?

Divine Ambrosia sits in a little strip mall looking pretty obscure itself. But inside, it's charming. It's a large rectangular room that seats about forty and has an overhead heater that works overtime in cold weather. The walls are textured and sponged gold and red. To one side is a small bar with a few stools. With some subdued lighting, wood furniture, and nicely spaced tables, it is reminiscent of the restaurants in small hotels across Europe.

The menu has overtones of small Euro-restaurants too. It's a blend of Italian dishes melded with global ideas into an Italian Fusion cuisine. Things like salmon and mint tortellini with a vodka rosé sauce. Or beef tenderloin with porcini mushrooms and cognac demi-glace. Nice ideas, well executed.

On a cold night we started dinner with a bowl of lamb-asparagus soup and a mixed salad. We were also served some of the tasty and complimentary house bruschetta. The lamb-asparagus soup was a creamy and delicate blend of flavours, a more elegant soup than I had expected. It had a velvety texture and subtle flavours that made me pay attention.

Next up was a bowl of pasta pescatore and a plate of lamb tenderloin wrapped in prosciutto and fresh mint with a Madeira demi-glace. The lamb was lovely, but those tenderloins are just so small that it would have been nice to have had more. This was Catherine's choice and she cleaned it up before I finished my pasta, which almost never happens. I was slowed down because the pescatore came with scallops, mussels, and prawns all still in their shells. Nice, fresh seafood, but I do think the menu or server should warn customers about the work ahead.

Aside from that, I was impressed with the service. The staff were exceedingly pleasant and professional. It was one of those meals where the food tasted just a little better because the service was so good. Two experienced staff ran the entire room and gave everyone personal attention. It's refreshing to see service of that quality and food that matches it.

So I'll try to get back to Divine Ambrosia more frequently. Altadore is not that far away.

Divino

Western Canadian Bistro

113 Stephen Avenue Walk SW
Phone: 410·5555
Monday – Wednesday 11 am – 10 pm, Thursday & Friday 11 am – 11 pm
Saturday & Sunday 5 pm – 11 pm
Reservations recommended — Fully licensed — Patio — Non-smoking
V, MC, AE, DC, Debit — $$ – $$$

A FTER a year and a half of renovation, the new Divino finally opened its doors in the summer of 2003. And those expecting the old Divino in a new location were quite surprised.

A mainstay of the downtown dining scene in the Grain Exchange building for years, the old Divino brought an elegant yet bohemian tone to the city core. But the new Divino has gone farther upscale, moved east, and introduced a bit more international flare to its food. The space is a sparkling redevelopment that features a 120-seat restaurant, a high-tech, second-floor function room, and a sandstone wine cellar and prep kitchen. The old brick walls of the building have been exposed, but aside from that, the rest of Divino looks brand spanking new.

The centrepiece of its open kitchen is a wood-burning grill that was built by the stylish Gramercy Tavern in New York. It imparts a rustic tang to the buffalo sirloin and the grilled tuna, and it adds a woody scent to the room. Next to the grill sits a large wood-burning pizza oven, and beside it on a chilled marble counter, a selection of cheeses is ready to serve. The new Divino is labelled a "Wine & Cheese Bistro" and, as such, offers an international cheese menu along with an extensive wine list.

The bulk of the menu is dedicated to a mix of French and Californian bistro items such as mussels and frites, an asparagus and green bean salad, and a lamb confit sandwich. Fans of the old Divino will find the trademark black-pepper linguine, but that's about the only carry-over. And prices have not escalated unreasonably— the sandwiches, pizzas, and pastas top out at $16, and only a few entrees, such as the rib steak with parsley-shallot relish and the buffalo sirloin, reach up to $30.

The food is rich and assured: the lamb confit is juicy and tender; the mussels are bathed in a robust, tomatoey sauce; and a bacon-roasted chicken sandwich is tender and zippy under a tomato relish. This is good food.

Divino is part of the Canadian Rocky Mountain Resorts corporate family, the others being Cilantro, The Ranche, Bin 905, Buffalo Mountain Lodge, Deer Lodge, and Emerald Lake Lodge. So the breads come from their corporate bakery, and the game meats are raised on their Canadian Rocky Mountain Ranch.

The old Divino was a great little place. But the new Divino is even better.

www.divinobistro.com

Dragon Pearl

Chinese (Szechwan)

1223A – 9 Avenue SE
Phone: 233·8810
Daily 11 am – 2 pm
Monday – Thursday 5 pm – 10:30 pm
Friday & Saturday 5 pm – 11 pm, Sunday 5 pm – 9:30 pm
Reservations recommended — Beer & wine only — Non-smoking
V, MC, AE, Debit — $$

I started going to the Dragon Pearl in Inglewood over twenty years ago when 9th Avenue SE was a pretty quiet place in the evening. Back then it was one of the few Szechwan restaurants around town, and it had the most arresting decor. On one wall was that fuzzy red velvet wallpaper, and on another, that shiny silvery-bronze stuff. Interspersed were gold-flake, mirrored tiles. Now that was a look.

But the Dragon Pearl never seemed too concerned about appearances. They were all about the food, a rich mix of forceful flavours backed up with loads of heat.

It's a new millennium now, and the Dragon Pearl has a lighter, more subtle look. But it remains mostly about the food. It's still one of the few Szechwan restaurants in town, and the food is still forceful and backed up by a big wallop of heat. And it is still served briskly by an efficient and friendly staff.

The spicier selections are marked by little dragons, and you should heed that designation. These dishes are hot. We had one of salt and pepper shrimp that was overloaded with chilies, too much actually for the delicate shrimp, and surprisingly lacking in flavour otherwise. Unfortunately, there was little indication of the salt and pepper side of the dish.

Much better was the black-pepper chicken on a sizzling platter. With this sort of dish, they bring the food on one plate and dump it onto a hot cast-iron platter at your table. What ensues is a big sizzling noise, a lot of smoke and released spices, a round of coughing if you inhale the fumes, and everyone else in the room staring at you. I think all the pepper that had been left off the shrimp had migrated to this dish. The sauce was strong and peppery, and the chicken was tender. A nice plate of food.

We also had the Szechwan eggplant mixed with minced pork in another rich, thick, spicy sauce. Tasty and again pretty hot—one of the best eggplant dishes I've had. But next time I won't order all my dishes from the dragon list.

Dragon Pearl remains extremely popular. Prices are good, with everything under $10 except some seafood dishes. The servings are huge and the ingredients fresh, the sign of a busy restaurant. So if you like it intense, Dragon Pearl will serve you well.

Dutchie's

Caribbean

#4, 3745 Memorial Drive SE
Phone: 204•8197
Monday – Wednesday 11 am – 8 pm, Thursday – Saturday 11 am – 10 pm
Reservations accepted — Fully licensed — Non-smoking
V, Debit — $ – $$

WHEN it comes to nondescript, they don't come much plainer than Dutchie's. The Jamaican posters and the stack of brochures announcing the next calypso party are about the only things that indicate it's Caribbean. That and the smell of jerk sauce sliding out of the kitchen and the throb of reggae on the stereo.

Dutchie's is the latest in a long line of Caribbean restaurants to have inhabited this strip-mall bay on Memorial Drive. First there was Lloyd's until Lloyd moved into the pattie business. Then there was Sam's. And now there is Dutchie's, named after the Dutch ovens in which much of Caribbean food is cooked.

Three small rooms have been cobbled together to make up Dutchie's, with about five tables placed in the main room. Daily specials are written on a small chalkboard to supplement a list of brown stew chicken, curry goat, and oxtail. Patties—made in-house—are sold individually or by the dozen, and hard-dough bread is available by the loaf. There's a constant flow of customers picking up takeout and catering orders while others dive into big plates of food. It's a lively place where everyone seems to know each other and the staff add to the friendliness and familiarity.

I am particularly fond of the chicken soup, available as a daily special. Thick with potatoes and chicken, the secret ingredient is a good dumpling. Nothing delicate about this dumpling; it's huge and one of the most dense I've seen in Caribbean cuisine. And the broth is good too. Just watch out for those chicken bones.

The same can be said for the jerk chicken. It's bony. But goo-ood. As in reach-for-the-fire-extinguisher good. I'm amazed when I see regulars adding hot sauce to their jerk. I'm ablaze with the dish as it is. Regardless, tender and meaty pieces of chicken are coated in fragrant spices, the nutmeg and cinnamon standing up to the heat. Served with a plate of rice and beans for $9.50, it's a hearty meal. If you're into milder things, try the brown stew chicken or one of their "Western" dishes such as the chicken fingers.

Dutchie's has a self-serve cooler filled with Old Jamaica ginger beer and sorrel, mango, and soursop beverages to complete the Caribbean taste. I usually go with water cold enough to numb my taste buds, even if just for a minute. Then I'm back for more. This is addictive food, even if it does hurt a little.

Eden

Fine French Cuisine with New World Influences

Mountain Avenue, Banff (The Rimrock Resort Hotel)
Phone: 762 • 1865
Daily 6 pm – 10 pm
Reservations recommended — Fully licensed — Non-smoking
V, MC, AE, DC, JCB — $$$

THE view from Eden is both stunning and surprising. Banff-dazzled tourists and locals alike are often unaware that the "main" floor of the Rimrock Hotel—which includes Eden—is actually the seventh floor. (Driving up to a seventh floor entrance always make me chuckle. I know, I'm easily amused.)

It's because the Rimrock clings to the side of Sulphur Mountain, and half the hotel flows down into the valley. Guest rooms and dining rooms all benefit from the architectural uniqueness of the building. At night, lighting illuminates the trees so that you don't miss the view even in the dark.

Eden is the main dining room in the Rimrock; it's a long, narrow space where all tables feature that view. It's similar to a cruise ship dining room: tables are lined in two long rows with a walkway down the middle. Likewise, service follows the best of cruise ships and hotels: it is impeccable from end to end. Servers know how to present and clear plates, how to suggest appropriate wines, how to make each diner feel comfortable and special.

Once ensconced in Eden, it is difficult to leave. We felt so well taken care of on our last visit that we hoped someone would just roll us back to our room and tuck us in. A meal here is not some dashed-off quickie. Allow a good three hours—we were there almost five hours that last time.

You are offered a choice between five multi-course tasting menus. Three of the menus are eight courses each ($95 per person, plus $50 for an optional flight of accompanying wines); the fourth is a nine-course blowout ($125, plus $60 for the wines); and the fifth is a ten-course degustation extravaganza ($500, but you get some pretty spiffy wines with that). A whole lot of bucks but a lot of very fine food too.

Lobster bisque with truffle foam, foie gras with celery root purée, seared scallop with porcini cream, Valrhona chocolate truffle cake, and more. All perfectly prepared and served in portions for savouring, not for gluttonizing. As much attention is given to the colour and style of the plate as to the taste. No effort, or price, has been spared to collect the finest ingredients for the menus.

Dining at Eden is a memorable event. It takes time and stamina and a healthy bank account, but it is worth it. Even if just for the view.

www.rimrockresort.com

Fleur de Sel

French Brasserie

2015 – 4 Street SW
Phone: 228 • 9764
Tuesday – Friday 11 am – 2 pm
Monday – Sunday 5 pm – last customer
Reservations recommended — Fully licensed
Non-smoking dining room, 4 smoking seats at bar
V, MC, AE, DC, Debit — $$ – $$$

W E Westerners like our wide open spaces, not only outside but inside too. And that includes restaurants. Cram us too close together and we get fidgety and cranky. But in a tiny brasserie like Fleur de Sel, the closeness is actually endearing.

Referring to restaurants back home, a Parisian friend once said to me, "We like to kiss zee elbows." Meaning they like to sit close together. I think that tradition has more to do with the general tininess of Parisian restaurants and the price of real estate there, but regardless, that tightness has been carried over into Fleur de Sel.

On a busy night, Fleur de Sel hums with activity as professional waiters slide through impossibly narrow spaces to deliver steaming pots of cassoulet and slabs of beef tenderloin glazed with a robust bordelaise sauce. The aromas flowing from the open kitchen meld together to pique appetites as the volume of sound increases. On special occasions, an accordion player may be perched on a small platform above the door, adding to the reminiscence of France. And as long as the few smokers stay to the far end of the bar, the scent is almost appropriate to the food style.

Owner Patrice Durandeau is almost always present, either in the kitchen or out front helping his staff. A native of the southwest of France, he embraces the rustic side of brasserie cuisine with ceramic bowls of choucroute (sauerkraut) and smoked pork chops and Spolumbo sausage. But he also shows elegance in his chicken with basil and his chocolate mousse and creativity in his beef served with pickled ginger and glace de viande. And if you're looking for a good lunch sandwich, his grilled salmon in a baguette with a side of greens is a bargain at $12.

The menu is reasonably priced, with an onion soup topped with three cheese-laden croutons for $8 (it's a meal in itself—and a good one too) and a combo of tuna and beef tenderloins for $23. The basic cassoulet and that choucroute are $21 each.

Fleur de Sel is a tiny 4th Street gem. Even the washrooms are worth a visit, but park any political correctness at the door; they are not for the meek. There is life here, character in abundance, and food quality that brings us back time and again, no matter how close the tables.

www.fleurdeselbrasserie.com

Galaxie Diner

Diner

1413 – 11 Street SW
Phone: 228 • 0001
Monday – Friday 7 am – 3 pm, Saturday, Sunday & Holidays 8 am – 4 pm
Reservations not accepted — No alcoholic beverages — Non-smoking
Cash only — $

Patience is a virtue, so they say. "They" obviously have never had to stand in line at the Galaxie Diner on a weekend morning, pangs of hunger clawing at their innards, shards of caffeine withdrawal poking at their brains. "They" must have room service or a private table or curbside delivery somewhere.

How can we be patient when we smell the bacon on the grill just centimetres away and see the mocha-scented steam wafting out of the coffee pots as staff wheel through the room? How can we be calm and kind to our fellow Calgarians when they're sipping their third refills and are not only reading their papers, but spreading them out on the tables? And they're still picking at their toast. (It's good toast too, thick and buttered and slathered with strawberry jam.) If they're not going to eat it, they should at least pass some on to one of us in line for heaven's sake!

The lineup at the Galaxie is not a place to test one's kindness to one's fellow man. The wait can be short or it can be excruciatingly long. The time varies inversely with the need. It's that kind of place: no reservations, cash only, keep smiling.

So what to do? Review the list of diner options posted on the menu board over the lunch counter. Look next door to see if the Palace of Eats is open yet—maybe a smoked meat sandwich would slake the appetite. Stare at the kitschy diner knick-knacks. Kibitz with your fellow lineup crew. Lean into the room, cough, and declare raspingly that you hope you are past the infectious stage by now (can't these people see we're in need here?).

But we are genteel Canadians. We only think about that last idea as we wait passively for our turn at the breakfast burrito. Eventually it arrives and we get to sink into a Naugahyde booth or park ourselves at two of the swivelling counter stools. It's our turn to dive into a hot breakfast and spread out the paper. It's our turn to sip our refills and wash away the gnaw of hunger and caffeine need. And it's our turn to ignore those less fortunate waiting in line and to pick at that last piece of toast.

They must learn to be patient. On my full stomach, I can now see that it is indeed a virtue. For others.

www.galaxiediner.com

Glory of India

Indian

515 – 4 Avenue SW
Phone: 263 • 8804
Monday – Friday 11:30 am – 2 pm, Monday – Saturday 5 pm – 10 pm
Reservations recommended — Fully licensed — Patio — Non-smoking
V, MC, AE, DC, JCB, Debit — $$

W E'VE got Mughlai, Bengali, Gujarati, and scads of Punjabi restaurants in Calgary. So the arrival of Glory of India in 2002 didn't make me sit up and notice. But when I sampled some of their tandoori chicken at a Taste of Calgary event, my interest was piqued.

We decided to pop in one evening and had one of the best Indian meals of our lives. The food was richly, intensely flavoured with a barrage of spices skillfully blended. The ingredients were fresh and of high quality, and the selection was intriguing. Glory of India really impressed us.

It is run by trained, experienced food professionals who describe their menu as Delhi-style, meaning that it's a collection of dishes from across India but with a strong Punjabi presence. We ordered four dishes, three of which were vegetarian— the paneer makhani, the aloo gobi, and the Pindi chole. The single meat dish we had was the chicken Chatinard.

The paneer, a house-made cheese, came in one of the most popular Indian sauces, the creamy, tomatoey makhani sauce. It was as rich and silky as I could hope for, a dense and complex dressing for the excellent, firm paneer. I was even more impressed with the Pindi chole, a chickpea dish that in some restaurants comes with a thin, one-dimensional sauce, as if the chickpeas don't really matter because, after all, they're just chickpeas. These chickpeas were well respected and elevated by a sauce that wafted mango powder and cinnamon to our noses. Then there was the aloo gobi of potatoes and cauliflower, the vegetables still firm in a dryish ginger-garlic coating. Nice, nice food.

Best of all was the chicken Chatinard, a dish from South India. Hot with chilies and dark with turmeric, nutmeg, and other aromatic spices, it was one of the most outstanding Indian chicken dishes I've ever had.

And the prices aren't bad. All the vegetarian dishes are under $10, with most meat and fish dishes under $16. They do not skimp out on the servings either. We had plenty of food to take home for lunch the next day.

Glory of India has also become popular for its lunchtime buffet. At $12.95 for a lengthy spread, it's an excellent deal and an efficient way to have lunch. If you can get a seat, that is. On lots of weekdays they turn away as many people as they can hold in their 120-seat restaurant.

www.gloryofindia.com

Golden Inn

Chinese (Cantonese)

107A – 2 Avenue SE
Phone: 269•2211
Monday – Thursday 4 pm – 3 am
Friday & Saturday 4 pm – 4 am, Sunday 4 pm – 2 am
Reservations accepted — Fully licensed — Non-smoking
V, MC, AE, Debit — $ – $$

My goodness, what has the world come to? The Golden Inn, long the grotty post-midnight choice of many Calgary night owls, has cleaned up its act. There is fresh paint, new carpet, dishes that aren't chipped, and what appears to be softer lighting. There's even an intriguing piece of sculptural art on the wall. And at certain times of the day, there are tablecloths. Can this be the same place?

The Golden Inn has been a Chinatown fave for decades. I remember going there in the seventies when I was still ambulatory in the wee hours. Back then and even as recently as a couple of years ago, it wasn't much to look at. But devotees have always sworn by the food, not the appearance.

The Golden Inn has maintained a high level of Cantonese cuisine over the years. The lengthy menu—over 150 items on the printed list with more items available for the asking—features the fresh, natural flavours of Canton. The seasoning is delicate, aimed at enhancing those natural flavours.

So the clams in black-bean sauce are not inundated with spice—the mollusks still have a presence under the saucy coating. And a dish of pea shoots in crab sauce allows the freshness of the greens to balance lightly with the creaminess of the sauce. These are subtle flavours, perhaps lost on those looking only for a big hit of Szechwan cuisine. Even the hot and sour soup does not have the intensity of the Western Chinese version. This one has a lighter background. It's still good, but your tongue won't be vibrating after a bowl of it.

The Golden Inn is a fine place to meet friends for a table-covering and stomach-filling meal. We ordered six dishes for five of us and had leftovers—these are large servings. The roasted rock-salt prawns and the roasted chicken Chinese-style were both big hits and disappeared quickly. And the clams, soup, pea shoots, and some Chinese broccoli in oyster sauce were all popular. It was nice food.

And I even have to compliment the service, a rarity for the Golden Inn. Most times it's perfunctory and utilitarian. Maybe we hit them on a good night or maybe it's just part of the upgrade. They were smiley and helpful and brisk, even in the face of a packed room.

So some things have changed at the Golden Inn. But I sort of miss the grottiness.

Grizzly House

Fondue & Exotic Game

207 Banff Avenue, Banff
Phone: 762·4055
Daily 11:30 am – midnight
Reservations recommended — Fully licensed — Patio — Totally smoking
V, MC, AE, Debit — $$ – $$$

I never lost The Faith. I bought my first fondue pot in 1973 when boiling small pieces of meat in oil was all the rage. I got my second in 1987 after a trip to Switzerland convinced my wife and me that coating bread in melted cheese is a great dinner-party activity. Both pots have been used frequently around our house.

Sure, there were those times in the 1990s when dinner guests would express surprise that we were still using our fondue pots. But I knew that sooner or later my Faith in Fondue would be recognized. And now fondues are back.

I was not alone in my years of fondue wilderness. Banff's Grizzly House has served fondues in various shapes, sizes, and tastes since 1967. On any given day, all 120 seats are filled with fork-wielding, oil-dipping, cheese-coating fans gorging on their favourite style. And I mean any given day—the Grizzly House is open every day of the year. (Not only are they unique in their commitment to being open all those days, but they are also the only place in this book that does not have even the tiniest non-smoking section. Fortunately, the smell of cooking meat usually dominates the room.)

A complete fondue dinner (for a minimum of two) is an easy way to enjoy a variety of styles. A soup or salad sets up your palate for an assault of three fondues. First there is an appetizer of either a cheese or a vegetable fondue. That's followed by a main course fondue, a choice of six meaty options, from the beef and either chicken or ostrich dinner ($32 per person) or the "Hunter" dinner of buffalo, wild boar, and venison ($39 per person) to the "Exotic" dinner of shark, alligator, rattlesnake, ostrich, frog legs, buffalo, and venison ($48 per person). A lower-oil option for this course is to cook the meats on "hot rocks," slabs of granite that have been heated in the oven. Instead of skewering and oil-dipping the meats, you add a bit of butter to the sizzling granite and toss your meat on. The main courses are served with five sauces, providing a tasty variety of flavours. To finish your meal, you get a Toblerone chocolate fondue with fresh fruit for dipping.

This style of dining remains a great way for visiting with friends. It takes awhile, but the staff keep the food coming. It's a fine feed and just reward for keeping The Faith.

www.banffgrizzlyhouse.com

The Gypsy

International Bistro & Wine Bar

817 – 1 Street SW
Phone: 263 • 5869
Monday – Thursday 11:30 am – 10:30 pm
Friday 11:30 am – 11:30 pm, Saturday 4:30 pm – 11:30 pm
Reservations recommended — Fully licensed — Patio — Non-smoking
V, MC, AE, DC, Debit — $$

WHEN Divino moved into its new digs on Stephen Avenue Walk in the spring of 2003, the old 1st Street Divino became The Gypsy. To freshen its look, owner Witold Twardowski (he had owned Divino in partnership with Connie and Pat O'Connor of Canadian Rocky Mountain Resorts) washed the old space in rich red paint and lit it with tasselled lamps. A friend of mine says it reminds him of the bordello windows in Amsterdam's red-light district. It's a tone that works with the dark wood and high ceilings of the building. And the Love Shop sign still hangs in the front window.

The layout hasn't changed—the chairs and tables are still worked around the basic floor plan of the two old stores that make up the space. But the wine bar has been reduced in size to create a little extra room. The restaurant is more open and airy in some spots, but remains tightly packed in others, which means those corners for quiet conversations or business discussions are still there. And thankfully, they have padded the chairs.

The menu has remained similar to that of the old Divino, but the theme has been reinterpreted a bit to represent the far-ranging, wandering nature of gypsies. So you'll find a variety of dishes, from penne with prawns and sun-dried currants to Thai green-curry chicken and eggplant with couscous. Many of the dishes are Divino favourites such as the black-pepper linguine and the ginger rotini with grilled chicken and red grapes. Daily specials bring more variation and seasonal specialties. It's a roving menu.

The service is pleasant enough and the food is fine, very much like the old Divino. A daily soup of butternut squash was a bit too thick but still tasty, and the lamb burger was freshly prepared. It could have been a little bigger and put together more evenly, but otherwise, the flavours were good. And there is a nice range of wines available by the glass and a list of daily desserts to round out the meal.

So The Gypsy sets up a lot like the old Divino—changes from the Divino days are mostly cosmetic. It remains a stylish, pleasant place that brightens with the sun at lunchtime and becomes sultrier in the evening. And it is still a reasonable place for a business lunch, a late-afternoon glass of wine, or a relaxing dinner.

Harbour City

Chinese (Cantonese & Peking)

302 Centre Street S
Phone: 269·8888
Sunday – Thursday 9 am – 2 am, Friday & Saturday 9 am – 4 am
Reservations recommended — Fully licensed — Non-smoking
V, MC, AE, DC, Debit — $$

WHAT would you call a group of restaurant reviewers? A gaggle? A murder? A glutton?

Occasionally, a gang of us food writers swarms a place for lunch so we can catch up on each other's finds, share inside stories, and nosh on some good food. One of the places where we have met is Harbour City, a sizable and unpretentious place on the shores of Centre Street.

Harbour City fits our needs. They have tables that can accommodate our group, they don't care who we are or what we're doing there, and the food is fast, furious, and flavourful. And at lunch they offer the option of ordering off an extensive 160-item menu or indulging in the quick decisions of the dim sum trolley.

There's something about dim sum that attracts the gamblers in us. Just what is going to be inside the next pile of steamer trays or under those metal lids? Will it be shrimp dumplings or duck feet? Some delicacy or another round of sticky rice?

Being a group, we just keep loading up the table. The steamers empty quickly. Salt and pepper squid and spareribs in black-bean sauce are disposed of in seconds. Rounds of dumplings come and go, and slippery rice pancakes are sucked back.

Dim sum requires not only lightning-quick choices but also table-management skills. Someone needs to remember if a particular dish has been ordered before and must also be sure that if new supplies are brought in, there will be enough for everyone. Pacing is vital. We don't want to overload on the first dishes if something better will be coming later. But neither do we want to miss any choice morsels that will disappear quickly. There's so much pressure.

Harbour City is set up well for dim sum. Tables are arranged so that the carts can easily flow through the room and deliver food efficiently. In most places, savvy dim summers will stake out a table near the kitchen door to get the food hotter, faster, and more reliably. But at Harbour City, that isn't as crucial. Tables seem to be served equitably.

Still, there is little room for dithering. The staff seem reluctant to stop moving, delivering the goods while on the go. They will pause briefly to display their fare, but any hesitation will see them head off to the next table.

Fortunately our clutch of critics barely skips a beat while ordering. We're pros.

The Highwood

Culinary School

1301 – 16 Avenue NW (John Ware Building, SAIT)
Phone: 284·8615
Monday – Friday for lunch, Monday – Thursday for dinner
Reservations essential — Fully licensed — Non-smoking
V, MC, Debit — $$

How can one of Calgary's most popular restaurants also be one of Calgary's most unknown restaurants? The Highwood is an enigma that way. Its location upstairs in SAIT's John Ware Building nominates it for obscurity to all except those who know the campus well. It has zero street presence and a limited marketing budget. But just try to get a reservation and you may well be told that the wait is months.

How is that possible?

The Highwood is the dining room attached to SAIT's Business and Tourism Department. So the cooks and the service staff are all students preparing for careers in the hospitality industry. They are trained and supervised by a staff of professionals, and they work hard to make dining at The Highwood a memorable experience. The food is always good, the culinary ideas are fresh, and the price is right.

As a student-run operation, The Highwood follows restricted hours. So lunch seatings are only weekdays from 11:30 a.m. to 12:15 p.m., except Thursdays when a buffet is rolled out at 11 a.m. The dining room is also open evenings from Monday through Thursday with reservations taken for 6 p.m., 6:30 p.m., and 7 p.m.

Prices have gone up in recent times, but cost recovery—with just a little profit—is the watchword. Overall, it's good value. A multi-course dinner is now $32.50 per person and typically includes a choice of appetizers, such as tempura vegetables and shrimp or smoked chicken agnolotti in a saffron sauce, followed by a freshly prepared soup. Then there's a choice of salads and a decision between six or seven main courses such as lobster bouillabaisse or a grilled vegetable napoleon with curried lentils. A final choice of dessert or a cheese arrangement finishes dinner. Lunch, except for Thursday's buffet, is à la carte with an asparagus and duck breast salad for $4.50; a beef, Merlot, and portobello pot pie for $8; and roasted monkfish for $9. All desserts are $3.50.

The food ideas are literally all over the map and the menus are in constant flux—this is a school after all. But the meals are interesting, and the kitchen is beautifully accessorized to accommodate any food style. If there is a downside, it's that the experience can be variable depending on the skills of the students and how far along they are in their studies. But that's a big part of the charm of The Highwood.

www.sait.ab.ca

Il Sogno

Italian (Neapolitan)

24 – 4 Street NE
Phone: 232 • 8901
Tuesday – Friday 11:30 am – 2 pm, Sunday 10:30 am – 2 pm
Tuesday – Sunday 5 pm – last guest
Reservations recommended, especially on weekends — Fully licensed — Non-smoking
V, MC, AE, DC — $$ – $$$

SUNDAY is a day for leisurely activity, and for me that includes relaxed dining. But much as I will wade into any buffet line during a weekday lunch, most Sunday buffet brunches leave me cold. Aside from my predilection for a calm, well-served brunch, I find so many Sunday buffets to be of inadequate quality or to offer too many food styles at one time to do any exceptionally. And few places put as much effort into the Sunday brunch as they do into the Saturday night dinner.

But one spot that continues to impress me is Il Sogno, the lovely Italian restaurant in Bridgeland. On most Sunday mornings, the owners—who are also the chef and the maître d'—are present, showing serious commitment to their à la carte menu, especially after a late Saturday night. They are there to ensure that the menu and the service are being executed in a way that makes them and their customers happy. (Just try to find an owner present at most Sunday brunches.)

This is no slapdash brunch. It matches the other efforts of Il Sogno. Chef-owner Giuseppe Di Gennaro creatively combines traditional styles and ingredients (like goat-cheese stuffed ravioli or grilled polenta) with global ones (like sablefish; cantaloupe and black-pepper marmalade; or dried cranberries) to create sumptuous dishes throughout the day.

And at brunch you'll find fontina melted over poached asparagus with prosciutto and a fried egg on the side. Or a frittata of zucchini, basil, and provolone presented with fresh greens. Or charbroiled wild boar sausage under smoked provolone and roasted peppers in a balsamic reduction. All served with a radicchio leaf filled with fresh fruit—a nice touch. It's forceful, colourful food, as satisfying to the eye as to the palate. The flavours fill the plate and bounce off the tongue with intensity.

If brunch requires an indulgent dessert, then Il Sogno is happy to accommodate. Crème brûlée, warm chocolate cake with vanilla ice cream, a trio of sorbets are all available. Plus Illy coffee, a fitting beverage for the food and the time of day.

The tone of Il Sogno is almost as important as the food. The two high-ceilinged, well-linened rooms are impressively simplistic and at the opposite end of the spectrum from the Italian checkered-tablecloth look. Which makes it softer on the eyes on a Sunday morning.

A treat for the eyes and the palate. Now that's Sunday brunch.

www.ilsogno.org

Indochine

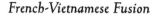

French-Vietnamese Fusion

315 Stephen Avenue Walk SW (+15 Level, Bankers Hall)
Phone: 263 • 6929
Monday – Wednesday 11 am – 7 pm, Thursday – Saturday 11 am – 9 pm
Reservations recommended — Fully licensed — Non-smoking
V, MC, AE, DC, Debit — $$

I love food that jumps up and grabs me by the tonsils. Food with flavour that makes me take notice. Food that can't be ignored.

That's one of the things I like about Indochine, the stylish restaurant in Bankers Hall. Their French-Vietnamese cuisine employs curries and lemon grass and ginger with force. They don't just hint at it: when you order lemon grass chicken, it comes coated with the stuff, plus some chilies to warm it up and loads of onion and green peppers to balance it off.

It's also sumptuous food that feels almost decadent in its richness. The coconut chicken curry, for instance, features tender chicken chunks swimming with potatoes and carrots in a flavourful, creamy sauce.

And it is almost too pretty to eat. It's plated beautifully with banana leaves curled around your rice and a flower decorating your plate. The combination of colours and textures is as tantalizing as the taste.

The flavours and the flowers come courtesy of owner Yvonne Nhan, who also operates the Garden Follies flower shop across the Plus-15 in Gulf Canada Square. You can see her sense of style in the elegant French bistro tones of the space too. Done in shades of brown and white, the restaurant could just as easily be serving duck confit and crème brûlée as green papaya salad and spring rolls. And in fact, they do make a fine crème brûlée. That's part of the French angle of their fusion cuisine, along with things like a good steak frites, the crepe d'Indochine, and a salmon niçoise.

Indochine's unique indoor patio bustles during weekday lunches as the crowds descend from the office towers above. Black-clad staff quickly satisfy customers who promptly buzz back to their offices at 1 p.m. (well, most do). Later in the day and in the evening, Indochine is a quiet and relaxed place for a meal.

Prices reflect the tony downtown location. This is no little noodle shop. The lemon grass chicken is $15, the steak frites, $19. An order of salad rolls is $6, more than they will cost in most Vietnamese cafés.

But it is sophisticated cuisine that is worth the price. Indochine has been packed for lunch almost every day since it opened in 1997, and for good reason. It seems a lot of people enjoy food that grabs you by the tonsils.

Indulge

Casual Gourmet

620 – 8 Avenue SW
Phone: 229•9029
Monday & Tuesday 7 am – 4 pm, Wednesday – Friday 7 am – 10 pm
Saturday 5 pm – 10 pm
Reservations accepted for evenings — Fully licensed — Non-smoking
V, MC, AE, DC, Debit — $ – $$

INDULGE started life as a catering operation that needed a downtown cooking facility. The owners found a space with a large kitchen in the back and a small café out front and they moved in, allowing them easier access to their downtown customers. They were surprised to discover how popular the café became almost instantly.

It doesn't have a flashy decor. It resembles a seventies granola bar with a counter cutting off the kitchen from the dining area, some square wooden tables, and minimal decoration. You step up to the counter to order from overhead chalkboards, which is difficult because, once you are close enough to order, you can't actually see the chalkboards anymore. So you have to do that shuffle of stepping back and forth to see the boards as you place your order. As I said, it's like a seventies granola bar. It's not complex, just a bit awkward.

But worth every moment of awkwardness. The menu follows a fairly simple format, but the chefs really know their stuff. A red-lentil soup was one of the best I've had. A carrot-apple soup was just as good. And sandwiches of grilled vegetables and ham with Asiago were great. There was nothing fancy about these preparations—they were just intelligent, simple, and not overworked. Sweets are much the same way: simple and intense. Their brownies are dense, rich, chocolatey squares, and the sun-dried cranberry scones are a buttery, flaky effort. The value is excellent too. It's easy to get away with lunch for under $10, and breakfasts are mostly under $7.

On the catering side, they do things like tequila-lime prawns; pear, Gorgonzola, and caramelized onion strudel; and crab cakes served with mango cream and whitefish caviar. But they also do breakfast quesadillas, sandwiches, and coleslaw. They can get as complex or as simple as their clients wish.

Indulge is a comfortable environment, the kind of place where it feels okay to sit for a while and read the morning paper or to catch up with friends over lunch. It's a fine place for a little indulgence in the heart of downtown.

Note: About the same time this book appears, Indulge will be expanding into evening tasting menus with table service. Featuring smaller portions for $7 to $15, the menu will include various pizzas, pastas, and whatever else inspires the chefs that day.

www.indulge-catering.com

Istanbul

Turkish

2005B – 4 Street SW
Phone: 229·0542
Monday – Saturday 11 am – 11 pm
Sunday 4 pm – 10 pm
Reservations recommended — Fully licensed — Patio — Non-smoking
V, MC, AE, DC, Debit — $$

THE ISTANBUL has managed to succeed in a space that has housed too many unlucky restaurants. This is a good 4th Street address, but for various reasons, at least four restaurants have come and gone from it.

When the Istanbul moved in, they made some good decisions. They kept the ceramic tile floor (I think that appeared during a Mexican phase), painted the walls in Mediterranean tones of off-white and deep blue, and topped the tables with linens. They draped some Turkish carpets on the walls and hired a belly dancer for weekend entertainment. And they introduced a solid and sensible Turkish menu that they had refined in their former 14th Street location.

The menu spans the familiar Eastern Mediterranean dishes of kebabs, stuffed grape leaves, calamari, and baklava. But it also presents less commonly seen Turkish specialties like white-bean salad, beef-stuffed baby eggplants, and Turkish-style pizzas called pide. All this means that customers can go as comfortable or as exotic as they want.

I particularly enjoy the white-bean salad for its blend of beans, tomatoes, onions, parsley, and sumac. It's a gentle salad—the balance is excellent. Don't expect it to be overly intense, just nicely fresh. The lamb kebabs, two skewers of marinated lamb interspersed with onions and green peppers, are well prepared. So many places use cheap and gristly meats on their kebabs, but not the Istanbul. This is good lamb and that makes all the difference. It's tender and tasty and not overcooked. Served with a pile of rice and various grilled vegetables, it's a great plate of food for a reasonable $14.

When I visit the Istanbul, I have to finish dinner with my favourite Turkish dish, sutlac (rice pudding). Theirs is as good as my years-old memory of the ones I had in Turkey, with creamy rice topped by crushed pistachios and cinnamon. Lovely.

The Istanbul is a family-run restaurant where there is skill in the kitchen and warmth in the welcome. It blends the richness of a home-cooked meal with the skill of professional restaurateurs. The service is always pleasant, and the wine list is short and intelligent. This is the kind of place where you can have a quick and light meal or a serious feast.

It was about time someone turned this ill-fated room into a winner. It is a much better location than its history reveals. And a great place for Calgary's only Turkish restaurant.

Jacqueline Suzanne's

International

1219–9 Avenue SE
Phone: 266•1005
Monday – Friday 11 am–close, Saturday & Sunday 10 am–close
Reservations accepted — Fully licensed — Non-smoking
V, MC, AE, DC, Debit — $–$$

OCCASIONALLY when I'm pressed for time and feeling culinarily challenged, I'll pop into one of the much-hyped sandwich chains for a fast bite. I'm not expecting anything great, just something reasonably edible, filling, and cheap. But when I paid over $7 one day for a mediocre sandwich stuffed into a plastic bag by someone with a surly attitude, I realized that this wasn't necessarily great value. And a nice lunch at Jacqueline Suzanne's the next day confirmed that.

First things first. No, Jacqueline Suzanne's has nothing to do with the steamy fiction writer, though the name is definitely an eye-catcher. Two women, Jacqueline Troughton and Suzanne Dale, own the place. Ergo the name.

Jacqueline Suzanne's is in an old storefront in Inglewood, a place with high tin ceilings and creaky hardwood floors. It was previously an Irish pub. The new team took it over in early 2003, and they have created a wonderful space, one that is visually interesting and relaxing. There are two levels to it—a thirty-six-seat main floor and a twelve-seat mezzanine. That mezzanine has a ceiling a little over six feet high, so beware all you tall folks. The room is done in brocaded greens and purples, elegant tones that fit the historic backdrop. And at the time of this writing, there were plans to include an antique shop as part of the business.

But back to my lunch. I had a sandwich made from beef tenderloin that had been roasted, sliced, doused with a horseradish-lime sauce, and piled into a whole wheat roll. It came with a bowl of tomato-based chicken and vegetable soup. The soup was deeply flavoured, a great concoction. And the sandwich was superb. The only problem? There was so much tenderloin that it kept falling out of the bun. And the price? All of $10.95. For that, I got to sit in a nice room, be served by one of the very pleasant owners, have as much water as I wanted, and leave feeling better than when I arrived.

That sandwich is the most expensive thing on the lunch menu. The sake-poached salmon sandwich with wasabi aïoli is $10, and the Asian noodle salad is $8.25. At dinner, the tenderloin is again the priciest at $18, and this time it's served in a peppercorn sauce and with vegetables. The seared Grand Marnier scallops are $16.75, and the porcini ravioli is $15.

Nice room, fine service, excellent food, decent prices. Now that is real value.

James Joyce & The Joyce on 4th

Irish Pubs

DOWN town
That's the Spot

114 Stephen Avenue Walk SW
Phone: 262·0708
Daily 11:15 am – close

506 – 24 Avenue SW
Phone: 541·9168
Daily 11:30 am – close

Reservations recommended — Fully licensed — Patios — Non-smoking sections
V, MC, AE, Debit — $ – $$

WHEN the Irish pub craze hit, the James Joyce was one of the first and the best. With its restored downtown bank setting, its solid Irish furniture, and its Guinness at three temperatures, it became an instant hangout for many Irish expats and others who had never been anywhere near the Emerald Isle. They had lively bow-tied service and a menu to match the atmosphere: shepherd's pie, ploughman's lunch, steak and Guinness pie, fish and chips. All the high-calorie food that goes with pubs.

The original Joyce became so popular that they opened a second location on 4th Street SW. The Joyce on 4th is a bright, active room that's been done in dark wood with some oversized chairs and couches that add an Alice-in-Wonderland quality. There's a raised area that doubles as a stage for live performances and some Irish memorabilia throughout.

And, of course, there is that pub menu: Irish stew, chicken curry, potato nachos, and Irish boxties (potato pancakes with various fillings). There are actually some salads, but predominantly this is a high-starch, high-fat list. There's something called a "Martello Mix," a plate of breaded mushrooms, stuffed potato boats, and bacon-wrapped sausages. Not exactly delicate fare.

Arriving for lunch about 1 p.m., I found the new place totally packed and very smoky. It has a non-smoking area in the back, but you do have to walk through the smoking area to get there. And these are diligent pub smokers. I find the Stephen Avenue Joyce to have better air—maybe it's the higher ceiling. (Both locations have excellent non-smoking patios however.)

I typically have a ploughman's lunch of bread and cheese with sliced ham and greens if I'm moderately hungry or a steak and Guinness pie if I'm really famished. But I thought I'd try something different on this visit. I started lunch with a bowl of good lamb-vegetable soup. Then, continuing the theme, I had the lamb-pistachio burger topped with onion marmalade and blue cheese. Nice idea, but the burger was a touch overcooked, and it could have used more cheese and onions. But it came with some decent fries of course. That's something the Joyce does with consistency. And they should. If you can't get good chips in an Irish pub, where can you get them?

That, and a cool pint. That's always perfect too.

www.jamesjoycepub.com

www.joyceon4th.com

JoJo Bistro

French (Provençal)

917 – 17 Avenue SW
Phone: 245·2382
Monday – Friday 11:30 am – 2 pm, 5:30 pm – 10:30 pm, Saturday 5 pm – 10:30 pm
Reservations recommended — Fully licensed — Non-smoking
V, MC, AE, DC, Debit — $$ – $$$

REVIEWING JoJo is tricky. I can write with assurance that it is in the 900 block of 17th Avenue SW. I can tell you that it is capably run by Mohammed Guelli and his daughter Nabila-June. I can also say that the service is professional, and I'm confident that the cuisine is French. But beyond all that, I'm a little less than certain.

That's because the look of JoJo frequently changes, albeit subtly. As does the focus of the menu, although it always stays somewhere in the realm of French cuisine. In the summer of 2003, JoJo made more changes, opening up the space a bit. And by the time you read this, they will have introduced a Provençal menu.

JoJo is a long and narrow room à la many French bistros. It's casually elegant, with tables that are close, though not Paris-close—they have been spaced to allow for Western Canadian comfort. In its latest iteration, two rows of tables still fill the room, and the banquette seating is pushed against the walls. The bar has been shifted around in one end of the space, and a large window has been cut into the wall behind it, exposing the kitchen and its activity. The new opening also allows for more of the good French aromas to issue forth.

JoJo's food is always skillfully prepared. On our last visit for this book, we encountered a menu that was more in line with Contemporary French Bistro cuisine than the Provençal fare you will now find. There was chicken breast in a marjoram beurre blanc; duck peppered with orange and star anise; sole with a shrimp and spinach mousse; pâté; and endive salad with Roquefort and walnuts. Good food, prepared with intensity.

Our spinach salad with pancetta and goat cheese was well dressed and executed with balance. There was enough pancetta and cheese to create a sumptuous salad and to justify the $8.50 price. Likewise, a pork tenderloin topped with an apple-ginger chutney ($22) and a steak frites with bordelaise sauce ($22) satisfied us with the flavours and volume. Not that we're looking for "big" food. We just want appropriate saucing on the food and reasonable amounts of the advertised ingredients.

That you will get at JoJo, plus fine service and a good wine list. And always the added mystery of what the latest menu and look will be.

Jonas'

Hungarian

937 – 6 Avenue SW
Phone: 262 • 3302
Monday – Friday 11:30 am – 2 pm, Monday – Saturday 5 pm – 9 pm
Reservations recommended — Fully licensed — Non-smoking
V, MC, AE, Debit — $ – $$

NAMED after its Hungarian owner, Jonas' Restaurant has an Eastern European café feel. The room is long and narrow and windowless except for right at the front. The cinder-block walls are hung with Hungarian weavings, and diners gather in groups large and small. As your evening wears on, conversations will grow louder and laughter will break out. Soon the room will be as lively as a gypsy violinist. The energy is contagious.

And then there is the staff, friendly ladies who explain the food in loving terms. And they have good reason to be proud. The menu is a collection of Hungary's favourite foods. There's chicken paprikash, cabbage rolls, schnitzel, and even goulash. All the hearty, robust dishes with all the calories that have made Hungarian an outcast cuisine. But for those who want to be careful, most of the dishes are offered in small portions as well as large.

The liver dumpling soup ($2.45 for the small, $3.45 for the large) features delicately light dumplings swimming in an excellent chicken stock. Nothing heavy about this. For that, you can try the Hungarian goulash, thick with beans and sausage, a large serving of which would be a meal in itself ($3.45 for the small, $5.45 for the large).

A small entree of paprikash or cabbage rolls or schnitzel will cost $7.45, and these are servings many places would call large. Large entrees start at $5.90 for the cabbage pasta and top out at $9.95 for the breaded catfish or the beef stew. The paprikash has a velvety sweet pepper sauce combined with tender drop noodles and chunks of chicken. And the schnitzel with pan-fried potatoes is everything I expect in a schnitzel.

For dessert there are palacsintas—crepes with various fillings such as chocolate sauce and ground walnuts. The apricot one is particularly tasty, especially topped with colourful sprinkles and a little slice of pineapple.

The food goes well with the selection of Hungarian wines by the glass. The list has some of my favourite bargains from university days, wines such as Szeksardi and the always popular Bull's Blood—it's as robust as ever.

So Jonas' Restaurant is very good. Don't expect the elegance of a grand Hungarian dining room. Instead, expect a cozy Budapest café. As a Hungarian friend told us the night we saw her there, it's cheap and cheerful and easier than cooking at home.

www.jonasrestaurant.homestead.com

Juan's

Mexican

807–1 Street SW
Phone: 266•0051
Monday – Friday 11 am – 3 pm
Monday – Saturday 5 pm – close
(closing December 31, 2003)

#7, 232 Stephen Avenue Walk SW
Phone: 266•0051
Monday – Saturday 11 am – 10 pm
Patio

Reservations recommended — Fully licensed — Non-smoking
V, MC, AE, Debit — $$

DOWNTOWN Calgary has become a dining destination with scads of shiny new eateries offering trendy cuisine in sparkling, spacious settings. But some places have been around since before downtown became popular. Like Juan's. When Juan's opened beside the Grain Exchange building in 1989, it was an innovative effort in an area that was pretty quiet after lunch.

Juan Cruz, a hospitality industry professional, left the hotel business and launched his eponymous restaurant on 1st Street while Calgary was still in the glow of the Olympic Winter Games. His small thirty-seat café became instantly popular—Calgarians familiar with the beaches of Mexico and longing for a tasty reminder flocked to Juan's. And they still do. They come for the food, the atmosphere, and the welcome. Juan is a master host.

And in the summer of 2003, Juan joined the throng to Stephen Avenue by opening a new location there with double the seating, a larger kitchen, and a patio. As this book goes to press, plans are to run both locations for the balance of 2003 and then to close the original 1st Street space on December 31, 2003.

Regardless, Juan's taco-dipping, enchilada-chomping, Corona-guzzling fans will follow him anywhere. They love his pinto-bean soup and his chiles rellenos and his huevos rancheros. Regulars wait for the days when he whips up a batch of tamales stuffed with chicken, capers, olives, and a spicy red sauce. And his fresh salsa disappears by the bucketful. Mighty tasty.

He arguably makes the best enchiladas in the city. Three chicken enchiladas covered in a rich mole sauce run about $12 and make a satisfying meal. The enchiladas are filled with a reasonable amount of chicken, and the mole is always fresh and forceful. For those looking for a little more intensity, he cooks beef tenderloin tips in a sauce piqued by habanero chilies. And for those who prefer something mild, his chicken quesadillas provide a tasty but lightly spiced alternative.

It's always a good idea to leave room for dessert at Juan's. His crepas con cajeta—crepes filled with a caramel spread—are sweet and sultry. And his flan is one of the best. He mixes a mean margarita too.

www.juansmexican.com

Kane's Harley Diner

Diner

1209 – 9 Avenue SE
Phone: 269·7311
Daily 7 am – 8 pm
Reservations accepted — Fully licensed — Patio — Non-smoking
V, MC, AE, Debit — $ – $$

POUNDING the Harley through the Foothills can build an appetite. Wrangling a few hundred pounds of American steel into Calgary traffic—the wind blowing on our faces, our colours emblazoned on our leathers, Steppenwolf blaring from the speakers—gives us the growlies. So we pull our chopper into Kane's parking lot and stride into the diner with our leather chaps rustling and our wraparound sunglasses gleaming in the light.

In our dreams.

More likely we will park the Toyota between the Harleys out back and enter quietly. No chaps, no sunglasses, no Steppenwolf (well, maybe just a little on the car stereo).

We're wannabe bikers, happy to soak up the tone and the taste of Kane's Harley Diner without risking road rash. This is not a synthetic, pre-packaged chain restaurant. Kane's is for real, an outstandingly authentic Harley diner. It's in the old Kane's Harley Davidson shop and is owned by bike dealer Mick Cawthorn. His new bike shop is just across the alley and is a mecca for any Harley fan.

Kane's Harley Diner is done in Harley orange and black with a Harley logo built into the flooring, Harley posters on the walls, and even a Harley jukebox filled with great diner tunes. The room seats about a hundred in booths, at tables, and at a bar where the kick-rail is a collection of old mufflers. Staff are appropriately diner toned too. A pot of coffee is permanently affixed to their hands, and they serve the food fast and hot.

Although we only ride the Harley in our minds, we can eat with the best of the real bikers. Kane's does a mean "Fatboy Classic," a sixteen-ounce burger loaded with everything and served with excellent fries. And the clubhouse is a jaw-expanding sandwich of fine ingredients. They also carry biker classics such as grilled bologna sandwiches and Campbell's soup (at least they state up front that it is Campbell's). They even carry a selection of salads, but I'm not sure anyone has ever ordered one.

Catherine likes to chow down on their heavy-duty breakfast, especially the pancakes loaded with syrup and butter. Me, I like to suck back a cool one in the form of a vanilla milkshake served in the metal container—but I want a dirty glass with it please! We may be cream puffs when it comes to riding the road, but we're hard core in the dining room.

Get your motor running!

Kashmir

Indian (Mughlai)

507 – 17 Avenue SW
Phone: 244·2294
Tuesday – Saturday 5:30 pm – 10 pm
Sunday 5:30 pm – 9 pm
Reservations recommended — Fully licensed — Non-smoking
V, MC, AE, DC, Debit — $$

SOME Indian restaurants are known for the abundance of their buffets. Others are known for their speed and value, and still others for their rustic charm and intense spicing. At the Kashmir, it's mostly about the elegance of the food and the uniqueness of the flavours.

The Kashmir is one of the few Mughlai restaurants in the city. Its menu has similarities to many of our Northern Indian restaurants, but the use of nuts, fruit, and dairy is much higher here. Cream is used to balance the heat, crafting lovely flavours. The Kashmiri prawns come in a mild cream sauce with grated apple, and the paneer pasanda is layered with mashed potatoes, nuts, raisins, and another cream sauce.

Those ingredients, however, do not infiltrate all the dishes. A non-creamy Madras lamb curry is rated "very hot," and the vindaloo chicken is "very, very hot." And they mean it. Even the dishes marked simply "hot" have plenty of zip.

The meat dishes at the Kashmir are as deep and rich and sultry as at any Indian restaurant in the city. The Kashmir offers almost forty meat entrees, including a tasty list of prawns. But they also list twenty-five vegetarian entrees, ranging from a thickly sauced jalfrazie of bell peppers, onions, tomatoes, cauliflower, carrots, peas, and spices to a dhal makhani of kidney beans and black lentils with cream and butter. Plus there's a lengthy selection of breads, including the deep-fried batura, the lamb-stuffed keema, and the buttered paratha. Excellent variety and all done with skill.

Beware the size of the dishes at the Kashmir. They look small but eat big. They can also add up quickly. The vegetarian plates are around $10, the meats are about $13, and the prawn dishes are all $15. Not exorbitant for the quality, but dinner here is not cheap.

The space and the service match the tone of the food. The Kashmir is actually two rooms, prettily decorated, with windows facing 17th Avenue. It is discreetly Indian in decor with staff who quietly go about their business. They are not stoic; they simply provide a calm, helpful atmosphere for dining.

The Kashmir also has a short but well-chosen and reasonably priced wine list. Markups are astoundingly low with few bottles over $30. And the selections match the food well.

When we feel like elegant Indian fare, this is the place we go.

The King & I

Thai

822 – 11 Avenue SW
Phone: 264·7241
Monday – Thursday 11:30 am – 10:30 pm
Friday 11:30 am – 11:30 pm, Saturday 4:30 pm – 11:30 pm, Sunday 4:30 pm – 9:30 pm
Reservations recommended — Fully licensed — Non-smoking
V, MC, AE, DC, Debit — $$ – $$$

THE KING & I is the mature father figure of the burgeoning Thai food scene in Calgary. The oldest of a growing number of Thai restaurants, it continues to impress with the quality of its food, the strength of its service, and the comfort level of its space.

The King & I exudes the confidence and assurance of its years. It doesn't give the impression of trying too hard; it impresses with subtlety and variety. It presents the longest Thai menu in the city, ranging from crispy Thai spring rolls and a Phuket fish soup to galangal cashew pork and a Mekong lobster curry. Rich, tasty dishes.

One of the best ways to explore The King & I is at lunch with their combo specials. I usually end up having the seafood one because it always sounds so good and it's a great deal. For example, on one visit I had some crisp Thai shrimp and squid on coconut rice, a bowl of prawn curry, and a second bowl of seafood salad. At $11, it was a bargain, especially considering the high quality and abundance. I particularly enjoyed the crisp shrimp and squid. The curry was also good—creamy and coconutty. And the salad's brininess balanced the coconut and curry flavours, enhancing the entire meal. There was no skimping on the ingredients either.

Ordering off the regular menu, look for some of those seafood curries to rub up against $20. But the value is still there. Chicken dishes are in the mid-teens as are the beef and pork ones.

You can also find a good tapioca dessert topped with mango. For tapioca fans, this is a must. But be careful of dishes prepared in advance: I've had salad rolls that were made ahead of time where the thin rice pancakes had dried out and become tough. I assume this pre-preparation was done because of the bulk of traffic passing through The King & I, but the result was an unfortunate side note of good planning.

Service has remained solid over the years, the product of owner Mel Sanders constant presence. Sanders has been there since day one, and he keeps a strong hand on the tone of the place. His staff are cheerful and professional at the same time.

So the look here is contemporary and sleek, and the air is always filled with rich aromas. I say, long live The King! (& I).

Kootenay Park Lodge

Mountain Home-Style

Vermilion Crossing, 42 kilometres south of Trans-Canada on Highway 93
Phone: 762·9196
Mid-May – late September: Daily 8 am – 10 am, noon – 2 pm, 6 pm – 8 pm
Reservations recommended — Beer & wine only — Veranda
Non-smoking dining room & veranda
V, MC, AE — $$

UPON occasion we head out to the Radium Valley to enjoy the beauty of the area. We try to coordinate our trip to pass through Kootenay Park at the same time that the Kootenay Park Lodge dining room is open.

We stop there for more than just a meal and the obligatory bathroom break after two and a half driving hours. It's a joy to park the car, step out, and inhale. The cool, mountain-pine air is intoxicating and revitalizing. Even the buzz of traffic on Highway 93 can't break into the serenity of the surroundings.

Kootenay Park Lodge was built in 1923 by Canadian Pacific Railway as a wilderness lodge to accommodate adventurous tourists who felt the Chateau Lake Louise and the Banff Springs hotel were too cushy. In the eighty ensuing years, the main lodge has changed little. Built from huge logs, it is centred around a large stone fireplace. Outside, a veranda wraps around two sides, allowing protected seating on warm days. Inside, there's a homey feel with comfy couches and racks of books among the dining tables. Just sitting in the room brings a sense of relaxation and a return to the tones of the 1920s.

But Kootenay Park Lodge is not just about the history. Francis and Paul Holscher— a mother and son team—have turned it into a popular destination in recent years. They have revived a group of log cabins nestled into the trees for overnighters and have built a modern convenience store and park information centre for those passing through. And they have worked up a pretty tasty menu for the dining room too.

The breakfast menu includes fruit- and yogurt-filled crepes and a sundae of layered granola, fruit, and yogurt. Lunch offerings include their definitive club sandwich of thick slices of chicken, bacon, and tomato on homemade bread, great with their mountain fries.

The dinner menu is a collection of burgers, crepes, and pastas with a few mountainy dishes such as rainbow trout with hollandaise sauce and sirloin strips with mushrooms in a red-wine sauce. The chicken breast with satay-style peanut sauce shows off the Holschers' Dutch heritage. And for dessert, there may be fruit clafouti with raspberry sauce and whipped cream.

It's good food, flavour-enhanced and appetite-aided by the mountain air. Those CPR lodge builders knew what they were doing.

www.kootenayparklodge.com

La Brezza

Italian

990 – 1 Avenue NE
Phone: 262•6230
Monday – Friday 11:30 am – 2:30 pm, Daily 5:30 pm – 10 pm
Reservations recommended — Fully licensed — Non-smoking
V, MC, AE, Debit — $$

MANY restaurants are in buildings that were never meant to be restaurants. A lot are in former bank buildings, and a big whack are in extinct retail shops. But there are also a few in old houses. The most charming of these is La Brezza in Bridgeland.

La Brezza is in an old 1940s bungalow, the kind that had small rooms to begin with. Most of the walls have been removed to create a forty-four-seat dining room and an open bar. The kitchen is hidden behind the one remaining wall. It's cozy and pretty funky. La Brezza has been renovated a few times since it opened in the eighties, and it's now a contemporary blend of taupey colours under stylish track lighting.

Tables are as generously spaced as possible in such close confines. But if you have discreet things to discuss, this may not be the place—sound travels easily here and it doesn't have far to travel. Tables are also well linened and adorned with simple white napkins and normal-sized dishes, an increasing rarity these days.

The food at La Brezza is lively, almost "extreme" Italian. In an era when many chefs are striving for subtlety, La Brezza stills pushes the intensity to the top. The Caesar salad bites back with garlic and lemon. The dressing is thick and forceful. Every mouthful grabs your taste buds and dares you to chew. (I should point out that I like this, but some may find it too intense.)

Continuing the theme of extreme cuisine is a bowl of penne con salsiccie, a robust combination of al dente penne with nicely peppered and sauced sausage. The flavours assault the mouth. There is a wealth of tomato and mushroom and more garlic. There is also a fair bit of oil in the dish, so beware.

On the dinner menu is a long list of pastas including linguine scoglio with clams, calalmari, escargots, and shrimp; fettuccine alla Brezza in a pancetta-mushroom cream sauce; and lasagna primavera. There is a range of beef, seafood, veal, and chicken dishes too—the small kitchen puts out a major effort. Lunch choices are similar though the list is shorter.

And then there is Marco Abdi, the ultimate host. The irrepressible owner of La Brezza is almost always on hand to ensure that his customers are well served. He is an even larger component of the La Brezza experience than the house.

www.labrezza.ca

La Chaumière

Continental

139 – 17 Avenue SW
Phone: 228 • 5690
Monday – Friday 11:30 am – 2 pm, Monday – Saturday 6 pm – midnight
Reservations recommended — Fully licensed — Patio — Non-smoking
V, MC, AE, DC — $$$

OVER the years, La Chaumière has established itself as one of the premier restaurants in Calgary. The service is impeccable, the room is crisp and comfortable, the food is creative and of the highest quality. Dining at La Chaumière is always a superb experience.

And the truly amazing thing about La Chaumière? It's not that pricey. One might assume that Calgary's foremost Continental restaurant would cost heavily. Now to be sure, it's not cheap, but the most expensive item on the menu is a rack of lamb with caramelized onions and pumpkin seeds for $29.75. Okay, there is a chateaubriand for two at $62, but even that seems quite reasonable in a market where the $40 entree barrier has been breached more than once.

Most dinner entrees are in the $20s—magret of Muscovy duck lacquered with honey and almonds at $24.50 and buffalo rib-eye with oyster mushrooms at $26.50 for example. And lunch presents remarkable food for comparative bargains—grilled tuna on a seafood and spinach brandade for $16 and veal kidneys with mustard seeds for $13.50. But La Chaumière is not all about price—it's just a nice surprise that they have not pushed as high as some other places.

La Chaumière is first and foremost about high-quality dining experiences. And much of that is related to service. Under the tutelage of owners Joseph D'Angelus and Joe Mathes, two masters of service themselves, the staff are attentive in a classic, friendly style: there when they need to be, invisible when not.

And then there's the food. Executive chef and partner Bob Matthews cooks up a creative storm with foie gras and Galloway beef and locally grown heirloom tomatoes. He brings great flavours to the table by combining his classic training with his experience cooking at places such as the Canadian embassy in Tokyo. A local boy, Matthews started his culinary career at La Chaumière before spending some years abroad. Now back in Calgary, he brings skill and talent to the kitchen.

Then there's flexibility. La Chaumière provides dining options ranging from intimate seating for couples and small groups in the dining room to a private room for up to a dozen. A larger room is available for functions, and a west-facing patio offers al fresco dining. Events are also held in the temperature-controlled wine cellar.

It all comes together at La Chaumière. It remains one of the best of the best.

www.lachaumiere.ca

La P'tite Table

French

52 North Railway Street, Okotoks
Phone: 938·2224
Tuesday – Friday 11 am – 1:30 pm, Tuesday – Saturday 5:30 pm – 10 pm
Reservations recommended — Fully licensed — Patio — Non-smoking restaurant & patio
V, MC, Debit — $$ – $$$

PERHAPS it's fitting that the oldest building to house a restaurant in our area showcases French cuisine. La P'tite Table is located in the old Okotoks Post Office, built in 1882, and it serves food whose origins are even older.

La P'tite Table is owned and operated by Paris Hotel School graduates Cidallia and Thierry Meret. They settled in Okotoks in 1996 to run their own restaurant and to raise a family. Since then, they have expanded the restaurant (it now has thirty-eight seats plus a patio) and built a loyal clientele from both the Okotoks area and Calgary.

The restaurant has been shaped by the post office building and an extension that has been seamlessly added. Windows splash sunlight in, and on pleasant days, there is seating on a small patio. The walls are covered with framed photos of France, and the ceramic tile floor creates a Mediterranean terrace look. It is casual and elegant, a perfect backdrop for the food.

The menu ranges from lunchtime omelettes, quiches, croque-monsieur sandwiches, and bouillabaisse to dinnertime duck breasts with orange and cranberry sauce and lamb loins with goat-cheese crusts. It's skillfully, classically prepared, but is neither the overweighted French food of decades past nor the ultra-light machinations of Nouvelle cuisine. The flavours are clean and sharp, the plates are full of intensity, and the vegetables are always treated as well as the meats.

At one recent lunch, I had an open-face sandwich of duck confit with melted brie and roasted walnuts on house-made ciabatta. Excellent ingredients, perfectly prepared to allow the confit to blend with the cheese and nuts.

Thierry Meret is a master of the subtle touch: My daily soup of ginger-tinged cauliflower was superb, not something I usually say about cauliflower soup. The lunch special that day was a wild sockeye salmon fillet on saffron- and thyme-flavoured rice with a sun-dried tomato and white-wine sauce. Nice ideas. And a pear clafouti dessert with house-made ice cream was another delicate delight.

Cidallia Meret's service matches the room and the clientele well. Her gentle smile and soft French accent welcome customers and assure them that this is no stuffy, pretentious café. It's professionally run, to be sure, but it is as relaxed as any good French bistro should be.

La P'tite Table is a fine blend of old and new—perfect for the retro-nouveau town of Okotoks.

www.la-ptite-table.com

La Tavola

Contemporary Italian

513 – 8 Avenue SW (Penny Lane Mall)
Phone: 237•5787
Monday – Friday 11 am – close, Saturday 5 pm – close
Reservations recommended, required for lunch — Fully licensed
Non-smoking dining room, smoking in lounge
V, MC, AE, DC, JCB, Debit — $$ – $$$

FOR well over a decade, a parade of hungry downtowners flowed into Dante's for weekday lunches. There is great access to the second-floor Penny Lane space through the Plus-15 system, and Dante's had a solid reputation for good food, reasonable prices, and a nice atmosphere. It was perfect for a casual corporate lunch.

But in the spring of 2003, Dante's was sold to Carmello Sangregorio and Michele Aurigemma, two restaurant professionals with years in the trade. It should be no surprise that the new operators transformed Dante's into an Italian restaurant.

Named La Tavola, it opened after only a few quick weeks of renovations. They laid down hardwood floors, repainted the room in a brownish tone appropriately called "osso bucco," and added granite tiles to the open kitchen. A corner space was curtained-off for small groups. They retained the exposed brick and skylight look and buffed up the ground floor lounge too. They also brought in comfortable new chairs and draped the tables in a double layer of black and pecan-coloured tablecloths. A V motif runs throughout the look, from the chairs to the folding of the napkins to the emphasized V in the spelling of La Tavola. It has a stylishly contemporary feel. They did a nice job in a short time.

That visual creativity is carried over onto the menu, a brief list of interesting dishes. A salad of roasted peppers, calamari, and prawns with greens and dollops of pesto and a balsamic reduction is a superb melding of delicate flavours. Another appetizer of a red-wine poached pear under prosciutto and shaved Parmesan with frisée is equally intriguing in its play of ingredients.

Five pastas are offered, including a plate of agnolotti stuffed with a purée of pork, spinach, and Parmesan and bathed in an herb and wild mushroom sauce. Simply resonant flavours. Seven non-pasta main courses round out the menu. One is sea bass with clams, grilled Genoa salami, black olives, and potatoes. Another is a chicken breast with a black-olive crust and a Gorgonzola potato pancake. Still another is a loin of beef that has been rolled around pesto and roasted before being served as a huge slab over polenta and eggplant. Stunning in its intensity.

This food is good. Strong ideas. Rich, intense flavours. They could do better in the bread department, but aside from that, La Tavola is high on my list. May it be around at least as long as Dante's.

www.latavola.com

Latin Corner

Latin American

2116 – 4 Street SW
Phone: 228 • 5377
Daily 11:30 am – close
Reservations recommended — Fully licensed — Patio — Non-smoking
V, MC, AE, DC, JCB, Debit — $$ – $$$

THE original Latin Corner was a lively, drafty former Dairy Queen on 4th Street SW. It was a lot of fun. The cramped space jumped with energy and frequently with live Latino music. In the winter when the door was opened, the temperature would drop ten degrees. Owners Gustavo and Nadia Yelamo were always present, ensuring their customers' satisfaction. They served simple Latin American food with gracious hospitality. It warmed the palate and soothed the soul at the same time. Eventually the Latin Corner moved to a larger space on Stephen Avenue and brought all that energy with it. Flamenco parties kept the place hopping into the wee hours.

But in early 2003, an opportunity to return to 4th Street arose, and now the Latin Corner is back just a few metres from where it started. It is firmly ensconced in what was part of the original 4 St. Rose, a two-storey house with a glassed-in alley.

The space works well for the Latin Corner. It has been opened up and brightened by fresh, tropical-coloured paint. It's a loud restaurant with hard surfaces bouncing sound around, but it works with the lively Latino tone. Performers squeeze themselves into available space, and their music adds a gloss to the sound, heightening the party atmosphere.

Gustavo is the ultimate host, there to greet his customers like long-lost friends. He oversees the action, leading the cheers when large "swords" of gaucho appear. (It's a South American tradition to cheer and whistle when the big hunks of chicken and beef, cooked on huge sword-like skewers, emerge from the kitchen. Yet another layer of sound.)

Nadia tends to the food rolling out of the kitchen: piles of rice and beans, the gaucho, the pollo Latino, and more, plus a list of tapas. She has created a list that ranges from artichokes stuffed with almond sauce and calamari in salsa to lunch sandwiches of cilantro-breaded beef and pork loin with ham and cheese. Major dinners include the gaucho, a full meal deal at $55 for two, and a seafood-laden paella at $45, also for two.

The food is matched with a list of Latino drinks, from Cuba libres and sangria to margaritas made with tamarind or guava and the currently popular mojito. They are the perfect accompaniments to the food and the atmosphere—the liquid side of *la vida loca* that the Latin Corner provides.

Le Beaujolais

French

Upstairs, Corner of Banff Avenue & Buffalo Street, Banff
Phone: 762·2712
Daily 6 pm – midnight
Reservations recommended — Fully licensed — Non-smoking dining room, smoking in lobby
V, MC, AE, Debit — $$$

L E BEAUJOLAIS is one of the classic restaurants of Banff. It has perched above the corner of Banff Avenue and Buffalo Street for over twenty-three years, serving French cuisine that is now also infused with some New World ingredients. It continues to wow global visitors and locals alike, and for serious food enthusiasts, it has become a necessary part of the Banff experience.

Le Beaujolais has been successful by flowing with the times. It used to be that a jacket and tie were *de rigueur*, but nowadays, a decent polo shirt is formal enough. Mountain chic, so to speak. And service has grown more subdued and comfortable over the years. Recent renovations have brightened the room and created a more open feel with a general tone of relaxed elegance. Owners Albert and Esther Moser have an uncompromising eye for quality and have found a balance that combines the weight of tradition with the freshness of the contemporary.

The current trend among high-end mountain restaurants is to prix fixe menus. Le Beaujolais has joined this movement and eliminated the à la carte menu totally. Guests may choose two or three courses from a table d'hôte list for $55 or $62 respectively. That list includes ostrich carpaccio with air-dried buffalo, lobster ravioli with veal sweetbreads, and venison tenderloin with quince-apple compote.

Or diners can upscale the experience with the three-course "Beaujolais Classic Dinner" at $75 or the six-course "Surprise Dinner" at $90. The Beaujolais Classic focuses on Canadian products with dishes like lobster salad, foie gras with pear compote, and a roasted rib-eye steak for two that is carved at the table. For dessert a choice of maple, Grand Marnier, or chocolate soufflés is offered. The Surprise Dinner features the chef's selection of various Beaujolais signature dishes. Wine selections can be paired with the Surprise Dinner for an extra $50. This is fine food, well prepared, and compared to some of its mountainy neighbours, a bargain.

Le Beaujolais also has one of the best wine cellars in the area, noted by the barrage of awards lining the walls and the stairwell rising up from the street. Among them is the much-vaunted Award of Excellence from the *Wine Spectator*. The cellar itself is an illuminated, temperature-controlled glass chamber situated in the middle of the dining room to add to the temptation. It holds over six hundred wines for a total of more than ten thousand bottles. It's just another corner of the continuing quality of Le Beaujolais.

www.lebeaujolaisbanff.com

Le Bistro Béni

French

5111 Northland Drive NW (Wrayton's Fresh Market in Northland Village)
Phone: 205•4253
Monday – Friday 11 am – close, Saturday & Sunday 9:30 am – close
Reservations recommended — Fully licensed — Non-smoking
V, MC, Debit — $$

I love a good French bistro. Forceful, elegant flavours. Nothing overworked, just good, solid food on the plate. Simply presented, expertly sauced, locally produced ingredients. A view of the Seine would be nice and the waft of good bistro coffee too.

But a bistro in a grocery store off Crowchild Trail? Just down from the Wal-Mart? With a big parking lot sprawled out to the McDonald's?

Well, why not?

Le Bistro Béni is such a place, an integral part of Wrayton's Fresh Market. Wrayton's took over one of the spaces that had been developed and subsequently abandoned by Debaji's. It's a full-service butcher shop, produce market, deli, bakery, dry goods store, flower shop, and restaurant.

Start-up chef Michael Allemeier developed the bistro menu before he decamped to Kelowna's Mission Hill Family Estate in the summer of 2003. Allemeier, who had been executive chef at Teatro prior to his Wrayton's stint, created a menu that includes some bistro classics: mussels with frites, duck confit, onion soup, and chocolate mousse. He dug pretty deep and also pulled out recipes for gribiche-sauced salmon and frog leg fritters with remoulade.

The preparations, now handled capably by chef Janet Lewis, are classic too. The confit is among the best I've had this far from the Eiffel Tower. The duck meat is permeated with just the right amount of luscious fat, and the skin is crispy. I like the potatoes at Le Bistro Béni too. The french fries are hot and crisp, the roasted potatoes have an oily crispiness similar to the confit, and the garlic mashed potatoes are creamy and savoury. Not particularly garlicky, but that's fine by me. Mashed potatoes don't need too much fussing to be good.

What could use a bit more attention is the boudin blanc, the veal sausage. Served with a thick and delightful onion gravy and those lovely mashed spuds, the sausage is too grainy and coarse. A smoother Alsatian weisswurst-style sausage would be preferable.

Desserts, however, are exceptional. The crème brûlée is about a half inch thick, crusted with a brittle topping, and served in a large tray. Great crème, fine brûlée. And the chocolate mousse is creatively layered between chocolate wafers in an amusing space-age design.

Le Bistro Béni also benefits from crisp service, another sign of a well-run room. The space is always well tended and soothing to the eye. Yet more reasons to like this bistro, even if the Seine is nowhere in sight.

www.wraytons.com

Leo Fu's

Chinese (Szechwan & Mandarin)

511 – 70 Avenue SW
Phone: 255•2528
Monday – Friday 11:30 am – 2 pm, Sunday – Thursday 4:30 pm – 10 pm
Friday & Saturday 4:30 pm – 11:30 pm
Reservations recommended — Fully licensed — Non-smoking
V, MC, AE, DC — $$

I don't get excited about chicken wings very often. I am typically unimpressed with all the effort that goes into the sauces draped over them and dazzled by the dedication some have to their favourite "wing night." Yet every time I go to Leo Fu's, I have to down a plate of their Szechwan chicken wings. Sometimes I'll even get a takeout order to demolish at home. Sure they are oily and incredibly bad for me, but they are soooo good. Huge wings, undoubtedly from twenty-pound killer chickens, battered and crisped in super-hot oil, coated with a Szechwan sauce so spicy that it's the only thing that slows me down. Mmm-mmm.

But Leo Fu's is about much more than their chicken wings. Those are just a single example of how tasty their food is. Leo Fu's has been my favourite Chinese restaurant of any style since I first reviewed it in 1987; I keep waiting for someone to come along and do it better, but no one has yet to exceed the skill here.

There are dishes on the menu that we almost never see elsewhere. There is General Tso's chicken in a spunky Szechwan sauce. There are string beans stir-fried in a black-pepper sauce. And there is orange-flavoured beef crisply fried and lacquered with a hot orange sauce (that's a really, really good one). There is also a zippy salt and pepper shrimp and one of the best versions of ginger beef in the city that birthed it.

Attention to quality and detail rarely waver at Leo Fu's. Owned by the Koo family, Leo Fu's is dedicated to consistency and to satisfying a long list of loyal customers. Many of their staff—including the ever-smiling Hua—have been there almost as long as the Koos and provide professional service.

The room itself is pleasantly done in blues and golds. A small function room fills a back corner, and windows along the front end provide a less than scenic view of an office building across the street. The small entryway is often clogged with hungry diners awaiting their tables or takeout orders as well as with those slowly making their way out after a hearty meal.

Leo Fu's can be a bit tricky to find the first time with its off-Macleod address. Just roll down your window and sniff out the Szechwan aromas. Those chicken wings are worth the search.

Lina's Italian Market

Italian Market & Café

2202 Centre Street N
Phone: 277·9166
Market: Monday – Friday 9 am – 7 pm, Saturday & Sunday 9 am – 5 pm
Café: Monday – Saturday 11 am – 2 pm for lunch, market hours for coffee/desserts
Reservations not accepted — Fully licensed — Non-smoking
V, MC, Debit — $ – $$

WHENEVER I need a bottle of balsamic vinegar, a slab of provolone cheese, a rich plate of grilled Italian sausage, or just an injection of high-decibel Italian energy with or without espresso, I head for Lina's. It's a market, a café, and a cultural experience all rolled into one.

Lina and her gang moved into their new and much larger digs in 2001 and, in the process, have helped redefine the Italian market in Calgary. The new space—which is right across the street from the one they opened in 1995—has been well designed for both customers and staff. It's bright, it's clean, and it's roomy.

The core of the space is filled with an array of Italian dry goods: the oils and vinegars and dried pastas and sweets. Around it is a flow of kitchen wares, produce, cheeses, fresh and cured meats, deli items, bakery fare, and finally, the café. The layout allows the staff to move freely between stations, bringing fresh sausage to the café when needed and rolling out boxes of peppers from the coolers in the back.

The café seats about fifty and is constantly filled with espresso-sippers, fatigued shoppers, and those indulging in one of the better Italian lunches in town. There's still no table service, so customers order at the counter, choosing their meals from the goods on view. Sometimes it's veal saltimbocca and grilled rapini. Sometimes it's pasta filled with goat cheese and spinach and draped with tomato sauce. And always there are cold cut sandwiches and flatbreads topped with roasted peppers and mushrooms and artichokes and such.

It's lively at the counter and there's usually a lineup, so it helps to be decisive. If you like the look of something, order it. Don't expect a lot of explanation. If you ask how a dish is made, the answer will likely be "in the oven." It's not that they are unfriendly—anything but. This is a cheerful bunch who just don't tend to use recipes and don't really talk about their food. It's good stuff. Leave it at that.

Prices have gone up a bit over the years, but you can still have a fine lunch for under $10, and that includes a well-pulled Italian espresso. Regardless of what you order, you'll leave freshly infused with Lina's unique form of Italian energy.

Lion's Den

Diner

234 – 17 Avenue SE
Phone: 265 • 8482
Daily 9:30 am – 9:30 pm
Reservations accepted — Fully licensed — Non-smoking
V, MC, AE — $

THE LION'S DEN is a bizarre little place, one of the few real diners remaining in a world of high-toned retro versions. Squeezed up against the Stampede Grounds at the end of 17th Avenue, it's been around forever and it never seems to change.

A row of stools is bolted down in front of a long counter, and butt-polished red vinyl chairs are parked at Arborite-topped tables. An eclectic assortment of prints, posters, and photographs dot the walls, newspapers are stacked on the ice cream cooler, a television lights up one end of the room, and a rogues' gallery of oddly shaped potatoes sits beside the cash register.

The Lion's Den continues to be popular for the food and the personality of the owners, Rose and Rico Festa. They are second-generation owners, and they and their family serve excellent homemade diner food with good will and bad jokes. I don't know where Rico gets his jokes, but it's worth the price of lunch just to listen to him. You'll leave smiling.

But don't miss Rose's soup. It was a bowl of tomato macaroni the last time we popped in, made with a real chicken broth and packed with flavour. Put this in a high-end Italian restaurant and you'd pay $7 for it. At the Lion's Den, you pay $2.50. And you get crackers with it too.

After that it's all over the map, with spaghetti and meatballs, veal cutlets, sauerbraten, hot turkey sandwiches, pizzas, and a pile of daily specials. I rarely get past the clubhouse sandwich, a diner classic of crisp bacon, freshly roasted turkey breast, lettuce, tomato, and mayo. With a pile of some of the best fries in town, it's all of $6.50. Every other diner chef in the city should drop by the Lion's Den for a lesson on how to make french fries. These are blazing hot from the oil, crisp and golden brown from the freshly cut potatoes.

The pizzas are huge, appetite-killing pies loaded with toppings, the perfect meal before a Flames game. The Lion's Den is also a great pit stop if you're on your way to the Stampede and looking for a calmer atmosphere than the grounds, especially if you have kids.

It's amazing how food tastes when it's done in-house from scratch. It just tastes real. And that's what the Lion's Den is all about.

Little Chef

Upscale Family Dining

555 Strathcona Boulevard SW (Strathcona Square Shopping Centre)
Phone: 242•7219
Monday – Friday 11 am – 8 pm
Saturday & Sunday 9 am – 8 pm
Reservations recommended — Fully licensed — Patio — Non-smoking
V, MC, DC, Debit — $ – $$

SOMETIMES we just want a nice, simple meal—nothing elaborate, but not fast food either. We might not feel like cooking at home, but we still feel like home cooking without a lot of glitz or high prices. And when that mood strikes us, one of the places high on our list is the Little Chef.

It has been around for over seven years now, but I'm always surprised at how many people have never heard of it. I think it gets forgotten in the much maligned category of "family restaurants." Many family restaurants are last resorts offering lacklustre service; frozen, pre-packaged food that lacks character; and industrial furnishings that are indestructible for even the most active toddler.

But the Little Chef epitomizes what a true family restaurant should be: Pleasant staff serve up tasty, freshly prepared food at reasonable prices, all in an atmosphere that is comfortable for everyone, from the local soccer team to a couple of seniors out for a nice dinner.

Now certainly, the Little Chef is no fashion plate with its mid-eighties pastel look. It's a large, angular room with a big overhead chalkboard announcing the specials and a pop cooler humming away behind the counter. But it's pristine and always active with staff trundling out plates covered with clubhouse sandwiches, bison stew, beef dips, and meat pies.

Those pies—steak and kidney, steak and mushroom, and chicken—are among the best we've had. That should be no surprise considering the chef and owner is Arthur Raynor, an expatriate Brit and former president of the Canadian Federation of Chefs & Cooks. His pastry is superb.

But more than that, the side dishes that come with the pies, such as a spinach or Caesar salad, receive excellent attention. The spinach salad is loaded with hard-boiled egg, real bacon bits, mushrooms, and a pile of excellent spinach, all bathed in a delightful vinaigrette. The Caesar salad has real croutons and Parmesan in a rich, creamy dressing. No bottles and packages here. The chefs actually prepare the food. And when a kitchen knows how to do things like that, the costs are reduced and the consumer benefits in value and quality. A meat pie with one of the salads or some fries comes in at only $9.

There are way too few family places like the Little Chef. That's a pity.

The Living Room

Contemporary Interactive Cuisine

514 – 17 Avenue SW
Phone: 228 • 9830
Monday – Friday 11:30 am – midnight
Saturday & Sunday 5 pm – midnight
Reservations recommended — Fully licensed — Patio — Non-smoking
V, MC, AE, DC, Debit — $$ – $$$

THE LIVING ROOM is an interesting name, suggesting a stylish casualness that is reflected on the menu. Its cuisine is labelled Contemporary Interactive to indicate a certain amount of customer interaction with some of the dishes. Like the fondues or the roasted chickens meant to be shared by two or more.

The owners have adopted a taupey, contemporary tone for the converted house in which the restaurant is situated. The space flows from a low table facing the fireplace past a large, raised communal table in the middle of the room to a semi-private room for twenty in the back. They also have one of the best patios on 17th Avenue.

Underlying this stylish appearance is a great depth. The menu is well conceived—it's somewhat ambitious without overreaching. And more importantly, it is well executed. The food quality can be attributed to both the ingredients they source and the diligence they take in preparation. When quail breasts are on the menu, the bones are trimmed from the whole bird and the leftovers are used to make stock. When you order bouillabaisse, the traditional provençale rouille is included—we almost never see this creamy, garlicky sauce served in these parts. When halibut and wild salmon are in season, they are included on the list.

The Living Room also pays attention to the vegetables, searching out purple kohlrabi, candy-cane beets, and baby bok choy to add colour and crunch to the plate. Each dish is subtly created with an eye to presentation as well as taste. An appetizer of seared scallops paired with pecan-crusted brie in a balsamic reduction brings a variety of textures and flavours to the start of a meal. Beef tenderloin layered with foie gras and doused with a black-truffle sauce adds more than a touch of decadence to any dinner.

Of course, all this goodness does not come cheap. The tenderloin is $38, and a butter-poached lobster for two in gazpacho cream runs $80. But there is a wide range of prices on the menu, with pasta and risotto dishes, for example, in the teens.

The Living Room carries one of the better wine-by-the-glass lists in the city. It is always changing and always focused on enhancing the food. And the staff are very good at offering suggestions.

So The Living Room is a fine restaurant with a chic look and some "interactive" cuisine. At last, it's "in" to play with your food.

Mango Shiva

Indian Bistro & Chai Bar

507 – 8 Avenue SW (Penny Lane Mall)
Phone: 290 • 1644
Monday – Friday 11:30 am – 11 pm
Saturday 5 pm – 11 pm
Reservations recommended — Fully licensed — Non-smoking
V, MC, AE, DC, Debit — $ – $$

RECENTLY we've seen a few new places where traditional Asian cuisines are being treated in non-traditional ways, partly with the food but even more with the packaging around it. These places are incorporating some of the style of Contemporary restaurants by presenting their food on spiffy plates in trendy settings. Restaurants such as Typhoon, Towa Sushi, and Sino are examples of those providing different looks on old food cultures. And the very fresh Mango Shiva is the first Indian restaurant that I would say is venturing over to the Contemporary side.

Many of Mango Shiva's dishes are prepared for individual dining rather than for sharing, and entrees are served with vegetables, rice, and nan. Colour, stacking, and contrasting elements add visual appeal to the plates. For example, a tandoori chicken breast is sliced in two and arranged over a pile of chickpeas with citrus-dressed salad greens sprayed around it. Very pretty. And a plate of three vegetable samosas is decorated with more greens and puddles of tamarind, mint, and hot chili sauces.

The presentation borrows from the Contemporary approach, though much of the food is still quite traditional. The tandoori chicken is good, the samosas an excellent version, the chili sauce as hot as I want. But a bowl of coconut chicken is a Thai-Indian hybrid of brightly flavoured chicken and vegetables with a robust coconut-chili seasoning.

This is good food: creative, colourful, and well priced. The tandoori chicken at $9, the coconut chicken at $12, and the samosas at $6 are all reasonable. The most expensive item is beef tenderloin in a truffle-scented mushroom sauce with curried gnocchi, vegetables, rice, and nan for $25.

Mango Shiva has also done extensive work on the look of the room. Formerly the Shehnai (and under the same owners), the new decor is modern with its taupe shades and sleek tables and chairs. The full name is Mango Shiva Indian Bistro & Chai Bar, words that give some indication of the tone. And of course they offer five different chai teas, from the traditional masala chai to one flavoured with hazelnut, along with lassi yogurt drinks and some creative desserts. The honey and cinnamon rice pudding is a delightful spin on a well-known sweet.

Mango Shiva serves a traditional Indian buffet at lunch for $13. But if you are looking for something different, check them out in the evening. It's almost like dining on a new cuisine.

Maple Leaf

Canadian

137 Banff Avenue, Banff
Phone: 760·7680 or 1(866) 760·7680
Daily 11 am−11 pm
Reservations recommended — Fully licensed — Non-smoking policy varies through day
V, MC, AE, DC — $$−$$$

THERE are loads of good ideas happening at the Maple Leaf. The room is lovely in a contemporary lodge way, the menu echoes the best of the True North strong and free, and the staff are so gosh-darned cute. It's meant to be comfortable for boarders looking for a quick bite and for international tourists searching out the latest cuisine. And in many ways it succeeds.

But despite its rugged good looks, I continue to have my quibbles with the space itself. The Maple Leaf is the result of a major renovation of the former King Edward Hotel (also known as the Eddy), and it has the look but not the flow. Too much of the two-storey room is consumed by a stairwell that cuts an immense hole in the place. This creates some small corners of comfort, but many tables are in awkward areas that increase traffic congestion. Once seated, it's best to stay put lest you risk being bowled over by dish-wielding staff. I must add, though, that the tables are well linened and spaced, and there are a number of private dining rooms for groups.

Enough about the space. The staff deal with it as best they can.

Food-wise I like the ideas of braised Alberta lamb shank and apple-crusted pork tenderloin and wasabi-crusted salmon. It's Canuck fare with a few global highlights, and it's reasonably well prepared.

A mushroom soup de jour is lightly creamy and seasoned. And the bison stroganoff is another creamy blend, this one with buffalo bits, mushrooms, pickles, noodles, and a dollop of sour cream on top. It is robust and filling, perfect for the après-ski crowd. But it's served in a bowl far too small to allow proper mixing of the sour cream and access to the noodles, which seems particularly odd in an era of oversized plates. When I had it, the tablecloth unfortunately bore the brunt of my pasta-stirring efforts. Again, the staff did yeoman work in toting and clearing and excusing my stains.

The menu carries a range of choices, from a ground buffalo, venison sausage, and air-dried buffalo pizza ($13) and a burger topped with Canadian cheddar ($11) for lunch to a bison tenderloin with Stilton ($38) and a rack of venison with saskatoon-Cabernet jus ($39) for dinner. How tastily nationalistic. Anyone care to join me in a rendition of "O Canada"?

www.banffmapleleaf.com

Marathon

Ethiopian

130 – 10 Street NW
Phone: 283 • 6796
Monday – Friday 11 am – 2:30 pm, 5 pm – 10 pm
Saturday 11 am – 11 pm, Sunday 5 pm – 10 pm
Reservations recommended — Fully licensed — Non-smoking
V, MC, AE, DC, Debit — $$

ANY vegetarian worth their tofu should be familiar with the Marathon and its Ethiopian cuisine. If not, they should hustle over to this Kensington restaurant for a real food treat. The Ethiopian calendar has over two hundred prescribed fasting days per year, days when it is forbidden to eat meat. As a result, Ethiopian is one of the most varied and interesting cuisines for vegetarians.

It also has some of the best food names this side of Thailand. There's shimbra asa (chickpeas in berbere sauce), yetimatim fitfit (chopped injera, tomatoes, and green peppers), and my personal fave, yater kik alicha (split peas in curry and ginger). Mighty tasty stuff too.

So then, what the heck are berbere and injera?

Berbere, a paste of hot peppers and spices, is one of the key flavourings in a culture that is rich with spices. It can be combined with niter kibeh, a spiced butter, or other seasonings to add zip to many of the dishes. Injera is a thin, crepe-like bread made from the tiny grain known as teff. It is literally and figuratively the base of Ethiopian fare. Most foods are cooked into various stews and served ladled over the injera. You then rip off a piece of the bread and use it to scoop up your food in a manner much as you do when using a nan or tortilla.

Carnivores needn't worry about the proliferation of lentils and cabbage. There are numerous meaty dishes, from yebeg wat (lamb braised in berbere sauce) to kitfo (ground beef seasoned with hot peppers). And if you are new to the cuisine, consider dropping in to try the variety on their lunch buffet.

The Marathon, named after Ethiopian Olympic gold medalist Abebe Bikila, is a modest room decorated with memorabilia from the owners' homeland. Many tables will likely be topped with *messobs*, the colourful covered food platters, and Ethiopian music from the stereo will soothe you. If you are looking for something different, this may well be the place. The staff are more than happy to talk about Ethiopia, its culture, and its food.

You can even finish your meal with the ultimate Ethiopian beverage. Made from roasted berries that have been ground into a powder and soaked with boiling water, the liquid is then decanted into cups and served with optional sugar and cream. You may have heard of this drink. It's called coffee.

Mekong

Vietnamese

2885 – 17 Avenue SE
Phone: 248•1488
Monday – Saturday 10 am – 9 pm
Reservations accepted — Fully licensed — Separately ventilated smoking room
V, MC, DC, Debit — $ – $$

THE MEKONG sits in a brightly lit strip mall on the south side of 17th Avenue just east of Deerfoot Trail. It's a nondescript place with glaring lights, about fifty seats, and a separately ventilated smoking room. It's also a constant buzz of pickup orders, large groups, and hockey games beaming off the television.

We started with the typical salad rolls and the cha gio spring rolls. I find that the quality of these two dishes usually indicates a restaurant's overall quality. And we were impressed. Although the spring rolls were wrapped in the won ton wraps that most places use (the Saigon is the only place we know that uses the lighter rice paper wraps), the filling of ground meats and vegetables was nicely flavoured and balanced. There was also a decent pile of greens to go along with them, something many places seem to forget and something I think is essential to round out the flavours and oil in this deep-fried appetizer. The salad rolls were also excellent, with a thoughtful eye to the balance of shrimp and noodles and especially some sliced pork. The dipping sauces enhanced the flavour in both appetizer rolls.

The Mekong's menu is a bit more varied than many of the popular Vietnamese noodle shops around town. There's pork and tofu in a tomato sauce; chicken curry with coconut milk and peanuts; and sweet and sour calamari, shrimp, and scallops. On the strength of our first two dishes, we next opted for the non-noodle side of the menu.

We ordered the caramel shrimp and the lemon grass chicken, both of which were under $10. We got three full chicken breasts, grilled skin-on, with a fresh lemon grass scent. The shrimp were also abundant—at least twenty on the plate in a rich, savoury sauce. Very good food and a lot less oily than I've found in many noodle shops. Even the steamed rice seemed particularly tasty.

The Mekong's food quality far exceeds the atmosphere of the room. It is not a place for lingering. I think we were in and out in about forty minutes, and in that time, a number of other tables came and went. Service is quick and mostly charmless in a functional way. It's not unfriendly, but is aimed at getting food on the table as fast as possible.

The Mekong is definitely one place where the "sizzle" does not exceed the "steak." But the food is good, fast, and cheap.

www.mekongcalgary.ca

Mélange

Fusion Food with a French Twist

#107, 721 Main Street, Canmore
Phone: 609·3221
Thursday – Tuesday noon – 3 pm, 5 pm – 10 pm (may vary seasonally)
Reservations recommended, especially on weekends — Fully licensed — Small patio
Non-smoking restaurant, smoking on patio
V, MC, Debit — $ – $$

WITH so many restaurant openings in Canmore, Mélange—which opened in 2002—seems like an old-timer. But it is still a pretty fresh concept.

Mélange, meaning a mixture of things, is a good-sized room seating about fifty. It seems older than it is because they took over an existing restaurant space and made minimal alterations. The window area offers comfy chairs and newspapers for lengthy lounging, and the open kitchen features a free-standing oven. It's a casual place suitable for hiking boots or business wear. Service is friendly and accommodating.

The owner was formerly the chef at the Baker Creek Bistro near Lake Louise, and he has brought his own style of eclectic, international cuisine to Mélange. The menu ranges widely from chicken and strawberry quesadillas and roasted duck breast with pine-nut couscous to seafood crepes and grilled veal steak with Armagnac butter. The prices also range here, from $5 to $9 for their tapas and up to $22 for dinner entrees.

We were in for lunch so we ordered a couple of items off the tapas list—some wild mushrooms with pancetta, garlic, and white wine and the warm scallops on a spinach salad with spicy pecans and an orange vinaigrette. Creative ideas and mostly successful. The balance was a bit off in the mushroom dish, with the wine coming through too sharply. Putting scallops and pecans together with spinach and an orange vinaigrette provided an intriguing blend of textures. We only wished that the dressing had been thoroughly tossed with the spinach so as to coat all the leaves with such good flavour. But the pecans and the scallops were exactly as we wanted them.

I also had a nice chicken burger, a tender breast of chicken with Swiss cheese and ham on a house-baked bun. A much simpler concept than the above dishes but well executed.

I think Mélange has great potential. We saw some nice flavours and some excellent ideas. And I have to give them credit for taking culinary chances. I can't remember the last time I saw falafel-crusted tofu on a menu or salmon coated with hemp seeds or even pork loin with a pineapple-coconut curry. They are reaching far at Mélange, as far as any restaurant in our area. They may not always succeed in their attempts, but they are definitely worth a visit.

Mescalero

Contemporary Southwestern

1315 – 1 Street SW
Phone: 266•3339
Monday – Wednesday 11:30 am – 10 pm, Thursday & Friday 11:30 am – midnight
Saturday 5 pm – midnight, Sunday 11:30 am – 2 pm, 5 pm – 10 pm
Reservations recommended — Fully licensed — 2 patios
Non-smoking restaurant, smoking in lounge
V, MC, AE, Debit — $$ – $$$

MESCALERO is one of the most attractive restaurants I've ever seen. Now, I'm very fond of New Mexico and Santa Fe in particular, so Mescalero leans toward my particular taste anyway. And the extensive array of rambling rooms and patios offers so many different spaces for intimate dining or blowout parties that I am always impressed.

Mescalero started life as a rebirth from a fire. This former bank building had housed a restaurant in the past, but was sitting empty when the building next door burned down. It survived, but sustained serious smoke damage. Seeing the cracked plaster and smoke-charred walls, owner Witold Twardowski decided to use the look to capture the trend to Contemporary Southwestern cooking. He installed a wood-fired stove, adding to the smoke, and hauled in furniture from Texas and Mexico. Old saddles and cattle skulls were hung on the walls, and a couple of plastered patios were built. The result is a restaurant that looks more like a Santa Fe restaurant than any restaurant in Santa Fe.

The stove has since been converted to gas, but the Southwestern theme has remained on a menu that includes tequila-lime salmon gravlax, corn-chip crusted crab cakes, and beef and chorizo burgers. Mescalero uses chilies judiciously rubbed onto chicken or worked into grilled scallops. This is richly flavoured food in the Southwestern style, a style that also incorporates fresh greens and vegetables. They do break from their Southwestern theme, however, with items like the "Tower of Terror" beef tenderloin.

Mescalero uses daily lunch and dinner menus and an all-day tapas list. Tapas run $5 to $12, with lunch dishes also up to $12. Dinner entrees top out at $30 for a rack of lamb. Portions are large, presentation is lovely, and service is usually good. Mescalero employs a number of staff who have been in the business for years and who know how to do the job.

We have had many memorable meals at Mescalero, ranging from great nachos on a sun-baked patio to bowls of thick black-bean soup when the weather is minus thirty. It may not be New Mexico, but it's a pretty good facsimile.

Mimo

Portuguese

4909 – 17 Avenue SE (Little Saigon Centre)
Phone: 235•3377
Monday – Thursday 11 am – 2 pm, 5 pm – 10 pm, Friday & Saturday 11 am – 11 pm
Reservations recommended for weekends — Fully licensed — Non-smoking
V, MC, AE, DC, Debit — $$

INTERNATIONAL (17th) Avenue SE is the longest smorgasbord in the city. Starting at Deerfoot Trail and heading east, you have Vietnamese, Central American, Indian, Jamaican, Italian, Cantonese, and so on, until you get to Calgary's only Portuguese restaurant, Mimo.

For a while the folks at Mimo had thought about moving into trendier downtown quarters, but a major expansion and renovation in 2000 solidified their presence on 17th Avenue. In the early days, Mimo was split in two with a bar at the front and a pretty but windowless dining room down a long corridor at the back. With the renovation, the dining room was moved out front and the floor space more than doubled. The result is a rectangular dining room lit by a full wall of windows and decorated in rich greens. It's much more pleasant than before, even if the view is only of the parking lot.

The kitchen was expanded too, but the food has remained the same. Isabel Da Costa's Portuguese cuisine is influenced by her native Azores. It is robust and lively, spiced with piri-piri sauce and lubricated liberally with azeite oil. Azeite is the hot-pressed olive oil of Portugal that can add a little spiciness to the food. Piri-piri is the sauce of chili, garlic, spices, and azeite that can add a lot of spiciness to the food. Da Costa keeps a gallon jar of the piri-piri within easy reach so she can mop it on the food.

Dishes range from the land-based frango no chorrasco (barbecued chicken) and bitoque (steak with a fried egg on top) to the seafaring sardines assadas (baked sardines) and paella with multiple shellfish to the odd crossover dish of carne porco à Alentejana (pork and clams). There are garlic shrimp, Spanish clams, and homemade sausage flamed with brandy. And with everything there are the wonderful, oily, salty fried potatoes, which must be horribly unhealthy but just taste so darn good.

As if that weren't enough, they serve the densest crème caramel going. Nothing delicate about it, it almost overpowers the taste buds with the sweetness of its dark syrup.

Mimo's food is well served by a pleasant staff, some of whom may be the progeny of the owners. It is a family operation with a high degree of professionalism. And they are quite comfortable right where they have been for years.

www.members.shaw.ca/mimorest

Moroccan Castle

Moroccan

217 – 19 Street NW
Phone: 283 • 5452
Tuesday – Sunday 5:30 pm – close
Reservations recommended — Fully licensed
Non-smoking on weekends, smoking section on weekdays
V, MC — $$

'M often asked where to go for something different, something that will break people out of their culinary ruts. One of the first places that pops to mind is the Moroccan Castle.

Why, you ask?

Cloth drapes from the ceiling to create a desert-tent tone. More draping separates dining areas that can seat up to six or eight people. Large brass tabletops are surrounded by cushioned benches. There's no Western table-and-chair seating here, and there's a suspicious lack of cutlery on the table. Because the style is Moroccan, and if you want, you can lounge back on the cushions and eat with your hands.

Well, more accurately, with your right hand. And even then, with just the thumb, index, and middle fingers of the right hand. (The left is used for, shall we say, other purposes.) Or you can just ask for cutlery. But where's the fun in that? As they say, "When in Rabat…"

The staff start your evening of Moroccan delights by bringing round a large silver basin, a pitcher filled with rose-scented water, and a towel. They then pour water over your hands in a cleansing gesture, a tradition inherited hundreds of years ago from Middle Eastern traders.

Moroccan cuisine is one of the more unique in our market, a descendant of the camel trains and the native Berber tribes of the desert. Much of it is made with dried fruits, nuts, and couscous, which were lighter for the trek across the sand, and it is flavoured with spices from across North Africa. And always there is sugar, answering the sweet tooth desires of the area.

The harira soup features lentils in a broth enriched by harissa sauce, a condiment made from the hot chilies and spices of neighbouring Senegal. The lamb tajine is a rich stew with prunes and almonds, and the couscous Fassi features chicken with raisins and chickpeas. Both can be scooped up with some Moroccan bread or with couscous pressed into an absorbent ball. (I never said this was easy. I also never said it wasn't messy.)

For the full effect, try the b'stilla pie. This is a mix of chicken, eggs, onions, cinnamon, ginger, and crushed almonds wrapped in phyllo pastry and baked. (Sounds good doesn't it?) Then icing sugar and cinnamon are dusted on top to add a sweetness to the pie. It's a gorgeous dish.

Now, how's that for something different?

Mt. Everest's Kitchen

Nepalese

1448A – 17 Avenue SW
Phone: 806•2337
Tuesday – Saturday 11:30 am – 2 pm, Tuesday – Thursday 5:30 pm – 10 pm
Friday & Saturday 5:30 pm – 11 pm
Sunday & Holidays noon – 2 pm, 5:30 pm – 10 pm
Reservations recommended — Fully licensed — Non-smoking
V, MC, AE, DC, Debit — $$

HERE's a cuisine that should be a natural for our mountainy section of the world—Nepalese. Considering how many folks from the Bow Corridor have climbed in Nepal, it's only surprising that we haven't seen a Nepalese restaurant here before now.

Mt. Everest's Kitchen is no little hole in the wall. The sparkling clean room, which seats about sixty, has been redone in a rich yellow with new chairs and linens. The yellow is called "pencil yellow," the same colour used for HB pencils. On one side of the room, they have a shiny buffet set out for the lunch crowd. And the staff look sharp too. They dress in black vests with black Nepalese topi hats adorned with Gurkha warrior symbols.

Nepalese cuisine has some similarities to Northern Indian food, seen in the curries and in the use of cream and fruit. For example, the "Chicken Fruity" incorporates cream, butter, mango, and almond powder. But some dishes, such as the momos, look decidedly Chinese. These are steamed dumplings offered either vegetarian-style or made with lamb—we had the lamb version and actually found the filling to be halfway between a Chinese dumpling and an Indian lamb dish. And like in both Indian and Chinese cultures, you'll notice that Nepalese dishes are typically served for sharing.

We also tried the Everest jeera chicken; the Nepalese tarkari of spinach, potato, and paneer (called cottage cheese on the menu); and a black lentil dish. All were spiced fairly mildly, but were still richly flavoured. We particularly enjoyed the jeera chicken, pieces of boneless, skinless chicken breast cooked in a tandoor and served in a sauce of cumin, ginger, coriander, and other Himalayan herbs and spices for which they tell me there are no good English translations. The tarkari (which means curry) was good too, but could have used more paneer. We also had some basmati rice and a couple of sweet nan breads, the nan perhaps being our favourite part of the whole meal. It was flavoured with coconut and raisins, just enough to give it a sweetness but not enough to make it cloying. We finished up with a Nepalese rice pudding and then rolled out with our leftovers—all for under $50, which included the tip.

So Mt. Everest's cuisine is a welcome addition to Calgary, not the least because we don't have to trek all the way to Nepal for it.

Murrieta's

West Coast Grills

808 – 1 Street SW
Phone: 269•7707
Monday – Friday 11 am – close
Saturday noon – close
Sunday 5 pm – 10 pm
Balcony

#200, 737 Main Street, Canmore
Phone: 609•9500
Monday – Friday 11 am – close
Saturday noon – close
Sunday 10:30 am – 10 pm

Reservations recommended — Fully licensed
Non-smoking dining rooms, smoking in lounges
V, MC, AE, DC — $$ – $$$

URRIETA'S has been packing customers into their Calgary location since they opened in 2001. Part of their success is due to the beautiful renovation of the historic sandstone Alberta Hotel. What was once an atrium now holds this second-floor, glassed-over dining room, which is surrounded on two sides by a lively lounge. In fact, things have gone so well for Murrieta's that, as I am writing this book, they are working furiously to open a second location. It also features a beautiful second-floor room, this time in downtown Canmore.

Aside from the look, the major reason for their success is the quality of the food. Murrieta's executive chef at both locations is Ned Bell, an energetic young chap who is one of the chefs on the Food Network's *Cook Like a Chef* program. He's a talent.

I started one lunch in their Calgary restaurant with an heirloom-tomato gazpacho, perhaps the best gazpacho I've ever had. It was intensely coloured with roasted peppers, piqued by habanero and tabasco chilies, topped with sweet and sour onions and jalapeno-marinated shrimp, and just packed with fresh tomato and cucumber flavours. Now you don't tend to pay $9 for a bowl of cold soup that often, but it was really good.

Then I had a cobb salad, again perhaps the best I've had. A sculpted pile of fresh butter lettuce sat overtop a lemon-herb dressing; the bowl was also filled with delicate pieces of avocado, blue cheese, crisp bacon, olives, tomatoes, hard-boiled egg, and green beans and was topped with slices of perfectly grilled chicken breast. Cobb salads are often thrown together as gooey piles of condiments in blue-cheese dressing, but this one had character and differentiation in flavours and textures. And price-wise, it wasn't bad at $11.96. Certainly worth every penny.

Other dishes to look at on the Calgary menu include the tuna burger with shaved fennel or the marinated sirloin sandwich with a creamy red-wine sauce at lunch and the bouillabaisse or the grilled scallops at dinner. And considering the neighbourhood, overall the prices aren't excessive. The Canmore location has a similar menu.

Service has been crisp on my visits and helps build an active, energetic ambience. It's an energy that's attractive to Calgary customers and is bound to win many fans in Canmore.

www.murrietas.ca

Muse

Contemporary International

107 – 10A Street NW
Phone: 670•6873
Sunday – Thursday 4 pm – 11 pm, Friday & Saturday 4 pm – midnight
Lounge open until late — Reservations recommended — Fully licensed — Patio
Non-smoking
V, MC, AE, DC — $$–$$$

I F you remember Café Calabash you can count yourself as a Calgary old-timer. Built in the early 1980s, it was one of the hippest restaurants of its day. But the Calabash eventually faded away, succeeded by a list of other restaurants and bars. Now the space is home to Muse, a multi-level room with private nooks and crannies that make it seem more intimate than a 125-seat restaurant would be.

Owners Brett Johnson and Christian Hurlburt have created a look that's part New Orleans Mardi Gras and part Cirque du Soleil. The colours are robust reds and deep yellows, the seats are upholstered with thick stripes, and Harlequin masks hang on the wall. It's a room with an attitude, one that is lively and comfortable. It is also a bit dim in places, so the menu can be hard to read.

But that menu is worth reading. It offers about a dozen each of entrees and appetizers, with a short daily list as well. It's rich Contemporary cuisine with dishes such as a blue-cheese apple tart, seared prawns with avocado pressé, and crusted rack of lamb with a portobello salad. Priced reasonably for Contemporary cuisine, appetizers are $6 to $13 and main courses, $17 to $30. It's not as expensive as some of its downtown cohorts, but is still one of the pricier places in the neighbourhood.

Executive chef David Cox is young, enthusiastic, and talented, with previous experience at The Belvedere and The Living Room. A potato and squash bisque with pesto is a silky bowl of soup perfectly balanced with the delicate flavours of the potato, the squash, and the pesto. A lamb shank in a meaty broth with barley and vegetables is deeply flavoured. An excellent dish. And the rack of lamb features eight ribs perfectly cooked. Very nice.

When Muse first opened I noticed a few flaws—underdone vegetables and imbalances in some dishes. But returning just a few months later, I saw great assurance in the kitchen, with strong choices and elegant pairings well beyond the years of the young staff. Such advancement in that short a period is impressive.

Muse's wine list is also impressive. It's an intelligent collection that offers value, quality, and intrigue both by the bottle and by the glass. Add to that attentive service that is knowledgeable without being pretentious and you have an attractive, dynamic restaurant. Certainly Muse has quickly become one of the bright new lights of 2003.

New Berliner

German

#19, 2219 – 35 Avenue NE
Phone: 219•0961
Monday – Friday 11 am – 2 pm
Wednesday – Saturday 5 pm – 10 pm
Reservations recommended for weekends — Fully licensed — Non-smoking
V, MC, Debit — $$

SCHNITZEL and rouladen fans were distraught when the Kensington Berliner closed in 2001. There's a general scarcity of German restaurants here because the food is perceived to be heavy and in opposition to leaner food trends. So for fans of the restaurant, there were no replacements.

The Kensington Berliner didn't close from lack of business. They needed a larger location, which they eventually found in the North Airways Industrial Park, not exactly a restaurant hotbed. But the New Berliner has great access off Deerfoot Trail and 32nd Avenue and also has loads of parking, especially in the evening when the body shops and printing houses around it shut down. The room itself looks nothing like the neighbourhood. It's done in soft gold and black, with about forty-five seats nicely spaced in what is still mostly a strip-mall bay.

Food-wise the New Berliner is as good as ever. Last time we stopped by for dinner, we tried a couple of schnitzels. One was a pork cutlet lightly breaded, fried, and topped with white asparagus, shrimp, and hollandaise. A chicken schnitzel was similarly prepared but with a sauce of double-smoked bacon, tomatoes, mushrooms, and paprika. Rich, intense sauces. Lovely. Both dishes came with braised red cabbage and a choice of either garlic spaetzle, potato dumplings, or fried potatoes. Not light food, but I have never found the Berliner's fare to be overly heavy. The contrast of the crispness of the schnitzels with the richness of the sauces is always a high point. Also good was the apple strudel, made in-house and topped with real whipped cream or ice cream. (Speaking of heavy, we had both.)

It's good value too. The most expensive dishes on the lunch menu are $11. That pork schnitzel was $17, but there were lots of shrimp and white asparagus involved. The chicken was a bargain at $15—there was enough left over for lunch the next day. Nothing on the dinner menu costs over $20. For $18.50 you can order eisbein, the marinated pork hock dish that John F. Kennedy ate before declaring "Ich bin ein Berliner."

Service is also sharp and professional and bilingual with both English and German. It's nice to see a restaurant that is successfully bucking current food trends with a strong adherence to a traditional style. The New Berliner may not be everyone's stein of beer, but when I get the urge for sauerbraten, it's where I go.

www.newberliner.supersites.ca

Oh! Canada

Canadian

815 – 7 Avenue SW (Nexen Tower)
Phone: 266 • 1551
Monday – Friday 11 am – 9 pm
Reservations recommended — Fully licensed — Patio
Non-smoking dining room, smoking in lounge
V, MC, AE, DC, JCB, Debit — $$

I admit to having a bit of a soft spot for Oh! Canada. I appreciate that this place wears its national pride on its shoulder, that it presents Canadian cuisine in a fun and customer-friendly fashion. But they are not slavish to the theme—if they need a pineapple, they use one regardless of the fact that none are grown in Canada. And they are not overly intense about it—there's no wild rice in deference to white rice. They just serve a surprisingly familiar looking menu with a Canadian twist.

It's a familiar menu because a lot of what we eat on a day-to-day basis is Canadian. Hamburgers, fish and chips, and apple betty all qualify as Canadian. But so do more flag-waving items such as cedar-planked salmon, bison steak, and AAA beef sandwiches. All are on the menu here plus much more.

They get a bit cutesy with the names. "The Gretzky" is a smoked turkey sandwich, and "The Friendly Giant" is a steak sandwich. I imagine that many a visitor wonders who or what "The Stompin' Tom" refers to (it's a chicken burger). Or why a seafood salad is called "Great Big Sea." But that doesn't stop the two hundred seats from filling up each weekday at lunchtime. And in the summer, outdoor types park themselves on the patio, sing lumberjack songs, quaff flagons of local ale, and trap beavers too! (Okay, I may be overstating it just a tad.)

Oh! Canada works partly because of the tongue-in-cheek menu and partly because of its location on the ground floor of the Nexen Tower. It is one of the better and certainly bigger places to lunch in an area surrounded by office towers. But their automatic audience has not caused them to become complacent. The food is fast, abundant, and reasonably priced, with most items under $15. It's not overly complex food, but just as straightforward as the country it represents.

Adding to the variety are seasonal specials that celebrate the regional cuisines of Canada. Recently, for example, they featured Nova Scotia with some crab cakes, lobster pitas, Atlantic halibut in maple syrup, and seafood lasagna.

So let's all put the video of the Salt Lake Olympic hockey victories on the tube, slap on the snowshoes, and pay our bill in loonies and toonies. We're Canadian, eh.

www.ohcanadarestaurant.com

Owl's Nest

Contemporary Continental

320 – 4 Avenue SW (The Westin)
Phone: 508 • 5165
Monday – Friday 11:30 am – 2 pm, Monday – Saturday 5:30 pm – 10:30 pm
Reservations recommended — Fully licensed
Non-smoking dining room, smoking in lounge
V, MC, AE, DC, Debit — $$$

A few decades ago the Owl's Nest was synonymous with "the best" and "the most opulent." It was regarded as *the* place to go for special occasions or major corporate functions. As the main dining room in The Westin—which also lays claim to creating the Caesar cocktail—it was a mainstay for visitors and locals alike.

But with the explosion of independent restaurants and the arrival of more food cultures over the past twenty years, the Owl's Nest was sometimes forgotten. With its windowless room, it was perhaps perceived as stuffy and unchanging. Good restaurants evolve with the times though. They incorporate new ideas and listen to their customers. So the Owl's Nest of today is different than the Owl's Nest of yesteryear, but it is also very much the same.

Many Owl's Nest customers love the cocoon of indulgent service that wraps around them the moment they enter. This is friendly, Western-tinged, classic service where the customer is king. Where you don't have to worry about servers dropping dishes or forgetting orders. They know their profession inside out.

The room looks brighter and more open than it used to. It's still windowless—not much they can do about that—but some enclosing walls have been removed, and the former conspiratorial lighting has been kicked up a few notches.

Much of the evolution has taken place in the kitchen where executive chef Martin Heuser has incorporated more of a Contemporary tone to the menu. Heuser's menu still contains the freshest, the best, and the most expensive ingredients, but there is greater variety and sensitivity on the list. "Smart Dining" items are available for high-protein, low-sodium, and low-fat diets, and several dinner entrees are available in smaller portions.

Lunch can be a chef's salad of smoked chicken breast, heirloom tomatoes, poached quail eggs, shaved Asiago, and mixed greens for $16 or charbroiled leg of lamb for $18. Dinner can rocket up to $42 for a free-range pheasant breast stuffed with cèpes and coated in a cloudberry sauce or for a mixed grill of beef tenderloin, buffalo, Arctic char, lamb, and prawns. And there are always large cuts of Alberta beef done to perfection.

The food at the Owl's Nest is very good and the experience exceptional, from the welcome right down to the finish with its silver bowl of chocolate-dipped cherries steaming with dry ice.

Some things never change—they're just tweaked. And that's not a bad idea.

Panorama

Canadian

101 – 9 Avenue SW (Calgary Tower)
Phone: 508 • 5822
Monday – Friday 6:30 am – 10:30 am, 11 am – 2:30 pm, 5 pm – 9 pm
Saturday 8:30 am – 10:30 am, 11 am – 2:30 pm, 5 pm – 9 pm
Sunday 9:30 am – 1:30 pm, 5 pm – 9 pm
Reservations recommended — Fully licensed — Elevation charge — Non-smoking
V, MC, AE, DC, Debit — $$$

THE PANORAMA DINING ROOM atop the Calgary Tower is thirty-five years old, it offers a striking view of the city, and it remains our only revolving restaurant. It's the kind of place where tourists go for the experience and locals go for special occasions such as birthdays and graduation dinners.

The Panorama has not been left to wallow in the mediocre fate that consumes many tower restaurants. The food quality has fluctuated from time to time, but the current management team has brought it to a new level and done some nifty renovations to perk up the look.

The best is a set of high-backed, curved booths that face outward, giving you almost total privacy from the rest of the room. If you're sitting at one of these, you see the scenery but no one else. That's nice. And the new grey and black tones add an elegance to the room that moves it out of the pastels of our Olympic era.

The Panorama food pushes gently into a Contemporary Canadian style that should please locals and intrigue visitors. Jumbo prawns and scallops are whipped into a chowder with Yukon Gold potatoes. Salmon is marinated in Alberta Springs whiskey while Brome Lake duck breast is roasted in a Grand Marnier glaze. And buffalo medallions are seared in a peppercorn crust and served with a saskatoon and port reduction. These are nationalistic food ideas with positive results.

I ordered something that I hadn't had in years, maybe decades—the surf and turf, a cut of prime rib and a three-ounce lobster tail. With some fresh vegetables, a baked potato, and a Merlot jus, it was a big, tasty plate of food. At a lofty $39 I might add, but it was good beef. The lobster, however, was bland and not worth the extra cost, but I still enjoyed the old-style dining experience. (I see that this combo came off the summer 2003 menu, though the prime rib remained on its own in a port and fresh horseradish reduction—more nice ideas.) Everything was well served throughout with a discreet, lightly friendly approach—nothing overly familiar.

Note: There is an elevation fee of $10 per adult, less for students, seniors, and families. If you go for breakfast before 8:30 a.m., that fee is waived. In the evening, you get two hours of free parking in the Palliser parkade. But you can still expect to spend nearly $150 for a couple.

www.calgarytower.com

Parthenon

Greek

8302 Fairmount Drive SE
Phone: 255·6444
Monday – Thursday 11 am – 10:30 pm, Friday 11 am – 11 pm
Saturday 4 pm – 11 pm, Sunday 4 pm – 10 pm
Reservations recommended — Fully licensed — Non-smoking
V, MC, AE, DC, Debit — $$

IT's amazing what can be done with an old donut shop. Chains such as Robin's and Country Style are floundering, but some of their old buildings—the ones with the prime locations—are being picked up by restaurant entrepreneurs. One case in point is the former Country Style shop on the corner of Fairmount Drive and Heritage Drive SE. It is at a high-traffic intersection with access off both roads, has a number of parking stalls against the side of the building, and is a bright, solidly built facility, perfect for a neighbourhood restaurant.

It's now the Parthenon, a pretty decent sixty-seat Greek restaurant, and it looks good. The ceiling tiles have been painted a mottled blue to resemble the sky, one raised area is sectioned off into a Greek temple, and small Greek columns adorn the tables as candle holders (small but heavy, these suckers must weigh five pounds each). It's a sunny room done in whites, blues, and browns. It may be a little kitschy, but it's not cloying. It's a fun place that has Greek music streaming through the room and a lively staff toting out platters of hearty food.

There is nothing kitschy about the food though. This is full tilt Greek fare prepared with skill. There is lamb in abundance, from souvlaki to roast lamb, lamb chops, and rack of lamb. And the menu features more than just the usual raft of Greek dishes. There is an entree of Greek sausage, penne, and tomato sauce baked with mozzarella and an appetizer of jumbo beans in an herb and tomato sauce. There are various appetizer and combo platters too. And there are dips of tarama, tzatziki, and hummus.

There's no wimping out on the flavours either. The fried calamari is crusted and served with sliced Spanish onions and a big bowl of garlicky tzatziki. It's crunchy and big enough to be an appetizer for two at $8. The coating is a touch too thick, making it oilier than it needs to be, but it's otherwise a good calamari dish.

The big lunch hit for me is the lamb souvlaki pita. Big chunks of lean, marinated lamb are grilled and folded into a pita with dressed greens and more tzatziki. The lamb is tender, and the pita is an absorbent cushion for all the juices. Sided with a crisp Parthenon salad, it's a fine lunch for $10.

And it's the best meal I've had in a donut shop.

Pelican Pier

Family Seafood Restaurant

4404 – 14 Street NW
Phone: 289 • 6100
Monday – Thursday 11 am – 9 pm, Friday 11 am – 10 pm
Saturday & Sunday noon – 9 pm
Reservations not accepted — Fully licensed — Non-smoking
V, MC, Debit — $ – $$

I am frequently asked where to find good seafood, especially decent fish and chips. I'm also challenged to offer up good places to eat in the city's Northwest quadrant. Both can be tricky questions, but Pelican Pier is one place that answers both desires.

Pelican Pier does a mean fish and chips, but it does much more too. It's a full-blown restaurant with loads of different seafood dishes, from shrimp bisque and breaded oysters to grilled salmon and Creole snapper. There's also a smattering of non-fishy things such as a chicken Caesar salad or fettuccine with chicken and mushrooms.

I've tried the creamy seafood chowder, the Manhattan clam chowder, and the shrimp bisque, but never purely on their own—the servers often suggest a blend of two soups to get a taste of more than one style. You'll find good quality seafood and crunchy vegetables in soups that are rich and gentle. No excess spicing here, just simple flavours.

The fish and chips are top notch. For $7.25, a couple of lightly breaded pollock fillets are served steaming hot over a pile of fries, with a side of coleslaw. The fish is lightly battered, not one of those three-inch-thick, doughy jobs that just traps all the grease. These seem halfway between being battered and being breaded, a great alternative for those who love fish and chips but don't really want all that heaviness. The pollock itself is fine too. (You can always upgrade to cod, haddock, halibut, or salmon for an extra few bucks, a great option. Halibut is my favourite.) They don't slack off on the fries either. Long, freshly cut, crispy chips—a perfect complement to the fish. They also offer seconds of these if you would like, at no extra charge. A nice touch. With some house-made tartar sauce on the side, these fish and chips are among the best I have had.

Pelican Pier is not a bad-looking place either. Split into two halves, it is appropriately coast-like with lobster traps and fishnets dangling from the ceiling and posters of fish lining the walls. Recent renovations have expanded the space a bit and given it even more of a wharf look. If you listen real hard, the traffic on 14th sounds like waves lapping the shore. I almost expect to see Captain Highliner waiting tables.

Pfanntastic Pannenkoek Haus

Dutch Pancakes

2439 – 54 Avenue SW
Phone: 243·7757
Tuesday – Friday 11 am – 8 pm, Saturday & Sunday 8 am – 8 pm
Reservations recommended Tuesday – Saturday, not accepted Sunday
Fully licensed — Non-smoking
V, MC, AE, Debit — $ – $$

FROM a food perspective, Calgary is first and foremost associated with good old Alberta beef. Perhaps the second food association is the pancake. Long affiliated with the Stampede and the abundance of pancake breakfasts held during that July event, the flapjack can easily call Calgary home.

Which may explain why Calgarians have embraced the Dutch pannenkoek. Sure, it's not the thick, fluffy pancake we grew up on in these parts, but there is a familial resemblance. The Dutch pannenkoek fits somewhere between a crepe and a flapjack in thickness. It's usually about twelve inches in diameter, and toppings are typically cooked into the batter.

And while the flapjack is traditionally considered to be a breakfast food, Dutch pannenkoeks span the day, slipping easily into lunch and dinner and sweetening up for dessert. Pfanntastic offers over seventy versions to please almost any palate.

Savoury pannenkoeks such as ham and cheese or shredded potato or bacon, onion, and mushroom are served at Pfanntastic for those looking for a meal. They are surprisingly filling. Then there are the sweet pannenkoeks for dessert—perhaps topped with warm blueberries or apple and cinnamon or maple syrup, all with powdered sugar and optional whipped cream.

For those who can't decide, there are combo pannenkoeks with both sweet and savory toppings—bacon and raisins or ham and pineapple and such. And for those who like their pannenkoeks just like back in Holland, a bottle of syrupy stroop sits on each table. Aficionados lace their savoury pannenkoeks liberally with the sweet stuff.

Pfanntastic also offers some open-face sandwiches, salads, and soups to round out the meals or to satisfy those who just don't want a pannenkoek. Although why that would be is beyond me—the pannenkoeks are a delight. Only a few of them break the $10 mark. So for price, variety, and quality, they are a popular family dining choice.

Pfanntastic is an accommodating place too. Owner Denice Greenwald bends over backwards to make her customers happy, and she has staff that keep up their end too. Tables are pushed together for larger groups, the coffee is non-stop, and there is a comfortable, energetic atmosphere. The room is simply decorated with a light Dutch tone, and their shift to a non-smoking atmosphere has made the room fresher.

It may not be a Stampede breakfast, but pannenkoeks at Pfanntastic taste mighty fine.

Piq Niq

Eclectic European

DOWN town
That's the Spot

811 – 1 Street SW
Phone: 263 • 1650
Monday – Friday 11 am – 2 pm, Wednesday – Saturday 5 pm – 11 pm
Reservations recommended — Fully licensed — Non-smoking
V, MC, AE, DC, Debit — $$ – $$$

THE Grain Exchange building plays host to a couple of dining options, one of which is Piq Niq Café. It's a small space that recently underwent an extreme makeover, changing its look from woody chic to contemporary chic. It still seats only a couple of dozen in its freshly mirrored and earth-toned confines though. A new bar juts into the room, but the old chandelier remains overhead. They've also kept the menu of skillfully prepared French Bistro fare. This is cuisine with backbone and elegance.

At lunch, the tiny kitchen produces excellent sandwiches of brie with roasted red peppers and onion confit or Gorgonzola with sautéed pears and leeks or shaved pastrami with Gouda and sauerkraut. The sandwiches are served on breads chosen to complement the fillings. Baguette is used for a roasted chicken and brie, and a walnut and pecan loaf is used for that Gorgonzola-pear sandwich. These are thoughtfully conceived and executed sandwiches, served with a choice of soup or salad for $10 to $12. They make an efficient, tasty, and affordable lunch, as do the salads and pastas.

In the evening, Piq Niq moves more firmly into the bistro domain with duck confit, pot-au-feu, and steak with frites. And they broaden out the menu with grilled salmon and a potato, snap pea, and artichoke salad; roasted pork tenderloin in a Calvados reduction; and linguine with chicken and pea shoots. It's always interesting food, prepared to order, as good as at many of the neighbours but at slightly lower prices. The lobster and spinach risotto is $17, the beef tenderloin in tamarind barbecue sauce is $26, and the confit—with a sauté of lentils, pears, and shallot— is $14. And portions are not insignificant.

The handcrafting at dinner can take awhile at Piq Niq, but lunches move briskly. Regardless of the time of day, staff always stay on top of customer needs.

It's a lively place, but I wouldn't use Piq Niq as the site for intimate conversations as it's such a small room. Your conversation, however, may be obscured by music drifting up through the floorboards. Because Piq Niq also provides (or hides) the entrance to a jazz club called Beat Niq. Located directly beneath the café, Beat Niq hosts live performances on a regular basis. It's not unusual to see an inordinate number of people entering Piq Niq to make their way to Beat Niq.

Fine food and good music. It's a nice combo.

www.beatniq.com

Post Hotel

Continental

200 Pipestone Road, Lake Louise
Phone: 522·3989 or 1 (800) 661·1586
Daily 7 am – 11 am, 11:30 am – 2 pm, 5 pm – 9:30 pm
Closed in November
Reservations recommended for dinner — Fully licensed — Non-smoking
V, MC, AE — $$$

WHERE to start? With the stunning view? Or the crisp service? Or the rustically suave dining room? With the string of accolades from influential magazines such as *Gourmet*, *Wine Spectator*, and *Travel & Leisure*? Maybe I should just say that the Post Hotel is superb in all aspects of the hospitality business from check in to check out. And that they do it effortlessly.

The Post is not an overindulgent spa for the rich and famous. On the outside, it has the appearance of a rustic mountain hotel where one could lounge by a fire or in a hot tub. On the inside, the dining room follows the same tone. It's a low-ceilinged log room that curls around the kitchen—it's quaint and cute and mountainy. It could easily pump out mediocre food and still be fairly successful.

But it doesn't. The Post Hotel provides one of the most uncompromisingly superb dining experiences in the Bow Valley. The food is outstanding, the wine list is unparalleled, and the attitude is service first and forever.

Brothers George and Andre Schwarz have built the Post into an international destination since purchasing it from original owner Sir Norman Watson in 1978. In 2002, they were honoured by *Wine Spectator's* Grand Award, given only to those places with the very best wine lists. In receiving the award, the Post became the fourth Canadian establishment to achieve such a high level. That's what a carefully selected list of 1,500 wines and 28,500 bottles will do for you.

The food side of the Post matches perfectly. Open from early morning to late evening for the assembled guests and any other visitors who happen by, the 120-seat room keeps the kitchen busy. Oven-warm bread appears, hearty mountain breakfasts roll out, handcrafted soups elicit oohs and aahs, and a fabulous burger and french fry lunch brings smiles of culinary joy to diners' faces. It's not precious in approach. It's just really, really good.

For the fully indulgent Post experience, a six-course tasting menu at dinner is hard to beat. There might be grilled squab with a truffle vinaigrette, salmon and halibut carpaccio with avocado oil and fresh horseradish, venison chops with a mushroom tower, Roquefort mousse, or a blueberry financier with champagne sabayon and mascarpone ice cream. At $90, it won't be cheap, but it will be surprisingly good value. And there will be no problem matching any of your food with wine.

Now, where to stop?

www.posthotel.com

Prairie Ink

Café & Bakery

120 Stephen Avenue Walk SW (McNally Robinson Booksellers)
Phone: 538·1798
Monday – Thursday 9 am – 10 pm, Friday & Saturday 9 am – 11 pm
Sunday 11 am – 6 pm
Reservations accepted — Fully licensed — Rooftop deck — Non-smoking
V, MC, AE, Debit — $ – $$

IT used to be a given that when you went to a bookstore, you did not eat food or sip on coffee. Then Chapters and Indigo changed all that. We were encouraged to kick back with a latte and scone and browse the stacks. Food service became a big part of the bookstore experience.

So when McNally Robinson Booksellers opened their spiffy new store on Stephen Avenue, it was no surprise to see a café component to it. But they've taken the food concept up a notch.

The café is called Prairie Ink, an appropriate name to come from a Western-based company. Situated on the second level of the store with a great south-facing view of the street, it seats about seventy-five on hardwood floors and in bamboo-backed chairs. It's casual and bright and covers a lot of territory—it's open during store hours, which means it's available for breakfast, lunch, brunch, afternoon tea, happy hour juices, and dinner. They offer a range of vegetarian dishes, and there's a bakery on-site. They are even licensed for alcohol, and there is live music on Friday and Saturday nights.

The menu itself is appropriate to the surroundings. It's a collection of salads, hot and cold sandwiches, pastas, pizzas, and a limited all-day breakfast. Plus a bunch of house-made desserts and a list of coffees and freshly squeezed juices.

I had a decent lunch combo of a pear and blue-cheese salad with a cup of mulligatawny soup for $8.25. Loads of toasted almonds and blue cheese were piled on a heap of greens with a mouth-puckering raspberry vinaigrette. The soup was pleasant but understated for mulligatawny—I expected more oomph. But it was served with a slice of house-baked oat bread, a nice touch.

I had to try one of their desserts, a coconut cake gussied up with apple and pumpkin mousse separating layers of the cake. An interesting idea—combining pumpkin, coconut, and apple—though not necessarily one that is going to set the world on fire. Let's just say I wouldn't have it every time.

But I'd be happy to eat here any time. The food is robust and thoughtful, meaty enough for the most avid carnivore while creative enough for those leaning to the soy side of the menu. And the setting is hard to beat. Prairie Ink is a great option for downtown lunchers and weekend bookstore browsers. I'm glad to see it.

www.mcnallyrobinson.com/bistros.php

Priddis Greens

Casual Clubhouse & Continental

Priddis Greens Drive, Priddis
Phone: 931·3171
Golf season: Daily 7 am – 10 pm
Off season: Friday 5 pm – 10 pm, Saturday 11:30 am – 10 pm, Sunday 10:30 am – 2 pm
Reservations recommended — Fully licensed — Sundeck
Non-smoking restaurant, smoking on sundeck
V, MC, AE, DC — $ – $$$

MANY golf course restaurants make a good clubhouse sandwich, and a number of the private clubs have excellent cuisine. But one of the few that has both great food and public access is Priddis Greens Golf and Country Club. Although you have to be a member to golf there, anyone can enjoy the food and the view.

And that view is worth the price of admission. The restaurant was smartly built to look over the course in a sweeping vista toward the Rockies. The high wraparound windows curve to the east too, adding a bucolic view of the Prairies. It's spectacular both in winter and in summer.

To answer the varying culinary desires of the members, food and beverage manager Bernard Duvette, the ultimate host, and executive chef Nicolas Desinai have created one of the most bizarrely diverse menus I've seen anywhere. It almost defies you to say there's nothing on it for you. There are burgers and salads and sandwiches, but there are also perogies, liver and onions, fish and chips, lemon chicken, seafood lasagna, escargots, rack of lamb, and mussels done three ways.

And there is duck confit, a classic French preparation and one of Catherine's favourite dishes. Duck confit is prepared by rubbing raw duck with salt and brining it for a while before cooking it in its own fat. Then it is stored in fat for anywhere from hours to months before preparing it for the table. The result is oh-so-tender meat with crisp skin and no shortage of oil. It's great. The confit at Priddis is the best I've had this side of Paris. I love classic French Bistro cuisine, but I don't necessarily expect to find it attached to a golf course in the Foothills.

At Priddis, you get two full legs of duck confit with a mâche salad and potato for $15.75. That is a stunning deal. I checked another local restaurant, and a single-leg confit dish there is $19. Priddis keeps all of its prices extremely reasonable.

The culinary diversity carries over into desserts of pecan pie, a warm chocolate cake, crème brûlée, and a cold fruit soup. The soup is a chilled broth of fruits with strawberries and blueberries floating in it. Not for everyone, but surprisingly refreshing. For the traditionalist, the crème brûlée is an excellent, classic version.

A stunning view, great food, fine service, good prices. Does it get any better?

www.priddisgreens.com

Puspa

Indian (Bengali)

1051–40 Avenue NW
Phone: 282·6444
Monday–Friday 11:30 am–2 pm, Saturday noon–2 pm
Monday–Thursday 5 pm–10 pm, Friday & Saturday 5 pm–10:30 pm
Reservations recommended — Fully licensed — Non-smoking
V, MC, AE, DC, Debit — $–$$

PUSPA is the kind of neighbourhood curry joint that I'd like to find in any area of the city. It's small, friendly, and well run; the food is good; and the prices are reasonable. It makes no pretense to grandeur, and over the past decade, it has built a loyal following for all of the above reasons.

Puspa is Calgary's only Bengali restaurant. As such, it features Northern Indian dishes such as butter chicken, aloo gobi, and rogan josh. You will also find the odd far-flung dish such as lamb Madras from South India. But in all these dishes you will find Bengali spicing and preparation, making them somewhat unique.

The Bengali style is less complex than some other Indian food styles. But less complex does not mean less intense. Although the food stays in a sane heat range, the forcefulness of the spicing is front and centre on your palate. It may not include a great deal of subtlety, but it still offers a satisfying wallop to your taste buds.

The bhoona chicken, for example, is cooked in a thick sauce of tomato, pimento, onion, and spices. The chicken stays tender, and the sauce bounces flavour into your mouth. Likewise, the saag lamb is served in a rich, medium-spiced sauce, its spinach melding nicely with the lamb.

Our favourites at Puspa remain the vegetarian dishes; for our palates, the spicing works best in dishes such as the mutter paneer and the tharka dhal. The dense cheese and the peas of the mutter paneer meld especially well with the spices, making it a perfect dish to scoop up with piping hot nan.

Add an excellent masala chai and some rice pudding and we are happy Puspa diners. And with most dishes under $12, we're not badly off in the wallet either.

Puspa will never win any interior design awards, but its bright, sunny corner location offers a great view of Northmount Drive. It seats only a couple of dozen people, and most evenings it becomes busy with those dining-in plus a steady stream of others picking up takeout foods. At lunch it fills with more diners indulging in bargain plates of great food for cheap. Service is fast, friendly, and accommodating.

Puspa remains a neighbourhood classic with its unique food and obscure location. I wish there was something like it where we live.

www.members.shaw.ca/dattaj/puspa

Quarry

International Bistro

718 Main Street, Canmore
Phone: 678·6088
Daily 7:30 am – 11 pm
Reservations recommended for evenings — Fully licensed — Patio
Non-smoking dining room, smoking on patio
V, MC, AE — $$ – $$$

CANMORE'S old Fireside Inn was perfect for its time. Dark, cozy, trimmed with brick, and warmed by a big fireplace, it was most popular in the 1980s when it was one of the few restaurants of note in town. We have an earthy ceramic jug in our china cabinet commemorating a visit during that era.

But things change. During the summer of 2003, in the middle of a Canmore restaurant boom, Quarry opened in the former Fireside spot smack in the heart of downtown. And like its predecessor, Quarry is perfect for its time.

Siblings and business partners Naomi and David Wyse, both of whom worked at the River Café in Calgary, gutted the place and reshaped it in the tones of today's trendiest restaurants. They kept the sloped, beamed ceilings, but removed the fireplace and filled the chimney hole with a skylight. Contrasting white walls with brown wood tables and chairs, they have created a sleek look that is comfortable to a broad cross-section of diners. Framed mirrors line one wall, and faux rock adds texture to another. Practical linoleum tile covers the floor. Outside, a boulder inscribed with the word Quarry welcomes visitors, and a street-side patio waits for those precious sunny days.

At the time of this writing, they had opened with a safe start-up menu to help determine their market. The list covered a range of comfort classics such as a big beef burger and linguine carbonara and got a little edgier with grilled lambsicles and duck-liver pâté with rhubarb jelly.

I tried a tomato and bread salad, a collection of classic Tuscan ingredients that included bocconcini, arugula, balsamic vinegar, and sea salt. All the elements were beautifully but individually arranged on my plate. This type of salad needs to be tossed, however, so that the bread can absorb all the flavours. Hopefully they are doing that now.

My scallops were prepared perfectly, seared and plated with pea shoots, pommes frites, and a caper aïoli. Nice contrasting tastes and textures. And another gorgeous presentation. My favourite dish was a blueberry and raspberry shortcake, layers of berries, whipped cream, and a dense, biscuity scone. Marvelous, pure flavours.

The Wyse's intent is to run Quarry as a dawn-until-dusk restaurant, starting with breakfast and flowing through lunch to dinner. This quarry is not going to be content with the traditional coal of Canmore mines. They're going for gold.

Rajdoot

Indian (Mughlai & Northern)

2424 – 4 Street SW
Phone: 245·0181
Sunday – Friday 11:15 am – 2 pm, Daily 4:45 pm – close
Reservations recommended — Fully licensed — Patio — Non-smoking
V, MC, AE, DC, Debit — $$

FOR over a dozen years, Rajdoot has been a fixture of the 4th Street dining scene. It has introduced many Calgarians to Indian cuisine, entertained us with tandoori cooking demos, and satisfied our palates with excellent flavours. It has also been the progenitor of many other Indian restaurants—a number of chefs have started here and eventually moved on to open their own places.

In the spring of 2003, the original owners retired, turning the reins of Rajdoot over to the Mall family. The kitchen staff remains, and the transition has been seamless. The lunch buffets and the Tuesday evening vegetarian buffet continue unabated. At $13, that vegetarian buffet offers a sumptuous array of choice. The Sunday and Monday evening buffets are $15 and include the addition of various meat dishes.

The buffets at Rajdoot are tempting because they offer so much variety and eliminate brain-racking decisions. They are also fast; it's easy to be in and out in less than thirty minutes at lunch if that is your need. But Rajdoot also offers a full menu at both lunch and dinner.

I've always enjoyed the saucing of the meat dishes here, from the dense, earthy flavours of the lamb rogan josh to the creamy, nutty taste of the beef korma. Some channa chandi chowk (chickpea curry) and a fresh nan and I'm happy.

Once upon a time, it was here that I had the hottest dish I've ever been served, a specially prepared paal vindaloo. That evening I was dining with a group who wanted a dish that really pushed the heat. I had been unaware that there was something hotter than a regular vindaloo, but there certainly is. Before cooking some prawns for us, the restaurant had marinated them in puréed habanero chilies. It took three bites for me to reach the depth of the heat, and by then, it was too late. This was a dish that was just too hot for me to eat. I did, however, consume a lot of mango lassi, the cooling yogurt drink, that evening.

Now typically, Rajdoot's food is flavour first and heat second. There are so many spices in Indian cooking, and Rajdoot uses them well. They don't obliterate the flavour with heat, but as I learned, they will adjust the heat to your taste.

Rajdoot literally means "ambassador." It's an appropriate word for a restaurant that has created many Indian food fans over the years.

The Ranche

Rocky Mountain Cuisine

Bow Valley Ranche, south end of Bow Bottom Trail SE
Phone: 225•3939
Monday – Thursday 11:30 am – 9 pm
Friday 11:30 am – 10 pm, Saturday 5 pm – 10 pm, Sunday 10:30 am – 9 pm
Reservations highly recommended — Fully licensed — Veranda — Non-smoking
V, MC, AE, DC, Debit — $$$

THERE are few Calgary culinary experiences more pleasurable than dining on the veranda at The Ranche on a warm summer evening. With the breeze rustling the prairie grasses and the sun setting over Fish Creek, it is a gorgeous setting, a perfect backdrop for the historic ranch house restaurant. (On a warm night, it's also much nicer outside than in, due to the absence of air-conditioning in the dining room.)

The Ranche is the beautifully restored former home of William Roper Hull, who built the house in the late 1800s. Hull sold the ranch to Pat Burns only six years after he built it, and it stayed in the Burns family until 1973. It then was acquired by the province and became part of Fish Creek Provincial Park. Returned to its glory in 1999 following years of planning and fundraising, the house is currently operated as part of the Canadian Rocky Mountain Resorts' group of restaurants.

Rocky Mountain cuisine is featured here, dishes such as BC halibut with an artichoke ravioli, confit of Alberta lamb shoulder, and house-cured Arctic char. With seasonal changes, the menu brings out the best of local flavours combined with global food preparations in things like grilled polenta, sablefish brandade, and sweet potato and chèvre galette. The traditional melds with the contemporary to create sharply flavoured dishes throughout.

Heirloom tomatoes and arugula are teamed with pancetta and Canadian brie to create a pleasant plate. A barbecue sauced free-range chicken is arranged over a pile of mushroom-infused risotto. Rhubarb and apples are baked into a savoury financier and served with a fireweed-honey ice cream.

If there is a downside to The Ranche's menu, it's that it is quite expensive. On the summer 2003 menu, that lamb confit was $36 and the halibut was $29. Most expensive was a buffalo tenderloin at $38. Appetizers ranged from $7 to $20, and desserts hovered around $8. So expect to drop at least $100 for two and possibly quite a bit more. And frankly, I'd like to see more food on the plates. But that view is worth a million bucks, so you may well get your money's worth.

The Ranche site also includes Annie's, a seasonal café a few hundred metres away (see "Little Eats" section). Between the two buildings sits a lovely garden laced with walking paths. It's a beautiful place, perfect for visitors and Calgarians alike and a tribute to our history.

Red Saffron

Persian

924B – 17 Avenue SW
Phone: 541 • 1041
Sunday – Thursday 11:30 am – 9 pm, Friday & Saturday 11:30 am – 10 pm
Reservations recommended for over 6 — No alcoholic beverages — Small patio
Non-smoking
V, MC, DC, Debit — $ – $$

RED SAFFRON has sleekly redesigned the space that for years housed Decadent Desserts. They have opened up the front with sliding windows, decorated in simple whites and wood-grained tones, and polished up the concrete floor. The look is sparingly contemporary and traditionally Persian at the same time. They've also got room for a few tables outside.

Red Saffron is a Persian kebab house, a café that specializes in grilled, skewered meats. This style is just one small corner of a complex cuisine that is rich with herbs, fresh flavours, and spiced meats. Traditionally, many Persian meats are skewered on long steel rods and grilled over red-hot coals. At curbside braziers they are folded into pitas with garlicky sauces, and in cafés they are served with rice and various vegetables. Red Saffron offers both styles, with kebab sandwiches at around $6 or $7 and full dinners at about $10 to $16.

Each full dinner here starts with a small plate of Persian nibbles to pique the appetite for the kebab—things such as sliced radishes, mint and basil leaves, parsley, green onion, walnuts, and goat cheese. The kebabs are quick and simple, but it is the pre-preparation that makes the difference. On my last visit, I had the sultani kebab dinner with one skewer of barg kebab and one of koobideh kebab. The barg is a good cut of beef, usually a sirloin or rib-eye, that they have marinated in saffron oil. The koobideh is ground beef that has been spiked with various seasonings. They both grill well, and sided with a pile of basmati rice combined with saffron rice and a whole roasted tomato, it's a flavourful meal.

Aside from the beefy kebabs, there are shrimp kebabs, salmon kebabs, chicken and lamb kebabs, vegetable and tofu kebabs, and even a Cornish hen kebab, all marinated and grilled. The rice and tomato remain pretty much the same throughout. They also offer a short list of appetizers such as grape-leaf wraps, a yogurt and spinach dip, an eggplant dip, and an incongruous Greek salad. But then there are also a few pastas, further showing a bit of an international spin.

What Red Saffron does not have though is alcohol. It's just not their thing. I only mention this because it is surprising how many people will leave a place when they find out they can't get a drink. So be forewarned and enjoy the food of another culture. It's worth it.

Restaurant Indonesia

Indonesian

1604 – 14 Street SW
Phone: 244•0645
Tuesday – Friday 11:30 am – 2:30 pm, 5 pm – 11 pm
Saturday 5 pm – 11 pm, Sunday 5 pm – 9 pm
Reservations recommended — Fully licensed — Non-smoking
V, MC, AE, Debit — $ – $$

INDONESIAN cuisine is one of the more uncommon styles in our neck of the woods. In spite of the petroleum connections between Calgary and Indonesia, we have only a single Indonesian restaurant in the city—Restaurant Indonesia. Fortunately, it is a good restaurant.

Residing near the mega-busy intersection of 17th Avenue and 14th Street SW, Restaurant Indonesia provides a calm and colourful contrast to the bustle outside. The walls are covered in carved, brightly painted flowers and masks, the products of a family business back in Indonesia. The colours and styles of the carvings indicate immediately that this is not like other Asian restaurants.

And a quick look at the menu shows that the food culture is different too. There's the ayam saus Java, a terrific dish of chicken in a creamy and spicy basil sauce. There's sambal goreng kambing, lamb done in an Indonesian curry. And there's aduk aduk tempeh, fried soybean cake and shrimp in a spicy, slightly sweet sauce. Now normally, fried soybean cake would be one of the last things I'd eat anywhere, but here, it is one of the first things I order. Soybean cake is not to everyone's taste, but this version is richly flavoured. The texture is similar to a very dense rice cake, and as a bonus, it is high in protein.

Indonesian food often contains the dense, salty-sweet tones of kecap asin, their own style of soy sauce. It's an intense flavour that provides the backdrop for that tempeh and many other dishes at Restaurant Indonesia. Also prevalent is sambal oelek, a chili paste that adds heat where necessary. Lighter tones are brought by ingredients such as lemon grass and pineapple. And there's coconut milk everywhere.

You may also indulge in a *rijsttafel*, or "rice table," that features twelve courses in a mini table-buffet of flavours. Rice tables harken back to the Dutch colonial days in Indonesia, and at Restaurant Indonesia it includes soup, an egg roll, satay, six more savoury dishes, rice, and fried bananas for dessert. That's a good deal for $22.50. For an even better bargain, Restaurant Indonesia offers lunch specials such as a satay combo with fried rice and noodles for $6.75.

It's always a pleasure to dine here, not just for the food but for the warm welcome and professional service. That and to get away from the traffic outside.

The Rimrock

Canadian

133 – 9 Avenue SW (The Fairmont Palliser)
Phone: 260 • 1219
Daily 6:30 am – 2 pm
Tuesday & Thursday 5 pm – 10 pm, Wednesday & Friday – Monday 5:30 pm – 10 pm
Reservations recommended — Fully licensed — Non-smoking
V, MC, AE, DC, JCB, Debit — $$ – $$$

A few years ago, I was asked by a CBC listener which restaurant was the oldest in town. I thought for a moment before realizing that the answer was stunningly simple—The Rimrock in The Fairmont Palliser hotel. Although it has been added to and renovated and had its name changed, there has been some form of food service facility at the west end of the Palliser's main floor since the hotel opened in 1914. I don't think there's another dining establishment in town that's been around that long.

The Rimrock is a grand hotel dining room with high ceilings, starched tablecloths, and beautiful hand-tooled, leather-clad pillars. One end of the room is highlighted by Charlie Beil's Rimrock mural, the artwork that gave the room its current name in 1962 (it was originally the Grill Room). The whole room reeks of Western history and always carries a sense of elegance.

Recent renovations have improved the ambience of The Rimrock even more. To expand the space, a private room and the entryway coat check were eliminated. Windows were punched in two small walls that separate the dining room from the lobby, creating an open feel to the space. There's now a greater sense of incorporation into the hotel. Instead of the room being closed in and dark, it is now bright and more inviting. And the view of the mural has been greatly enhanced.

The increase of space has allowed The Rimrock to move its popular lunch buffet into the room itself. It had previously extended into the lobby—admittedly a tempting sight, but traffic flow around it had been difficult. The buffet is rolled out each weekday, and for $21, features a range of salads and hot dishes, often including some carved-on-the-spot roast beef. Then there are the requisite decadent desserts (this is the place that holds "Death by Chocolate" evenings every Tuesday and Thursday too).

Beyond the lunch buffet, the menu offers an eclectic midday selection of items such as braised buffalo with Yorkshire pudding and linguine marinara, both at $19. In the evening, things get serious with pork tenderloin wrapped in wild boar bacon ($25), flax-crusted lamb ($32), and cedar-planked salmon ($26). It's fine food, well presented and sold at hotel prices.

The Rimrock menus always stay current with market trends, and the room is updated frequently. It is a historical masterpiece and will likely be around long after most other local restaurants pack it in.

www.fairmont.com

DOWN
That's
the
Spot
town

River Café

Seasonal Canadian Cuisine

Prince's Island Park
Phone: 261·7670
Monday – Friday 11 am – 11 pm, Saturday & Sunday 10 am – 11 pm
Closed in January
Reservations recommended — Fully licensed — Patio — Non-smoking
V, MC, AE, DC, Debit — $$ – $$$

THE most preferred patio for many Calgarians is that of the River Café. It's a greenery-swathed terrace on Prince's Island and has a view across a small Bow River channel to Eau Claire. The River Café is the only ongoing business on Prince's Island, giving it a monopoly on the beauty of the place. The patio has been lovingly landscaped, and outside of poplar-fluff season, is a fabulous place to dine.

It's hard to believe that the River Café was once a dowdy, concrete City of Calgary Parks building. That old building is still there somewhere, but it has been buried under elegant renovations. The interior now has the rustic charm of a five-star fishing lodge. With weighty wooden chairs and crisply linened tables, wraparound windows and stone fireplaces, it is outdoorsy and sophisticated at the same time.

The food style spans a similar theme with a strong dedication to natural Canadian ingredients. The chefs search out the best of local and Canadian food products, choosing them first over imports. Natricia feta cheese from Ponoka is combined with grilled portobello mushrooms in a torte. Local pheasant is teamed with dried blueberries and fennel in salad rolls. Red lentils from the Prairies are puréed into hummus. And Northern Alberta wild boar prosciutto tops flatbread with Parmesan from Camrose.

The wood-grilled buffalo burger with aged cheddar and chokecherry jelly is not just local, it's one of the best burgers I've ever had. Meaty and rich, set off by the tartness of the jelly and the bite of the cheddar, it elevates burgers to a new level. And you can't get much fresher and healthier and even tastier than their stinging nettle and leek soup. (Don't worry, the sting of the formic acid has been cooked out of the nettles.) I've had some pretty wonderful desserts here too, from a wild rice pudding to a creamy panna cotta.

But these dishes do not come cheap. Salads are $9 to $11, with other appetizers in the $8 to $19 range. The Lake Winnipeg pickerel with potato and leek salad and smoked oyster vinaigrette is $28, while the locally raised Arctic char with a lobster couscous is $27. A beef tenderloin with oyster mushrooms, bacon vinaigrette, and foie gras emulsion tops the list at $39.

It's unique food in a unique setting—a truly fine and very Canadian experience.

www.river-cafe.com

Rose Garden

Thai

207 Stephen Avenue Walk SW
Phone: 263•1900
Monday – Friday 11:30 am – 10 pm, Saturday noon – 10 pm
Mid-April – late September: Also open Sunday 5 pm – 10 pm
Reservations recommended, especially at lunch
Fully Licensed — Patio — Non-smoking
V, MC, AE, Debit — $ – $$

A lot of high-toned and flashy restaurants have opened on Stephen Avenue over the past few years. And many of them have great food and wonderful ambience. But in the middle of all the splashy places is an unassuming Thai restaurant that is packed every weekday for lunch. The Rose Garden offers a full lunch and dinner menu, but also sets out a great midday buffet of red-curry beef, Thai barbecued chicken, and spring rolls that often has the restaurant full before noon. This is one of downtown's favourite hangouts, a place to meet friends and a place for good Thai food.

The lunch buffet is $11, a bargain compared to many of the neighbourhood menus. It's especially a good deal when you look at the quality of the food you are getting. The buffet is constantly tended. Bowls of scorching hot calamari are delivered as quickly as they are devoured.

And devoured they are. Many fans of the Rose Garden are, to be charitable, hearty eaters. Big guys from oil companies tuck in and make numerous trips to the buffet. But many lighter eaters are here too, going more for the freshness of the food. Some dishes are deep-fried, but lots are stir-fried and come across as quite light in a world of greasy buffets.

I've never found skimping on the quality. The tom yum goong soup is well structured and packed with shrimp and mushrooms. The cuts of meat used in the red-curry beef and the ginger chicken are always good—you don't have to pick through bones and gristle here. And there is more than just broccoli and green peppers in the various vegetable dishes.

While customers are pillaging the buffet, Rose Garden staff swoop down on the tables, tidying them and bringing fresh water and napkins. It is unobtrusive, professional service that is always done with a smile.

The quality and care flow into the look and tone of the room. In spite of being a hectic lunch buffet place, it comes across as calm, even serene. Tables are spaced as well as possible in the long, narrow room, allowing almost everyone a certain amount of privacy. The decor is mildly Asian, and the room always strikes me as well maintained.

So the Rose Garden is not big and loud, and it's easy to miss with all the other distractions of Stephen Avenue. I think that's just the way its many fans want it.

Rouge

Calgary Cuisine with a French Twist

1240 – 8 Avenue SE
Phone: 531•2767
Monday – Friday 11:30 am – 2 pm, Monday – Saturday 5:30 pm – 10 pm
Reservations recommended — Fully licensed — Patio — Non-smoking
V, MC, AE, DC, Debit — $$ – $$$

THIS historic home of A.E. Cross sits quietly by the Bow River, surrounded by a caragana hedge. It's a small but stately Victorian wood frame with a huge yard and garden, the river along the back adding to the pastoral charm. Cross, a major mover and shaker in the early 1900s, purchased the house in 1899, wisely choosing a residence that was just a few short, upwind blocks from his brewery. Today, the yard rolls back from a patio to flower beds and shady elms. On a warm twenty-first century evening, there are few more private patios on which to enjoy a meal.

The site gained historic status in 1977 and has been a restaurant since 1991. In the summer of 2001, Paul Rogalski, a former head chef at La Chaumière, and Olivier Reynaud, an experienced restaurateur from Provence, took it over. Together they have been reshaping the restaurant, which had been called The Cross House until the spring of 2003, into a delightful destination now dubbed Rouge.

They have moved Rouge away from the former tea-house look and toward a more contemporary feel. The exterior has been repainted a deep burgundy, and the dining rooms reflect new tones of sage and more red. A huge bellows, a souvenir of Reynaud's homeland, hangs on one wall, and new cutlery and chairs tie the look together.

Rogalski's experience at places such as La Chaumière and in Asia shows on the menu. There's a lobster dumpling consommé with fresh lemon balm, seared foie gras on walnut French toast with a port syrup, and tempura tuna with a gingered sake broth. Rogalski is one of the most talented chefs in Calgary, and he can draw exquisite flavours from the most unusual combinations. His prairie roots show in a white-bean and bacon cassoulet and a buckwheat risotto, and his global sophistication shines in a white-asparagus soup with a black-truffle froth. It's a soup that has diners squeezing the bowl for the last drop.

Meanwhile Reynaud runs the service side of Rouge with Gallic charm and professionalism. His team perfectly complements the standards set by the kitchen.

And you can't beat that patio on a warm summer day. Rouge is an elegant blend of contemporary and traditional, of local and global, one of the best of the best. I think A.E. Cross and his family would be pleased.

www.rougecalgary.com

Sage Bistro

Canadian Bistro

1712 Bow Valley Trail, Canmore
Phone: 678·4878
Sunday – Thursday 8 am – 11 pm, Friday & Saturday 8 am – midnight
Reservations recommended — Fully licensed — Deck
Non-smoking restaurant, smoking on deck
V, MC, AE, Debit — $$

O N the Bow Valley Trail entrance to Canmore, there's a big log building that's been there for about twenty years. For the past fifteen of those years it's been called The Kabin restaurant. It was popular on the tour-bus circuit for its woodsy ambience and "safe" menu. But recently the owners decided to change the concept. They renamed it Sage Bistro and added a Contemporary mountain tone to the menu. And the result is impressive.

I've always liked the look of the place. What's not to like about huge logs and a view of the railroad tracks from a sheltered patio? But now I really like the attitude of the menu. So many places open in the Bow Valley with little sense of the surroundings. But Sage Bistro captures the mountain-fresh-and-friendly tone of Canmore perfectly with buffalo lasagna, a roasted carrot and goat-cheese terrine, and quail stuffed with wild rice and cranberries.

The menus have a hearty approach and a socially conscious undertone. They lure the meat eaters with lamb burgers and whitetail deer medallions, but satisfy the vegetarian crowd with asparagus, roasted squash, and pea risotto and eggplant Parmesan with pesto spaghetti. They indulge both sides with desserts of maple syrup crème brûlée and caramelized banana and vanilla cream pie. As a bonus, prices aren't as high as the Three Sisters out the window. Most items are well under $20.

I had a bowl of roasted red-pepper soup with fresh basil and goat cheese that was sublime. Thick and velvety, packed with black-pepper heat, the goat cheese and basil brought lightness and freshness to the soup. Marvelous.

Then a venison meat loaf sandwich exceeded my expectations. The meat loaf itself was exceptional, two slices of well-spiced and well-cooked loaf. Placed over a toasted slice of sourdough bread, glazed with a thick mushroom gravy, and topped with beer-braised onions, it was one of those rare dishes where all the elements work together to create something superb. Not only that, the sweet-potato fries were an inspired addition to the plate with their colour, texture, and flavour.

As a final touch, service follows the current "no worries" style of Australian itinerants. Unfailingly cheerful, the band of Aussie boarders and bikers that populate the mountain service industry provide an appropriately energetic backdrop to the room.

Sage Bistro is a bold change from the tried-and-true, and it works wonderfully.

Saigon

Vietnamese

1221 – 12 Avenue SW
Phone: 228•4200
Monday – Saturday 11 am – 10 pm
Reservations recommended — Fully licensed — Non-smoking
V, MC, AE, DC — $ – $$

COMFORT food comes in many forms. Sometimes for Catherine and me it comes as plates of imperial rolls and bowls of bun at the Saigon. The food is delicately, beautifully flavoured with nuoc mam and lemon grass and fresh mint, the service is quick, and the price is low. And if we want it in a hurry, we can be in and out in about twenty minutes.

Vietnamese cuisine has been one of the biggest global food trends over the past decade, but in spite of the proliferation of restaurants, the Saigon has remained our favourite for its freshness and quality. They offer a huge list of dishes—about 170 in all—from the imperial rolls to the tamarind sautéed chicken, with great variety in between. Of the many main dishes, the satay sautéed shrimp and the la lot beef remain among my favourites. The shrimp are done to crunchiness in a peanut-chili sauce. The la lot beef is an unusual dish of meatballs wrapped in fragrant la lot leaves and charbroiled. The lemon grass chicken is always good, and then there is the caramel sautéed shrimp or the barbecued pork chop on rice. All excellent.

For those interested in working for their dinner, there are the Genghis Khan grills. A curved, perforated metal grill—reminiscent of Genghis Khan's helmet—is delivered to your table along with plates of onion with raw beef, shrimp, or calamari, rice-paper wraps, and fresh greens. Burners go under the helmet to create the grill effect, and you toss the raw stuff on to cook. When it's done to your taste, you roll it in the wraps with the greens and some hoisin sauce and gobble it down like a barbarian. Loads of fun and tasty too. The grills come for two or more and start in the low $20s.

Otherwise the most expensive single dishes hit $12.75. Five imperial rolls cost $4.25, and the la lot beef is $9.75, as is the lemon grass chicken.

The Saigon is filled with glass-topped tables and brightened by some north-facing windows offering a scenic view of 12th Avenue traffic. It will never win any awards for design, but it is comfortable and simple. It's a family-run operation where there is a great deal of skill in the kitchen and friendliness out front. And the food still offers you some of the best quality for your dollar in the city.

St. James's Gate

Irish Pub

207 Wolf Street, Banff
Phone: 762 • 9355
Sunday – Thursday 11 am – 1 am
Friday & Saturday 11 am – 2 am
Reservations accepted for over 7 — Fully licensed — Non-smoking section
V, MC, AE, DC — $$

I was sitting near the front door of St. James's Gate enjoying a fine plate of fish and chips when the door flew open. Spilling in with the early afternoon light came three Brits, a fiftyish fellow with his wife and daughter. The male of the group lunged to the bar, pulled himself up, and declared in a thick Yorkshire accent, "I'm all right now, Mutha." Pints were poured, shepherd's pies were ordered, and the small group relaxed.

I watched for a while as a procession of middle-aged Americans, youthful Australians, and a host of Canadians flocked into St. James's Gate in a similar fashion. Victims of vacation overload and tour-bus cuisine, they were revived by the familiarity of the frosty lager and the pub-food menu.

St. James's Gate (a reference to the Dublin address of the Guinness brewery) is a lifeline to many visiting Banff. It's woody and smoky and pubby, there is no view of the mountains anywhere, and there are thirty-three beers on tap. It's just what the doctor ordered for those in need of an Irish pub fix.

Which is why St. James's Gate is always busy. That and a menu that exceeds the norm. Having achieved official Guinness certification, St. James's Gate has a high standard of cuisine, albeit within the confines of the Irish pub genre. The fish and chips, served with stinging hot french fries, is genuinely fine, the best halibut version I've had outside Alaska. Sure it's high fat, but this is a pub after all and that's what the beer is for, to cut the oil.

Filling out the list are pub classics such as steak and Guinness pie, Irish stew, various boxties (potato pancakes), and a lamb curry. And in deference to Banff's eclectic nature, there are offerings of Szechwan green beans, meat loaf ciabatta, and an Asian noodle and tuna salad. Prices are fair with most items under $14 and a Jameson-laced steak topping out the list at $18.

On the downside, service leans to the pub style of things too. It's not unfriendly, but it can be erratic and somewhat impersonal. I'm confident that everything will arrive as ordered, but not necessarily in a well-timed fashion. The other note is that smoke does permeate the room, even the non-smoking section. So beware.

But if a lifeline to your favourite pub back home is needed, St. James's Gate is more than capable of filling the bill. And the glass.

Sakana Grill

Japanese

116 – 2 Avenue SW (Harmonious Centre)
Phone: 290 • 1118
Daily 11 am – 2 pm, 5 pm – 11 pm
Reservations recommended — Fully licensed — Non-smoking
V, MC, AE, DC, Debit — $$

SOMETIMES it's easy to forget that there's more to Japanese food than just sushi. Every time I think the sushi craze is fading, I see another sushi bar opening. But one place that has always presented a balanced approach to this cuisine is the Sakana Grill in Chinatown.

Part of that approach is due to the sheer size of the place. The Sakana Grill is, I believe, the biggest Japanese restaurant in Calgary, allowing it space for teppan grills, a sushi-boat bar, tatami rooms, and a variety of other booths and tables. Customers can dine discreetly in a booth or have a lively group party wrapped around one of the grills. Wherever you sit, however, the energetic tone of Sakana will likely invade your space.

The Sakana Grill had the first sushi-boat bar in town (nowadays there are many fleets plying the waters of Calgary) and still serves a good round of sushi. For big sushi eaters there's the $29 "Love Boat" dinner for two, which comes with soup, salad, ice cream, and a whole whack of sushi and sashimi.

But the parties happen around the teppan grills where the chefs wield their knives skillfully. They slice, they dice, and they toss their knives in the air while the meats and vegetables and noodles sizzle away. Sauces are added with flare, and the food is scooped onto plates and served bracingly hot. Sure it's just a fancified version of the mall-based Edos around town (or more accurately they are a simplified version of the teppan grill), but it's entertaining and pretty darned tasty.

For those looking for more cooked food, there is an evening list of tempura, noodles, and various dishes ranging from chicken baked in seaweed and salmon teriyaki to beef tenderloin Kobe-style. And at lunch there are lots of combo specials for $7 to $9 in addition to more noodles, gyoza dumplings, and other good things.

Service can bog down a little when lunch gets rolling. That's due to the instant crush of lunchers descending from nearby office towers and the strain it puts on the kitchen. Otherwise, though, service is efficient and pleasant, performed by traditionally clad staff.

The Sakana Grill also offers classes for those who want to make sushi at home or for those who just want a little more knowledge about the food they're eating. I guess the sushi craze still has some staying power.

www.sakana.com

Saltlik

Steak House

101 Stephen Avenue Walk SW
Phone: 537·1160
Monday – Friday 11 am – 11 pm, Saturday 5 pm – 11 pm, Sunday 5 pm – 10 pm
Reservations recommended — Fully licensed — Patio
Non-smoking dining room, smoking in lounge areas
V, MC, AE, Debit — $$ – $$$

SALTLIK is from the new school of steak houses, a place that is bright, airy, and has a lively, contemporary atmosphere. It is also from the Earls Restaurant group, their own take on a steak house. I have a lot of respect for what Earls does; they've come a long way since the fluorescent purple and orange days of Fuller's. They seem able to capture the mood of the market and create restaurant concepts that are immensely popular. Just look at the success of Joey Tomato's.

Plunked into an old bank building, Saltlik has a look that is part swanky Western and part upscale steak house—lots of big booths, a fireplace, and elegant lamps. Plus a huge hanging glass sculpture that's part Mardi Gras and part jellyfish. It's a large space filled with smiling, Earls-trained staff.

The menu showcases steaks, from a prime sirloin and a New York cut topped with Ermite cheese to a straight-ahead tenderloin with Béarnaise sauce. Starters include dry ribs and calamari and smoked-salmon bruschetta. Add in rotisserie chicken, seared tuna salad, and pork chops to round out the list and you've got a crowd pleaser.

We tried one of their small tenderloins and a combo plate of chicken and ribs. But first we had a tasty bowl of yesterday's rotisserie chicken in a chunky, herb-filled tomato broth. The tenderloin was a perfect medium rare, as requested. The chicken and pork ribs were well prepared, though the chicken was a little more cooked than I would have liked. The ribs were excellent, glazed in a chipotle barbecue sauce that our server cautioned might be spicy. I found it more sweet than spicy— on a heat scale of one to ten, it was about a three.

My only concern with Saltlik is their pricing. The tenderloin was $27 and a peppercorn strip loin is $32. With those you get a baked potato. If you'd like some asparagus or scalloped potatoes or such, you can add on another $3 or so per person. Sorry, that's too much. Saltlik gives the initial impression of being priced more moderately, but it can quickly become expensive.

Not that Saltlik does a bad job. It's a culturally appropriate place to have a good Stampede meal any time of year. It's a fun room and our server did a superb job. But those prices are still too high for what it is.

Note: There is a Saltlik franchise in Banff with a similar menu.

Sandro

Italian

431 – 41 Avenue NE
Phone: 230·7754
Monday – Friday 11:30 am – 2 pm, 5 pm – 10 pm, Saturday 5 pm – 10 pm
Reservations recommended — Fully licensed — Non-smoking
V, MC, AE, Debit — $$

YOU'LL notice that the pizza recommendations in this book are pretty scarce. We're picky about our pizza, and there is a lack of good ones around. (If you find one, please let me know.)

But we do like the pizza at Sandro. A lot. Enough that they don't even give us a menu any more. They just ask us if we want the "Dom Special," extra large, with crisp pancetta and no shrimp. We always tell them yes, but we add that we want it Italian-style, meaning light on the cheese.

Then we're happy. With a window seat, a glass of red wine, and our Dom Special, we are transported for a few moments from the corner of Edmonton Trail and 41 Avenue NE to a place where all pizzas are works of art. We forget that we're sitting in a crowded café on the second floor of a nondescript strip mall above Wheel Pros and Hitchez Trailer Accessories.

All the elements of Sandro's pizza work. The crust is good enough to eat on its own—no cardboard taste here. And the tomato sauce tastes like real tomatoes were used. The toppings, including the cheese, are high quality and intelligently distributed. And it's cooked properly and thoroughly, without gummy textures or burned spots. Good pizza is so simple.

We understand that Sandro does other Italian food too. We see people order pastas and veal dishes as we scarf back our Dom, and we've even gone so far as to order appetizers of Caesar salad and shrimp in a lemon and white-wine sauce while waiting for our pie. But in truth, we've never had a full Italian meal here. We've thought about it, and we always say to each other that those other dishes look great. And then we order our Dom.

Sandro is always full, so call ahead. Fans from bikers to business suits to big Italian families gather here for their favourite dishes, and they all cohabite easily. Partly it's the oddly conspiratorial location and partly it's the professional staff who take everything in stride.

That's another big reason we like Sandro. By now, the staff know I review restaurants, and they couldn't care less. They give us no extra attention, and treat us the same as everyone else. And that's just how it should be.

Santorini Taverna

Greek

1502 Centre Street N
Phone: 276•8363
Tuesday – Thursday 11 am – 10:30 pm
Friday 11 am – 11:30 pm, Saturday noon – 11:30 pm, Sunday 4 pm – 9:30 pm
Reservations recommended — Fully licensed — Patio — Non-smoking
V, MC, AE, DC, Debit — $$

EVER since the success of *My Big Fat Greek Wedding*, there has been a resurgence in the popularity of Greek restaurants. The public has returned to the fragrant foods of the Greek isles and the lively atmosphere that accompanies it. And no place does it better than Santorini Taverna.

Santorini looks the part of the typical Greek restaurant with an exterior of white plaster and blue trim. Inside there's a patina to the wood floors and more plaster walls; plants have overgrown parts of the room, and a small fountain trickles in one corner. It looks like it's been there since the days of Odysseus. It's really only been there since the mid-eighties, but that practically rates it as an antiquity in Calgary restaurant terms.

Quality has never wavered over the years—the food is uniformly excellent. The arni kleftiko (roast lamb) is consistently tender and moist. It pulls apart in long, juicy strands. The calamari is among the most skillfully prepared we've ever had. They pay attention to it, cooking it twice in hot oil and changing the oil frequently to ensure clarity of taste. With a little tzatziki for dipping, it is a superior squid dish. The moussaka is a comparatively light dish of potatoes and ground meat. Some versions are heavy and oily; this one is not. Then there is the pastichio, a fairly uncommon dish on Greek menus. Similar to moussaka, the potato is replaced with pasta, but it is still layered with béchamel—a sauce claimed by the Greeks as their own. It's a savoury blend of creamy flavours and textures.

The difficulty is in deciding what to have at Santorini. So the owners have also created various combination plates ranging from a collection of cold appetizers ($12) through to seafood appetizers ($16) to a big dinner platter for two with six dishes ($45). But the best way to sample their food is with the mezethes special at $26 per person. It combines smaller portions of eight dishes, providing a broad array of tastes. It's a lot of very good food—we speak from experience here.

Throughout the Santorini experience, there will likely be fine Greek wine, a little ouzo, and lots of music and dancing. Owners Andreas and Maria Nicolaides say that every day is a party at Santorini and that everyone is invited. It's no wonder they have survived the test of time.

Shikiji

Japanese

1608 Centre Street N
Phone: 520•0093
Monday – Thursday 11:30 am – 10 pm
Friday & Saturday 11:30 am – 11 pm, Sunday 11:30 am – 9 pm
Reservations accepted — Fully licensed — Non-smoking
V, MC, AE, DC, Debit — $ – $$

THE new Shikiji is a fine example of a Japanese noodle shop, albeit with a strong side of sushi. Most of the menu is focused on the udon, the ramen, and the soba noodles of Japanese cuisine. Udon are wheat-flour noodles done here in two sizes (fat and skinny), ramen are egg noodles that have become quite popular in Japan in the last few decades, and soba are buckwheat-flour noodles that are common to the northern islands of Japan.

Shikiji, which means "the way of the four seasons," is a small, unassuming room that seats about forty around a central service area. The tabletops are loaded with the usual soy sauce as well as bottles of rice vinegar and chili oil and jars of dried garlic. Depending on which noodles you order, you'll receive more stuff—maybe a dish of sesame seeds or a wooden ladle or an assortment of additional bowls. In the latter case, you can eat directly out of a big noodle bowl or you can remove some of the noodles to a smaller bowl and add in the other ingredients that have been delivered to your table. It's complex, so go, order, ask some questions, and have fun. This is a style that gives the customer options.

I've tried both the thick udon and the ramen on two visits to Shikiji. You get a lot for the price tag. Noodle dishes range from about $7 to $11, and they are packed with stuff. The Nabeyaki udon had mushrooms, green onions, sea legs, and an egg swimming in a broth with the noodles. And a bowl of ramen was filled with barbecued pork, nori, slivered vegetables, and more broth. Both dishes had a variety of textures and flavours, and the broths, expertly prepared on-site, were great.

One note about the food at Shikiji is that it is quite salty. Those stocks are highly salted, and they don't offer low-salt soy sauce, even with the sushi. But I admit that it is part of the food culture. The sushi, by the way, is quite good. They offer a reasonable by-the-piece menu and a list of combos, including a nine-piece selection for about $9.

Service at Shikiji is pleasant. I think I confused them a bit by asking lots of questions about how to manage the food, but they were unfailingly helpful.

Just remember, you're dealing with long, slippery, wet noodles here, so expect a dry-cleaning bill to go along with your meal.

Silver Dragon

Chinese (Cantonese & Szechwan)

106 – 3 Avenue SE
Phone: 264·5326
Monday – Thursday 10 am – midnight
Friday & Saturday 10 am – 2 am, Sunday & Holidays 9:30 am – 10:30 pm
Reservations accepted — Fully licensed — Non-smoking
V, MC, AE, DC, JCB, Debit — $$

WAITING in line at the Silver Dragon, I was reminded of my first visits to this Chinatown classic almost thirty years ago. My roommate and I would come down here for dim sum, the Silver Dragon being one of only two restaurants serving it at that time. And back then, it was only on Sundays. The place was mostly red, and there were few other Occidental faces in the crowd. We enjoyed the experience and brought many people here over the next few years. In spite of dim sum's growing popularity, we never made a reservation, lining up only occasionally.

So when we dropped in on a Sunday evening, I didn't even think to reserve ahead. Wrong. We were added to a long list with an unlikely estimate of twenty minutes. So we waited and watched the goldfish swimming in the tank by the door.

The Silver Dragon has changed a bit from the seventies. The room still has a distinctive L-shape, and there's still a long staircase leading up to it, but they have redone the interior with natural wood, adding skylights and gold trim. It appears successful and a far cry from the utilitarian fluorescents and worn carpet of the early days.

But many long-lived restaurants survive on reputation rather than on current product, so I was interested to see how the Silver Dragon would fare. We were seated after only fifteen minutes and presented with the menu, a collection of 235 mostly Cantonese dishes. The prices have gone up a bit over the years, and they now include a few non-Cantonese dishes like the Szechwan beef, but most looked surprisingly familiar.

We ordered some grilled dumplings ($7.95), prawns in black-bean sauce ($16), spicy palace-style chicken ($10.25), and stir-fried vegetables ($8.50). And we were impressed. The dumplings were perhaps the best we've ever had, fat and flavourful with a tasty pastry and two dipping sauces. The prawn dish featured at least a dozen and a half huge crustaceans, perfectly cooked, and the chicken was crunchy and crisp. (But spicy? Well, it was actually pretty mild.) Even the vegetables were excellent, a combo of baby corn, pea pods, bok choy, broccoli, and mushrooms.

All the flavours were gentle but sincere, allowing the natural taste of the ingredients to come through. On top of that, service was pleasant, brisk, and professional. Once seated, we were fully fed and on our way in about forty-five minutes.

Which made the next folks in line very happy.

Silver Inn

Chinese (Peking)

2702 Centre Street N
Phone: 276•6711
Tuesday – Friday 11 am – 2 pm
Sunday, Tuesday – Thursday 5 pm – 10 pm, Friday & Saturday 5 pm – 11 pm
Reservations recommended — Fully licensed — Non-smoking
V, MC, AE, Debit — $$

FROM the outside the Silver Inn doesn't look much like a historic site. It sits perilously close to the traffic buzzing by on Centre Street, quietly doing business as it has every day since the late seventies. Inside it's a simple collection of dining rooms created from an old retail building and a house. First-timers look for signs of notoriety and fame but find none.

But Silver Inn regulars know that they are dining in hallowed culinary halls. That they are at the epicentre of the most Calgary of foods. That they have journeyed to the storied home of ginger beef.

The true origins of ginger beef have been lost in time. The Silver Inn owners insist they did not invent it. Rather, they say, they dug out a recipe and adapted it for the Calgary market when the Silver Inn opened in its first location in 1974. They just wanted this "new" Peking cuisine to have a good beef dish for their meaty market. It quickly became popular both at the Silver Inn and at their sister restaurant, the Home Food Inn.

Since then, ginger beef has become a standard dish in most Peking restaurants. Everyone has a version of it, and I've known tourists to travel thousands of miles to dine in the city of ginger beef.

And it's still good at the Silver Inn. They start with a decent cut of beef and go from there. Occasionally it gets a little too sweet for my taste, but when the kitchen is "on," it's a flawless blend of chilies and ginger and sweetness. (Remarkably, the same chef as day one is still at the helm.)

The Silver Inn is far from being a one trick pony. Other classics here include a definitive chicken and cashews in yellow-bean sauce featuring chunks of boneless, skinless chicken and loads of cashews in a salty, savoury bean sauce. I always have an order of it. It's the perfect foil to the ginger beef. And the grilled dumplings are better than most. More ginger is used and it comes through, along with the taste of green onion. These dumplings are not overworked or undercooked.

The Silver Inn staff always seem dazzled and a bit shy about their ginger beef notoriety. There are no flashy signs or claims to fame. They just smile when asked about it. And then they serve the food and let you decide how good it is.

Sino

Vietnamese Fusion

513 – 8 Avenue SW (Penny Lane Mall)
Phone: 503 • 0474
Monday – Wednesday 11 am – 5 pm, Thursday & Friday 11 am – 9 pm
Saturday 5 pm – 10 pm
Reservations recommended — Fully licensed — Non-smoking
V, MC, AE, DC, JCB, Debit — $$

PENNY LANE used to be a death trap for restaurants, especially the ones that didn't have street presence. But right now there are some pretty busy places in the eventually-to-be-demolished mall. Perhaps the hottest is Sino with its fusion of Vietnamese, Thai, and French cuisines.

Sino opened in 2000 and quickly built a loyal following. In fact, they expanded just one year after opening. Their popularity is due to the culinary talents of chef-owner Ken Nguyen and the service skills of his partner Donna Malonzo. At any given lunch, every seat is taken, including those that spill into the hallway. Service may not be as fast as at a traditional Vietnamese noodle house, but the staff buzz around and the food still rolls out quickly. If you want a quiet meal at Sino, it's better to go in the evening, but lunch provides an energetic midday event. A meal at Sino can lift the spirit and satisfy the palate at the same time.

Nguyen's food jumps with flavour. Crispy prawns are seasoned with pepper, cloves, onion, and garlic. Salmon is wrapped in rice paper with prawns and dipped in a chili fish sauce. Chicken is poached in a creamy curry, and green papaya is shredded into a salad with cucumber and carrot. It's beautiful food, often served with flowers adorning the plates.

All around Sino there is a sense of style. The room is done in subtle greens and off-whites to compensate for the lack of natural light. Nguyen also runs the Itinerante Flower Boutiques in North Hill Centre and Bow Valley Square, and his creativity flows easily from the food to the bouquets of orchids throughout the room.

Sino is not cheap. Appetizers run $5 to $10, with entrees rolling into the teens. But then, this is not cheap food. There are no shoddy ingredients here, and you won't find yourself scraping off unnecessary bits of bone and skin. The food is high quality throughout.

If you have room, try one of Sino's crème brûlées. They always have the basic vanilla brûlée, one of the best versions in the city. But if you are a chocolate fan, ask if they have any chocolate brûlée. It's not to everyone's taste, but it alone is enough to bring back some people.

Sino goes against the grain by serving a unique cuisine in an invisible location and packing them in every day. I guess the market knows a winner when it sees one.

Sobaten

Japanese Noodle House

#105, 550 – 11 Avenue SW
Phone: 265 · 2664
Monday – Wednesday 11:30 am – 10 pm, Thursday & Friday 11:30 am – 11 pm
Saturday 3:30 pm – 11 pm, Sunday 3:30 pm – 10 pm
Reservations accepted — Fully licensed — Non-smoking
V, MC, AE, JCB, Debit — $ – $$

I had noticed Sobaten after it opened in late 2002, but I think I'd been avoiding it because the space had housed so many poor restaurants over the years. But then Stephen Wong, a food writer from Vancouver, told me how much he had enjoyed the house-made noodles there. So I went. He was right.

Sobaten (which means "heavenly buckwheat noodles") has taken over the west side of the space, hiving off a long, narrow section that seats about eighty. The look is minimalist contemporary with solid, straight-backed chairs, black-topped tables, big windows, and simple overhead lamps. The view of the busy streets and the glaring sun is dampened by large pull-down blinds. Very sleek.

At the north end of the room, in a glass booth, sits the noodle machine. Imported from Japan, it pumps out soba and udon noodles on a daily basis. The udon flour mix comes from Japan too, ensuring the most authentic texture for these wheat-flour noodles. The soba are a blend of North Dakota buckwheat flour and Alberta wheat flour. Both noodle styles are popular in Japan, served with various toppings and either hot in broth or cold with sauce on the side.

Sobaten also does some donburis, rice dishes with toppings such as salmon or breaded pork. You will find a limited amount of other things like tempura and yakitori and a list of sushi too, but the menu is mostly about noodles.

So I tried a bowl of soba in a hot broth topped with broiled duck breast, grilled green onions, spinach, and watercress. The broth is marvellous—a rich, deep brown that is still clear, filled with soy and seafood flavours. It's the perfect backdrop for the al dente soba noodles. Soba are not soft like many wheat and rice noodles; they have a denseness to them. It's like the difference between fluffy white bread and dense multi-grain. The grilled greens add lightness and more flavour to the bowl. It's marvellous food with only two downsides. The main one is that it is salty. The other is that it can be messy, flipping the broth around as you slurp up those noodles.

But for soup and noodle fans, Sobaten is a must-visit. It may just set a new standard for how you view your soup. I know I'll be back for more.

www.sobaten.com

Spolumbo's

Italian Deli & Sausage Makers

1308 – 9 Avenue SE
Phone: 264•6452
Monday – Saturday 8 am – 5:30 pm
Reservations accepted for private room only — Fully licensed — Non-smoking
V, MC, AE, Debit — $

IT used to work like this: People searching for a sausage place they'd heard about in Inglewood were told to head to the south end of the Zoo bridge on 12th Street SE, keep going south a block or two, and then look for a big brick building at the corner of 9th Avenue. Now it works like this: People searching for the Zoo are told to head for Spolumbo's and then go north across the bridge. Easy.

It's fascinating that a sausage factory cum café has become a culinary landmark for Calgary. The energy of the owners, combined with the intensity of the food, is a perfect fit with the personality of the city.

Spolumbo's is owned and operated by three large, retired Calgary Stampeders, brothers Tony and Tom Spoletini and teammate Mike Palumbo. (Get it? *Spol*-etini and Pal-*umbo*?) They have managed to parlay some family recipes for sausage and meatballs into a mini-empire of sausagedom. They started out in a small deli with a rudimentary sausage machine in the back and a single ordering station. When the lineups extended into the parking lot, they decided to build their own place a few blocks away. Not being into half measures, the boys built a hundred-seat café with a large federally inspected sausage plant attached. The lineups are still long but move pretty quickly (now there are two ordering stations).

Spolumbo's is crowded most days with avid Spolumbites, eyes glazed over, mouths caught in a rictus of tomatoey delight. It's not a pretty sight. They're diving into meat loaf sandwiches, big piles of cold cuts stacked into Italian rolls, and tomato-sauced sausages. And they are loving it.

They are not alone. In 2002, *Gourmet* magazine writers Jane and Michael Stern visited Calgary and found the sausages equal to those back home in their sausage-savvy neighbourhood. That's lofty praise from people who know their meats.

Spolumbo's twenty varieties of sausage can be found not only in their deli, but also in local grocery stores and at community events around the city. And one of their promotions takes them to Eskimo games at Edmonton's Commonwealth Stadium where they grill sausages on the sidelines for the fans. Occasionally they make a foray into the end zone, unfamiliar territory for former linemen. Once there they do a little dance, but so far have resisted the temptation to spike a sausage into the turf.

www.spolumbos.com

Stranger's

Caribbean

#9, 2650 – 36 Street NE
Phone: 248 • 4012
Monday – Thursday 11 am – 9 pm
Friday & Saturday 11 am – 10 pm, Sunday noon – 8 pm
Reservations accepted — Fully licensed — Non-smoking
V, MC, Debit — $ – $$

I love Caribbean spicing when it is handled with skill. The cinnamon, the nutmeg, the cloves, and all the other fragrant spices, perked up with habanero heat, assault the mouth and make the diner sit up and pay attention. I'm not talking about stupid-hot food that blows the flavour away with chilies. I mean skillfully prepared jerk chicken and curry goat and beef roti like you'll find at Stranger's.

Stranger's food is good because of owner Everol Powell, a professional chef from the Caribbean. He has trained and worked in various restaurant and hotel kitchens and is now fulfilling his dream of running his own restaurant. He has a subtle hand at the stove and produces an excellent version of the cuisine.

His jerk chicken is a symphony of flavours. Each bite spreads various spices over your palate with just enough heat to make you take notice. His brown chicken is softer in tone, a more delicate version of Caribbean cuisine for the heat-averse. And his culinary skill is obvious in the rice and beans. They are not just an extra side starch; they have taste and substance too.

Stranger's also offers some of the more unique fare of the Caribbean such as oxtail, callaloo, and ackee with codfish. And a freezer sitting by the counter is filled with soursop, rum and raisin, grapenut, and mango ice creams. Specially imported, they bring another tone to Stranger's. Beside the freezer is a cooler of island drinks with the requisite beers and ginger beer and Ting, the grapefruit drink. If you can handle the sugar, these are tasty beverages.

Stranger's does lunch and dinner, but one of the best ways to try this cuisine is at a leisurely $16 Sunday brunch that is held on the last weekend of each month. It's a laid-back island experience that can warm the coldest January day.

Many people have never heard of or been to Stranger's. If it were on 4th Street or 17th Avenue, it would be packed every day from the moment it opened. But it's a little off the beaten restaurant path in the quiet neighbourhood of Dover. Not that it's quiet inside though. Stranger's seats about sixty under ceilings colourfully draped in Appleton rum and Carib beer banners. It's bright and friendly and understated, with reggae on the stereo and skill in the kitchen.

And where else can you find grapenut ice cream?

Sugo

Contemporary Italian

1214 – 9 Avenue SE
Phone: 263 • 1115
Wednesday – Friday 11 am – 2 pm, Tuesday – Saturday 5 pm – 10 pm
Reservations recommended — Fully licensed — Non-smoking
V, MC, AE, DC, Debit — $$

THE arrival of Sugo has brought more variety into the Italian food scene. Not that there's anything wrong with the abundance of Calabrese- and Abruzzese-style restaurants. But Sugo's Contemporary tone is welcome.

Their Inglewood building has high ceilings and a bay window, giving it a sense of maturity and airiness. It's narrow so the owners have painted it off-white and mounted a bank of mirrors along one wall to generate the sense of a larger space. The look is neutral and clean; white tablecloths, wood chairs, and a bar at one end add to the spare, simple look.

Sugo prepares a new menu each day and it's fairly short, reflecting the fresh ingredients available. We started dinner with a grilled eggplant and portobello salad in a balsamic reduction and a bowl of rabbit and root-vegetable soup. Both were huge servings—the salad was big enough for two and should have been for the $11 price tag. The soup, filled with chunks of rabbit and crunchy vegetables, was a bargain at $6. It was a hearty winter soup, not over-the-top on flavour, but just right for a cool evening.

Then we went on to the pastas, the menu giving four choices: linguine with fennel, mushrooms, and prawns; a simple spaghetti with garlic and olive oil; and the two we chose, penne with sausage in a pepperonata sauce and gnocchi in a roasted red-pepper cream. Both came in skillfully prepared sauces. There was a lot of sausage in the penne, and a light cream with the gnocchi set off their lightness. Well worth the $17 and $18 prices.

We didn't indulge in any of the meatier plates such as the grilled tenderloin with sun-dried peaches or the sea bass with a mandarin-mint-basil compote. But we did find room for a hot-out-of-the-oven torta that showed a deft balance of apples, chocolate chips, and cranberries with a flaky almond pastry.

The service was professional and accommodating. One comment about a few flecks of cork in our wine had our server bringing us new glasses. Most of their wines are sold by the glass too, so you can have a taste of Zenato Amarone, albeit for $14, or a Pinot Grigio for $7. And they pour healthy servings at Sugo.

All round, we were impressed with the quality of the experience at Sugo. They offer the delicate side of Italian cuisine with an abundance of intricate flavours woven into a relaxing and comfortable meal.

Sultan's Tent

Moroccan

909 – 17 Avenue SW
Phone: 244•2333
Monday – Thursday 5:30 pm – 10:30 pm
Friday & Saturday 5 pm – 11 pm
Reservations recommended — Fully licensed — Non-smoking
V, MC, AE, DC — $$

O NE of the big restaurant trends of the day is to open everything up—to knock down walls to the kitchen and add windows and skylights. We want air and light and vision. That's all fine and dandy, but sometimes we want discretion and a cocoon of privacy. We want to sink into a swaddle of brocade fabric and indulge in the food and customs of an exotic culture. That's when we want the Sultan's Tent.

There are few restaurants that take us away from the stress of daily life quicker than the Sultan's Tent. Just steps off the buzz of 17th Avenue, it surrounds diners in the mystery of the casbah and bathes them in the aromas of couscous and Moroccan tajines. The ceiling is draped with bands of cloth reminiscent of a tent, and dining areas are dimly lit and defined by hanging carpets. Low, padded benches wrap around large brass tables in spaces ranging from intimate corners for two to larger areas for twenty. The enclosures provide visual privacy—you can only glance at other diners from a distance.

The room is filled with Moroccan memorabilia: brass water bottles, colourful bread baskets, intricately decorated lamps, and ornate silver teapots. The theme carries over into the service as staff pour water over diners' hands in a ritual cleansing before dinner. (Diners are encouraged to eat with their hands—actually just their right hand—following the traditions of Morocco.)

And then there's the food. The b'stilla is a favourite starter, a layering of chicken, eggs, onions, ginger, saffron, and almonds baked in phyllo and dusted with icing sugar and cinnamon. Sweet, savoury, crisp, and soft, it is a medley of flavours and textures. Other appetizers include more phyllo pastries stuffed with lamb sausage or spinach.

Next up are the tajine and couscous specialties, which arrive in ceramic dishes also called tajines. Food is piled high under the cone-shaped lids of the tajines, and wonderful scents waft out when these are removed. The flavours are rich and cooked deeply into the stews of tender meats and vegetables. Some may contain olives and wedges of preserved lemon, others may have almonds and prunes and honey. Still others may be made in a spicy paprika or tomato sauce.

To finish, there are glasses of mint tea and sweet desserts. And the regret of having to leave. The Sultan's Tent has successfully seduced again.

Sumo

Japanese

200 Barclay Parade SW (Eau Claire Market)
Phone: 290 • 1433
Sunday – Thursday 11:30 am – 10 pm, Friday & Saturday 11:30 am – 11 pm
Reservations recommended — Fully licensed — Patio
Non-smoking dining room, smoking in lounge
V, MC, AE, DC, Debit — $$

PETER KINJO is a man with a big knife. He knows how to use it too. And in a world of quiet, discreet sushi chefs, Kinjo is lively and constantly in motion. He laughs and tells bad jokes and has fun with his customers.

Kinjo is also a man with a mission. Arriving as a partner at Sumo early in 2003, his task has been to make a less-than-successful sushi bar profitable. His approach is to try to fill every seat and to make sure his customers leave happy. I overheard a customer telling Kinjo that her teriyaki chicken had too much skin on it (an odd complaint, I know); he presented her with a gift certificate to bring her back. He's really not kidding about pleasing his customers. And almost every day since his arrival, Sumo has offered free sushi samples at the main entrance to the restaurant in order to draw people in. It also gives some presence to the long, narrow corridor that announces Sumo too quietly to strollers in Eau Claire Market.

Inside, the entrance opens up to a big metal sushi-boat bar, a couple of dining areas, a lounge, and a large patio. It's been decorated colourfully and a bit outlandishly. Huge, theatrical samurai swords impale the ceiling, a dragon dances above the sushi bar, and red lanterns dangle over the patio. It's a tone that fits Kinjo and offers a casual introduction to sushi for many.

The sushi is well cut and of excellent quality, but is not the most adventurous. The traditional wasabi swab on the nigiri is left off so as not to offend first-timers. That's a bit too timid for me so I always mix more than usual of the hot green stuff into my soy sauce.

Kinjo says that at least 70 percent of Sumo's customers order sushi, but there is still a long list of cooked foods available. There are grilled teppan yaki meats, various tempura dishes, a small collection of Chinese dishes, plus the odd Western one. It's an eclectic list served with enthusiasm.

So Sumo's dedication to service has taken a great leap forward lately. Attuned to the needs of quick lunchers and after-work relaxers, Sumo delivers the goods promptly and effectively. For those most pressed for time, the sushi-boat bar offers almost instant gratification.

Just watch out for Kinjo and his big knife.

Sushi Ginza

Japanese

10816 Macleod Trail S (Willow Park Village)
Phone: 271•9642
Monday – Thursday 11:30 am – 10 pm, Friday & Saturday 11:30 am – 11 pm
Sunday noon – 9:30 pm
Reservations recommended, especially for tatami rooms — Fully licensed — Non-smoking
V, MC, AE, Debit — $$

YOU have to like a place when you can get from behind your desk to scarfing back sushi in about five minutes. That's me and Sushi Ginza. If I hit the lights right and go directly to their sushi bar, it takes about that long. Some days you just need sushi on the run.

Sushi Ginza has probably the best sushi in the southern part of Calgary. I realize there may not be a lot of competition for that title, but regardless of location, Sushi Ginza puts out a reliably high level of sushi—good selection, clean cuts, fresh fish, everything we like to see in sushi.

It is also a pretty place with spacious booths and tatami rooms for groups large and small, a little waterfall, and a sushi-boat bar. Whether I'm in a hurry or not, the bar is usually where I end up, trawling for nigiri and tekka as little boats float by. The sushi flows around a large oval prep area where a couple of sushi cutters diligently ply their trade. Preparing the various cuts, they plop their finished products onto trays and place them on the floating boats. The trays are colour-coded to indicate prices ranging from $3 for six tekka rolls to $5 for a couple of scallop nigiri. Don't be surprised to see that small pile of dishes add quickly to $25. Customers can also order from a long list that includes the always-popular rolls and cones.

One interesting aspect of the sushi at Ginza is that they don't swipe the rice with wasabi when they build the nigiri pieces. I've been told that they feel the wasabi may be too much for some people. Yet many of the orders I hear being called out to the sushi cutters are for Cajun shrimp rolls and spicy tuna cones. Seems we like it hotter than some may think.

Sushi Ginza also offers a full list of cooked Japanese foods including rice bowls, udon noodles, tempura, and teriyaki dishes. But we're so deeply in the throes of sushi that almost everyone orders at least an appetizer of the stuff.

I am always impressed with the professional service at Ginza, no doubt due to the diligence of the owners. They have kept the place and the staff sharp since they opened. That consistency has paid off for them with loyal customers from across the southern part of the city.

Teatro

Modern Italian Food

200 Stephen Avenue Walk SE
Phone: 290•1012
Monday – Thursday 11:30 am – 11 pm
Friday 11:30 am – midnight, Saturday 5 pm – midnight, Sunday 5 pm – 10 pm
Reservations recommended — Fully licensed — Patio — Non-smoking
V, MC, AE, DC, Debit — $$ – $$$

TEATRO is the eastern bookend to what has become an amazing stretch of eateries along Stephen Avenue. Looking west through its huge windows, the sight of dozens of other restaurants rolls out.

But I try not to get distracted because Teatro demands some attention. Located in an old Dominion Bank building, Teatro is both lovely to look at and delightful to dine in. It is a mature, well-run restaurant that continues at the forefront of the Calgary dining scene. Owned by Sal Howell and Dario Berloni, Teatro is the sister restaurant of the River Café. It has more of a buttoned-down look than its Prince's Island cohort, but is far from stuffy. Comfortable for a pre-CPO snack (the entrance to the Jack Singer Concert Hall is just a few steps away) or for a corporate lunch (city hall is not much farther), it's still possible to enjoy a casual lunch on the patio in one's shorts.

The menus match the seasons at Teatro. A summery lunch menu offered a green-pea soup with pancetta and sour cream. It had great depth of flavour, the saltiness of the crisp pancetta setting off the freshness of the peas. The sour cream added just a touch of fat and tartness to the mix. Other summer appetizers included a Caprese salad of heirloom tomatoes and buffalo mozzarella, romaine lettuce with a tarragon and mint dressing, and grilled calalmari with smoked paprika.

Main courses included a selection of wood-fired, individual pizzas, a list of pastas, and some bigger-ticket items such as halibut with a morel ragout, grilled wild sockeye, and brick-roasted chicken. The grilled chicken panino with tomato, basil, and mozzarella was a good sandwich, not so much because of the preparation but because of the high-quality ingredients. That's a constant at Teatro—their food sourcing provides exceptional products.

It also provides variability in pricing. Although the pea soup was a reasonable $7, the Caprese salad was excessive at $15. That's a lot for a few tomatoes and some cheese, as good as they were. In the evening, some dishes brush up against the $40 mark, keeping Teatro at the higher end of local eateries.

There is strength and creativity at Teatro, backed up by the calm assurance of years of success and the weight of a stellar wine list. Teatro has already seen some of its flashier neighbours come and go. I suspect they will continue to do so for quite some time.

www.teatro-rest.com

Thai Boat

Thai

#108, 2323 – 32 Avenue NE
Phone: 291•9887
Monday – Friday 11 am – 2 pm
Monday – Thursday & Sunday 5 pm – 10 pm, Friday & Saturday 5 pm – 11 pm
Reservations recommended — Fully licensed — Non-smoking
V, MC, Debit — $ – $$

I get excited about food when I taste something that redefines my concept of a particular cuisine. And in just a few visits to Thai Boat, my perception of Thai cuisine has been irrevocably changed.

Thai Boat is an offshoot of Thai Sa-On, my favourite Thai restaurant for about a dozen years. Thai Sa-On is a family-run operation that consistently provides excellent Thai cuisine. But when Term Chanhao, the oldest son, opened Thai Boat in a northeast strip mall, he didn't copy the original place; he created something quite different.

He started with a different look, that of a Thai boat. The place is done in a nautical theme with dock-like booths and a bar that's shaped like a boat. The room is also filled with lots of decorative elephants, including some cute teacups with elephant handles. It's very attractive. He also introduced a new food style when he brought in a Thai chef from the Oriental Hotel in Bangkok.

On my first visit, I had the best pad Thai noodles I'd ever had and a definitive yam nua beef salad with fresh mint and grapes. I also had a dish called "Crying Tiger" that brought tears even to my eyes with its rich flavours of grilled beef, lemon grass, chilies, and roasted rice. Everything I've eaten at Thai Boat has been outstanding. The flavours are intense and bright, and there is a strength and clarity to the food. They don't add MSG—they use palm sugar to amplify the taste instead. It adds a little sweetness, but it balances the flavours too.

I'm also impressed that the most expensive dinner item is only $13 and that's for a whole fish. The main dishes generally fall in the $9 to $12 range. They offer combination dinners at reasonable prices too if you prefer to let the experts choose.

At lunch there is a longer list of noodle dishes topped with things like barbecued pork or green curried chicken for around $7. You can add side dishes of satay or spring rolls or some of that Crying Tiger for another $4 to $6 and make a rich, filling meal.

Service is pleasantly professional in the warm Thai style. They are a welcoming bunch, the perfect complement to a kitchen that has redefined my palate for Thai cuisine.

Now the most difficult decision is whether to go to Thai Boat or Thai Sa-On (we alternate).

Thai Place

Thai

1947 – 18 Avenue NE (Best Western Airport Inn)
Phone: 291·4148
Daily 11:30 am – 1 pm, 5 pm – 10 pm
Reservations recommended — Fully licensed – Indoor patio by pool — Non-smoking
V, MC, AE, Debit — $$

OVER the years I have reviewed some restaurants in odd locations, and the Thai Place is right up there. We don't see a lot of Thai restaurants in Best Western hotels.

But the Best Western Airport Inn doesn't really have a true restaurant space of its own. What it does have is one of those generic breakfast rooms with industrial-sized cereal containers, stacks of coffee cups, and big signs imploring customers not to swipe the cutlery. There are no windows, and cruel lighting makes your breakfast compatriots look like the living dead.

And that's where you'll find the Thai Place. After the breakfast mess is cleaned up, the Thai Place staff move in to create daily lunches and dinners. They bring in linen tablecloths and napkins, white ceramic bowls, and a lengthy list of Thai dishes. They are super, offering both menu suggestions and Thai travel books to look through while you wait for your food.

The breakfast room is small (it seats about thirty), so the Thai Place also uses the plastic tables by the swimming pool. This is where we sat so we could absorb some humidity and scent our meal with a little chlorine. How often can you say you've dined poolside in Calgary in February?

And the food was good. We ordered a red-curry vegetarian dish, some green-curry prawns, and a masaman chicken dish with a half-order of spring rolls. It all had a lightness and clarity to it and was well balanced. The chicken was tender, the green curry was packed with basil, and even the tofu had a freshness to it. I also liked the bowls that the food was served in. They kept the dishes hot and contained the sauces much better than the plates we usually see.

So there is talent in the kitchen here. That's because the owner is a former cooking instructor. Her skills are obvious in the food as well as in the photo albums that are filled with pictures of her food layouts and carvings.

We were in a curry mood when we visited, but the Thai Place also offers a range of Thai stir-fries, noodles, soups, and desserts (we had a warm-from-the-oven Thai taro root custard that was just superb). For those not into Thai, you can get fish and chips, beef dips, and clubhouse sandwiches.

But if you're looking for a little Thai poolside dining and can't afford the flight to Bangkok, the Thai Place can do the job.

DOWN
town
That's
the
Spot

Thai Sa-On

Thai

351 – 10 Avenue SW
Phone: 264·3526
Monday – Friday 11:30 am – 2 pm, Monday – Thursday 5 pm – 10 pm
Friday & Saturday 5 pm – 11 pm
Reservations recommended — Fully licensed — Non-smoking
V, MC — $$

TENTH Avenue across the tracks from downtown is not prime restaurant territory. It's largely populated with places that attract the after-work crowd for a drink or six. But in-between all the busy bars is one place that is very much about food—Thai Sa-On. It has been Calgary's best Thai restaurant since it opened over a decade ago. (The only other place as good is their new sister location, Thai Boat.)

Thai Sa-On has built a substantial following over the years. It's highly advisable to reserve well ahead to ensure a table. Although it's a large room, it's always full and almost impossible to just walk in most days.

So what makes Thai Sa-On so popular? Partly it's the gracious service that includes a willingness to meet customers' wants. Partly it's the calm Thai decor, the lovely green plates, and the filigreed tin rice pots. But mostly it's the food, a collection of "heating" and "cooling" dishes all freshly prepared.

This fare is actually good for those who like Asian food yet don't want the heat. Although Thai cuisine produces some of the hottest, most chili-filled dishes in the world, it is designed to balance those hot dishes with cool ones that are flavourful in different ways. The pad pug tua (stir-fried vegetables in a peanut sauce) is a fine example for the mild of palate. The goong narm mun hoi (shrimp with oyster sauce) is another richly flavoured dish without extreme heat.

For those into the heat, Thai Sa-On has curries in green, yellow, red, and masaman styles, and they can be inflamed to any degree. I don't suggest going to ridiculous lengths though; Thai cuisine has so many lovely flavours, you'd hate to lose them under excess chilies.

Thai Sa-On is constantly changing their menu, incorporating new dishes to keep the regulars intrigued. But they maintain a long list of favourites too. Over 140 dishes are offered to satisfy everyone. They also have one of the best wine lists of any Asian restaurant in town. Although it can be a challenge to match Thai dishes with wines, Thai Sa-On has spent much time and effort building a list that works well. That's just another sign of a fine restaurant doing its best for the customer.

Sa-on means "to have a passion for something." In this case, the passion revolves around presenting the best Thai food and service possible.

Thomsons

Regional Canadian Cuisine

700 Centre Street S (Hyatt Regency)
Phone: 537·4449
Daily 6:30 am – 1:30 pm, 5 pm – 9:30 pm
Reservations recommended — Fully licensed — Patio — Non-smoking
V, MC, AE, DC, Debit — $$ – $$$

WHEN the Hyatt Regency hotel opened in the heart of downtown, it was obvious they had made some smart decisions. One was in preserving as much of the old sandstone buildings in the area as possible. Another was in incorporating a classy Western theme that reflects the tone of the city without getting kitschy. And yet another was in creating a single dining space, a one-size-fits-all restaurant.

That dining room is called Thomsons, after the Thomson brothers who built the original structure in 1893. It's a lovely room, encased in old brick and sandstone, with wrought iron and wood highlights throughout. Discreet dining areas have been created for private business meetings while other spaces can be opened up to accommodate groups. It's a large, flexible room that fills many needs.

Which is important for the Hyatt. When you've set up shop on a busy restaurant stretch with neighbours like Catch and Centini, it can be difficult to compete. And the old-style, enclosed, demure hotel dining room is currently out of vogue (remember the windowless Conservatory at the Delta? It's gone). So Thomsons has been created with street presence and a leafy patio for the summer months. If you don't look too closely from the outside, it doesn't even appear to be part of the hotel.

But once inside, the Hyatt service clicks in, and it is quickly obvious that this is a serious operation. There always seems to be twice as many staff as necessary at any Hyatt dining room, and Thomsons is no exception. There is a constant buzz of staff as they pour water, whip out napkins, and hustle food to tables.

And the food is good hotel fare, adventurous enough to satisfy tourists looking for a local experience and traditional enough to please those who just want it plain. So at lunch you'll find a tasty caribou burger and a platter that includes air-dried buffalo and venison salami alongside a clubhouse sandwich and beef tenderloin. With a dinner menu that includes maple-glazed Brome Lake duck with cherry confit and a sampler plate of grilled venison, crab cakes, and sautéed prawns, there's enough variety to tempt visitors to dine at the hotel and enough quality to draw Calgarians in too. Pricing is not out of line, perhaps a little on the high side, but considering the neighbourhood and the level of service, quite palatable.

Thomsons is a fine combination of the old and the new, a smart decision for the Hyatt.

www.thomsonsrestaurant.com

Ticino

Swiss-Italian

415 Banff Avenue (High Country Inn), Banff
Phone: 762 • 3848
Daily 7 am – 10 am, 5:30 pm – 10 pm
Reservations recommended — Fully licensed
Non-smoking dining room, smoking at bar
V, MC, AE, DC, JCB — $$ – $$$

INCREASINGLY Banff is becoming a more interesting place to eat. But while food quality has gone up substantially, service remains inconsistent. Sometimes service is superb, other times it's spotty. That's the downside of a tourist town and the itinerant nature of many service personnel.

But one place where the service never disappoints is Ticino. It is a rock of reliability; some of the staff have been with the place since well before Ticino relocated to the High Country Inn in 1995. The food and the ambience are also comfortably reliable, making Ticino a place we like to go.

Ticino is adorned in the trappings of the Swiss canton it is named after. Lamps are shaded by stained glass motifs of the Swiss and Ticinese flags, cowbells and ski memorabilia dot the walls, and a large alphorn hangs over the room. It's a little bit of Switzerland on Banff Avenue.

The menu follows the theme with appetizers of air-dried beef and melted raclette and main courses of veal with wild mushrooms on pasta, grilled pork tenderloin with Gruyère, and venison with pear and caramelized chestnuts. And then there are the fondues—beef cooked in oil, beef and shrimp cooked in broth, or bread dipped in cheese—for those who want to play with their food. It's all hearty, rich, indulgent fare made for satisfying the appetite after a long day of hiking or skiing.

To start the day off with enough fuel for those activities, Ticino's breakfast buffet fits the bill perfectly. The cold buffet at $9 is a Swiss assortment of cold meats, croissants, cheeses, muesli (of course), yogurt, stewed fruit, fresh fruit, juice, and coffee. For an additional $2.75 you can add on some hot items such as scrambled eggs, bacon, and sausage. It's a quick, efficient, and pleasant meal. I have one caution though: watch out for tour groups starting their day. They can descend en masse from the hotel and clog the dining room for brief periods. Larger groups, however, are handled in a room in the back with a separate buffet.

Seated in the bright east-facing sun room, it's tempting to sip another coffee and enjoy the pleasant service rather than head out into the mountains. But we know that is our only way to work up enough of an appetite to justify dinner at Ticino.

www.ticinorestaurant.com

Towa Sushi

Japanese

2116 – 4 Street SW
Phone: 245•8585
Tuesday – Sunday 11:30 am – 2 pm, Tuesday – Thursday 5 pm – 10 pm
Friday & Saturday 5 pm – 11 pm, Sunday 5 pm – 9:30 pm
Reservations not accepted — Fully licensed — Patio — Non-smoking
V, MC, AE, DC, Debit — $ – $$

DOES 4th Street really need another sushi bar? Sushi Kawa and Hana Sushi have been doing a good job there for a few years now. And for that matter, does Calgary need another sushi bar? There are boatloads of good sushi available.

To be impressive, a new place must provide something better or something that sets it apart from the crowd. Towa Sushi does just that.

It opened in the spring of 2003 in the north part of what used to be 4 St. Rose. It's gorgeous, designed by Robert Sweep Interior Design in tones of saltwater and natural cherry. There are tables and a sushi bar and a counter that overlooks a patio. There are no boats or trains here, no cute delivery gimmicks, just good sushi.

And it is some of the best—and largest—sushi I've had. Towa has moved away from the small-sized sushi that has only a few bites to it. They have reverted to a larger style which was popular in Japan a hundred or more years ago and which I've seen more of in the States. Each piece of fish on the nigiri sushi is about four times the size we usually see. But it is not just big—it is fresh, well cut, high-quality fish. And they do little things such as topping the nigiri with sprouts and sliced pickles, creating plates that are as gorgeous as the room itself. At $2 to $3 a piece, it also costs more, but it is still a bargain for what you get.

Towa uses a couple of automatic sushi rollers to make their rice balls. This allows them to use less water and create a slightly denser ball. These machines can work exceptionally well, but need to be tended carefully. When sushi chefs loose the hand touch of making rice balls, they must ensure that the machines are intricately adjusted. So far so good at Towa.

The only thing I can fault Towa on was some damp nori inside my tekka rolls that made them tough to bite through. This then made them fall apart. Other than that, I had excellent sushi. Especially a spicy tuna cone. And I have to commend them on having three kinds of soy sauce—regular, low salt, and sweet. More attention to detail.

Towa Sushi will change some people's perceptions about sushi and may well alter the sushi scene on 4th Street.

Trong-Khanh

Vietnamese

1115 Centre Street N
Phone: 230·2408
Sunday – Thursday 11 am – 9 pm, Friday & Saturday 11 am – 10 pm
Reservations recommended — Fully licensed — Non-smoking
V, MC, Debit — $

IT hasn't been that long since Vietnamese was a mystery cuisine in these parts. Only fifteen years ago there were less than a handful of Vietnamese restaurants, and those few struggled for customers. One of the first was the Trong-Khanh.

I remember trudging up the concrete steps to the Trong-Khanh back in the late eighties. It was a homely room then with worn carpets and glaring lights. But they stuck it out and helped popularize bowls of bun and salad rolls. And they seem to have been packed solid for at least the last five years as a reward for their tenacity.

The look has improved a lot since the early days. The walls are now soft pastels lit by trendy wall and ceiling lamps. The ceiling itself has been opened up to give more height, and it's painted deep blue. They've even fixed the washroom doors (part of the Trong-Khanh's early charm were washroom doors that tended to lock people in). They have, however, retained the pop cooler that dominates the tiny room with its size and its incessant hum.

The tables are all numbered, as are the dishes on the menu. That way regulars can reserve their favourite table (say, number eight) and order their favourite dishes (perhaps a number four and a number fifty-five) with greater ease. It's a very user-friendly place. And fast. It's the kind of restaurant where you can easily be in and out for lunch in a half-hour. And feel good about it.

The food is always tasty at the Trong-Khanh. The salad rolls (number four) are a classic. The shrimp is tender and crunchy, the greens fresh, and the noodles lightly al dente. With a spiked brown-bean sauce, they are among the best in town.

The bowls of bun are likewise filled with freshly prepared ingredients and topped with richly grilled meats. The barbecued pork (number fifty-five) is a salty partner to the rice vermicelli, the greens, and the light nuoc mam. Occasionally I've found the meats a touch oily here, but that is a minor complaint.

The prices continue to amaze me. Most dishes remain under $10, like the deep-fried quail with chopped egg on broken rice for all of $8.50. And that brisk service remains friendly.

The Trong-Khanh is nothing fancy, but it is fresh, hot, fast, and cheap. And you won't get locked in the washroom anymore.

Tropika

Malaysian

#171, 1518 Centre Street N
Phone: 230•3330
Monday – Saturday 11 am – 11 pm, Sunday 11 am – 10 pm
Reservations recommended — Fully licensed — Non-smoking
V, MC, AE, DC — $$

Now where can you get a drink in a fresh coconut these days? Why, at the Tropika restaurant of course! The Tropika, a new Malaysian place inside the Madison building on Centre Street, has coconuts by the grove and a tangy menu to help work up a thirst.

In spite of our passion for Asian cuisines, we haven't seen a lot of Malaysian food in Calgary. It has similarities to Chinese, Thai, and Indian fare. There are rich curries, coconut milk in abundance, seasoning with lemon grass and tamarind, and as much or as little heat as you'd like. It is a fine cuisine.

Malaysian dishes are pretty unfamiliar to a number of us, so the Tropika has developed a colourful menu with photos of many of them. This at least gives you an idea of what they look like. We tried the Assam prawns, one of the dishes where lemon grass and tamarind are used, here in a marinade with star anise and chilies. Crunchy prawns and a delicate sauce made for a nice dish. We also had the sayur lemak hotpot where peppers and onions are cooked in a spicy coconut sauce along with more prawns. This was rich and creamy, a little oily perhaps, but tasty. And we had the terung udang kering, an eggplant dish they tout. Stir-fried with a sambal sauce and sun-dried shrimp, it was definitely one of the best eggplant dishes we've had.

The portions are generous too. With those three dishes and some coconut rice, we had lots of leftovers for lunch the next day. And the prices aren't bad either. Most dishes are in the $7 to $15 range. But they do satay for $1.50 each—I wondered why they were so expensive until I saw them. They are huge. As an appetizer, I'd be careful about how many skewers I ordered (though the minimum order is six).

The Tropika is a sizable place, seating about one hundred in a rich, well-appointed Asian setting. The staff wear tropical shirts to add colour and to match the Tropika name, and the chairs are an attractive Asian hardwood. It's a comfortable place with just a hint of the old Tiki lounge. I note that they also have restaurants in Vancouver and Edmonton, so they are an experienced operation. Which helps explain the good service and excellent food.

And where else are you going to get a drink in a coconut?

www.tropikagroup.com

Typhoon

Eclectic Asian

211 Caribou Street, Banff
Phone: 762•2000
Daily 11:30 am – close
Reservations accepted — Fully licensed – Non-smoking
V, MC, AE, Debit — $ – $$

I F you're as adept at Banff addresses as I am, here's how to find Typhoon: it is just down from the Mount Royal Hotel and across from Coyotes. It's in a small space that has had a few different personalities in the past, but Typhoon seems a logical choice to stick around.

Typhoon does Asian food in a market where there has been little beyond sushi bars and a few Cantonese places. There is the Asian Express across the street, but it's more of a cafeteria. And Typhoon is definitely not that.

It is done in fresh tropical tones, strung with colourful ribbons and silk fabrics and lit by Oriental lamps. Huge flowery paintings, the work of one of the owners, cover the walls. It is run by a couple of former Rimrock Hotel staffers, one an Aussie, the other a Quebecer. A quick look at them and the menu and my first thought was that Typhoon must be a Westernized version of Asian cuisines. And it is. The food brushes along Thai, Szechwan, Indian, Japanese, Indonesian, and Vietnamese lines. Normally menus like this send me running quickly in another direction because there are too many cultures going on for there to be much authenticity.

But Typhoon's version of Asian is not meant to be authentic, and it is an approach that works for them. They make all their sauces in-house, and while they do tame them down for their perception of the Western palate, the effort is earnest and the food is not bad. The dinner menu tops out at $22, with appetizers in the $4 to $6 range. Entrees at lunch are all under $10. So it's attractive to those who like Asian cuisines, a pleasant atmosphere, and good prices. That's pretty broad appeal.

The Szechwan spicy squid on crispy noodles features tender squid rings in a gingery, garlicky sauce arranged over fried vermicelli. With their crispiness, the noodles are almost impossible to eat, but the squid is excellent. A Thai grilled chicken salad has a lovely lime-cilantro dressing. All its elements were too cold when I had it, but the intent was still there. And the Shanghai noodles with chicken and vegetables in a spicy peanut sauce are also quite tasty. Lots of flavour in the sauce. Sure, it has a Western tone, but it still tastes good. And I give full marks to the creamy mango pudding. That's where the Western influences are at their best.

Vintage

Chophouse & Tavern

322 – 11 Avenue SW
Phone: 262 • 7262
Monday – Saturday 11:30 am – close, Sunday 5 pm – close
Reservations recommended — Fully licensed
Non-smoking dining room, smoking in tavern
V, MC, AE, DC — $$ – $$$

A good chophouse is a joy to behold. It should have a dark, leathery look highlighted by crisp linens and wood trim, immaculate waiters with white shirts or jackets starched so they whiffle when they walk, and a menu that spells out meat in all its gory glory. It should be a place that makes carnivores salivate and vegans quiver and shake their heads. Above all, it should be uncompromising in quality.

These concepts were firmly in mind when Vintage opened. But it has not been trapped by the stale, windowless tones of old-style steak houses. They have kept the leather and wood, but have incorporated a contemporary, brighter look and a broader menu selection.

Vintage has consumed the Vintage Building—ergo the name—where a Santa Fe Grill had been of late. A major overhaul opened the space and provided that sumptuous leather look that flows from the dining room into the tavern. The unfortunate allowance of smoking in the tavern brings tainted air into some seats, so beware of where you are placed. But other than that, the room is lovely, with windows wrapping around the east and south sides.

The staff are appropriately outfitted in sharp white jackets and are quick with the chair pulling and the napkin snapping. They are also adept at tableside preparations of Caesar salads and bananas Foster and such. These are classic dishes whose time has come again.

Now to the meat. Vintage does a prime rib at dinnertime that can bring a tear to the eye of the most dedicated beef fan. Using Certified Angus Beef that has been aged twenty-eight days, it is crusted on the outside, fork-tender on the inside, and served with tonsil-searing horseradish and a great beef demi-glace. This is a serious meat-lover's dish, as is their full range of beef steaks. Other evening options include fresh oysters, grilled tuna, braised lamb shank, pork chops, and planked salmon.

The bill is not for the meek either. Expect to drop at least $100 for two at dinner, more if you indulge in their lengthy wine list. Lunch will be substantially less with an eight-ounce steak sandwich at $15 or an eight-ounce burger topped with double-smoked bacon, Asiago cheese, and a chipotle aïoli for $12.

Regardless of whether you go for lunch or dinner, you can expect some of the best beef in the heart of cattle country.

Waldhaus

German

The Fairmont Banff Springs, Banff
Phone: 762•6860
Daily 6 pm – 9:30 pm
Reservations recommended — Fully licensed — Non-smoking
V, MC, AE, DC, JCB — $$ – $$$

MOST families have a restaurant or two that they frequent for special occasions. When I was a kid, it was the old Blue Willow Chinese restaurant in Edmonton. But for some strange reason, in recent years, it has become the Waldhaus at the Fairmont Banff Springs. I say strange because our family tree has no roots in Germany (not that we have any in China either). But German cuisine is one style of food that most everyone in my family seems to enjoy, and the setting at the Waldhaus is unbeatable.

So we go there for big birthdays, anniversaries, and other major family gatherings. They graciously pull together enough tables to seat everyone and we have a grand time. We eat a lot of schnitzel, drink too much wine, and sing along to the lively oompahpah music. And when we have kids along who aren't quite up for the good German food, they graciously allow us to order nachos and such off the pub menu from downstairs.

The Waldhaus is one of the Springs' restaurants that is actually not in the Springs. It's located on the upper level of the old golf clubhouse just a short stroll down the mountain from the main hotel building. When the Springs built a new clubhouse in the early nineties, this high-ceilinged, rough-hewn room became the perfect location for a German restaurant. Seating about ninety, it has the full *gemütlichkeit*, or good times, feel. Banners fly overhead, a fire crackles in the huge fireplace, and hearty German fare rolls out.

The jägerschnitzel is a hunger-stifling pork escalope covered in a mushroom and cream sauce. Sided with red cabbage and spaetzle, it's as tasty as it is filling. The roasted duck is a hearty Teutonic turn on classic cuisine with its cider sauce, caramelized apples, and grapes. And their fondues—both beef broth and cheese—are popular, especially with the après-ski crowd.

There are also rich appetizers such as pheasant ragout with wild mushrooms and sautéed prawns done with garlic-herb butter and Riesling. And, of course, there are the typical strudels and cobblers for dessert. The lightest dish on the menu is a tomato and butter lettuce salad, so be forewarned.

Service has always been excellent on our visits, no small task with a group as diverse as my family. So we will continue to return for our special occasions. At least until they suggest we don't.

Wildwood

Rocky Mountain Cuisine & Brew Pub

2417 – 4 Street SW
Phone: 228·0100
Monday – Sunday 11:30 am – 2 pm
Sunday – Thursday 5 pm – 10 pm, Friday & Saturday 5 pm – 11 pm
Reservations recommended — Fully licensed — Patio
Non-smoking restaurant, smoking in pub
V, MC, AE, Debit — $$ – $$$

PART of the Creative Restaurants group, Wildwood provides the rustic game and beer tone to the family. Bonterra is more upscale Mediterranean, Catch is into the downtown seafood thing, and Wildwood is the strong, solid older brother who brings home the bacon. And it's probably wild boar bacon too.

I think that's partly because Wildwood is imbued with the spirit of Franzl's Gasthaus, the lively German restaurant that served sausage and rouladen and buckets of beer here for years. Sure, Wildwood looks nothing like Franzl's. It's been redone in woody overtones with a fireplace and banks of windows. But if you listen closely when the beer taps start flowing, you can hear the sound of an oompah band.

And the beer taps flow freely here. Seven house-made brews are on tap, brews that can also be had at the other Creative Restaurants. They go perfectly with Wildwood's gamey menu of Alberta pheasant and bison short ribs.

It might be best to warn your vegan friends away from Wildwood. It is possible to find vegetarian meals here, but mostly it is one meaty place. An appetizer of wild boar sausage on potato rösti is a carnivore's delight, the fennel glaze and smoked tomatoes adding just a hint of lightness. And the veal tenderloin medallions layered with Cambozola cheese and topped with a wild mushroom sauce is a superb blend of gentle flavours. Those mushrooms are fresh, not reconstituted dried ones. There are lots more gamey things too, from braised rabbit risotto and elk steaks to pine-nut crusted trout and grilled Arctic char.

Wildwood offers a variety of atmospheres in which to dine. The main room has a lovely lodge feel that matches the food. There is also a private room suitable for a couple of dozen at one end. Downstairs the brew pub is a dark and cozy hideaway, perfect for a few cool ones. And a south-facing patio offers a pleasant al fresco experience.

Service has always been outstanding on our visits. Wildwood employs a professional staff who appear happy to work there. They know the food, they pace it well, and they create a pleasant atmosphere.

So whether you're dining in style on the main floor, kicked back on the patio catching rays, or buried in the basement with a brew, Wildwood is a delightful operation. I think Franzl's would be happy with the service and the *gemütlichkeit* that carry on their fine tradition.

DOWN town
That's the Spot

Yuzuki

Japanese

510 – 9 Avenue SW
Phone: 261 • 7701
Monday – Friday 11:30 am – 2 pm, Tuesday – Thursday 5 pm – 9 pm
Friday & Saturday 5 pm – 10 pm
Reservations recommended — Fully licensed — Non-smoking
V, MC, AE, Debit — $$

A LL aboard the sushi train! Leaving from the sushi bar at the Yuzuki and traversing the wilds of a dining room filled with ravenous lunchers, the sushi train delivers rolls and cones and tuna and salmon from its flatbed cars. I don't know why I think the train is so darn cute, but every time I go to the Yuzuki, which is pretty often, it gives me a chuckle. And I'm not the only one. With every delivery of sushi, smiling customers turn to watch. Sure it's a gimmick, just like the sushi boats and double-decker conveyor belts at other places.

The point is, no gimmick is good enough if the product is poor. But the Yuzuki's sushi is very good. Fans of the Yuzuki are a loyal bunch. Most will try out new places, but they are almost always drawn back to one of the oldest Japanese restaurants in the city.

It's never been about the decor. From the outside, the Yuzuki is easy to miss as you buzz by on 9th Avenue. The front is nondescript and the entry is dark and empty. Inside it's improved lately with fresh paint and new chairs imported from Japan. But while many of the new joints are either overly busy or understatedly elegant, the Yuzuki remains among the plainer of the Japanese restaurants.

I'm one of those regulars who is always checking out the new places. And there are loads of good ones. Still, I'm always impressed with the diligence and expertise of chef-owner Sam Oshiro's work. His cuts are clean and even, there are few ragged edges, and the flavours and textures all balance perfectly. His attention to quality and food safety is paramount. Not only does his food taste great, it is handled as safely as any place around.

I particularly like his salmon-skin cone. With its thick, meaty, toasted skin wrapped in a nori cone with rice and greens, it surpasses all local competitors. And he never lays back on the wasabi either. Expect at least one wasabi head rush with every meal.

There are cooked dishes on the menu too, mostly eaten by those who are dragged along by the regulars. These are the requisite tempuras, teriyakis, and donburi dishes found in most Japanese restaurants. All are prepared well, but it's the sushi that really draws people in. That and the train.

www.yuzuki.com

Little Eats

A & A Foods & Deli

1401 – 20 Avenue NW, 289 • 1400

AT any lunch hour you'll likely find a lineup flowing out the door of A & A. A lineup at a convenience store? Why?

It's all about the fast Lebanese food of donairs and tabbouleh and falafel. And the floor show provided by the owner. Jimmy Elrafih, a master of the one-liner, zings out jokes as quickly as he wraps pitas in tinfoil.

There are tables outside, and in 2003, they splurged by covering them with small marquee tents. But most of A & A's food is for takeout. The chicken shawarma laced with garlic sauce, tomatoes, pickles, and greens is the big seller. One caution though—don't drive and eat this at the same time. It's messy.

Annie's

Bow Valley Ranche, south end of Bow Bottom Trail SE, 225 • 3920

THE old foreman's house at the Bow Valley Ranche in Fish Creek Provincial Park provides seasonal sustenance to the area's bikers, hikers, strollers, and their dogs. An adjunct to The Ranche restaurant a few hundred metres away, Annie's is rustic and cozy with creaky wood floors inside and a couple of porches outside.

Some of the mostly light food is prepared on-site, and some comes from the kitchen of The Ranche. The fruit muffins and scones are always a hit, and the homemade soup goes quickly. Annie's is the perfect place to kick back and enjoy a sandwich or a piece of pie and coffee while watching the prairie grasses rustle.

Atlas Specialty Supermarket & Restaurant

116 – 16 Avenue NE, 230 • 0990

IF you're in the mood for a jojeh kebab or a fesenjan stew, where are you going to go? Likely to a little store cum forty-seat café on 16th Avenue called Atlas. There you'll find some fine Persian food, some friendly people, and a quiet escape from the traffic outside.

Atlas has a large gas and charcoal grill where kebabs of koobideh (ground beef), barg (beef tenderloin), and jojeh (chicken) sizzle away. And they have a cooler where house-made yogurt, various salads, and the fesenjan stew of walnuts, pomegranate seeds, and chicken await hungry customers.

Atlas is also the perfect place to pick up those hard-to-find Persian ingredients such as sour-grape molasses and wild rue.

Baba Ka Dhaba

3504 – 17 Avenue SE, 207•5552

L OOSELY translated as "old man takeout," Baba Ka Dhaba offers Calgary's only Pakistani fast-food that I know of. There's little in the way of decor, there's only one table, and it's ridiculously hard to spot even though it's right on the corner of 17th Avenue and 35th Street SE.

But the smell of fine Pakistani cuisine rolling out of the kitchen is marvelous. The dishes are similar to the many Indian restaurants around. The curries are forceful, the nan is steamy and dense, and the seekh kebab is particularly flavourful. If that table is free and you decide to eat in, don't be surprised if there's no cutlery. Just use the nan.

The Better Butcher

385 Heritage Drive SE (Acadia Centre), 252•7171

S OMETIMES I just like to stand in front of the counter and look at all the chops and roasts and sausages. They don't have a huge meat cooler at The Better Butcher, but it's always filled with excellent slabs of meat.

The beef and the pork are particularly well cut here, and the cold cuts—especially the ones prepared in-house—are always of high calibre. The Better Butcher has also been my choice for the holiday turkey for years. They know how to source meat, how to age and trim it, and how to serve it with a smile. So what if they always have big knives in their hands?

Boca Loca

1512 – 11 Street SW, 802•4600

F INDING just the right chili for that mole or some fresh cactus paddles for that pork stew can be difficult in Cowtown, so Renette Kurtz opened Boca Loca. Fans of Central and South American foods flock to her store for tortillas, chipotles, and epazote. Each day she makes a couple of fresh salsas, such as the basic pico de gallo or her popular mango one. She also does enchilada sauces with tomatillos and roasted poblanos and carries tasty tamales from local chef Norma French. Her guacamole is outstanding and her meals-to-go have saved many a Friday night. Look for cooking classes and cookbooks too, all focused on the warmer side of the Americas.

Boogie's Burgers

908 Edmonton Trail NE, 230•7070

A H, the smell of the open grill, the lingering waft of the deep fryer. The heyday of the independent burger bar is past, but a few soldier on, defying the big chains with (gasp!) quality. One of the best is Boogie's, an Edmonton Trail institution for decades.

Boogie's has changed hands in recent years, but the style has remained much the same. The made-to-order burgers and shakes and the blazing hot fries remain a treat, and they now serve beer and wine with their food. The mushroom burger is popular here, but the chicken burger is right up there too. And the move to a totally non-smoking room is a real plus in the confined space.

Brûlée Patisserie

722 – 11 Avenue SW, 261•3064

B RÛLÉE resides just downstairs from The Cookbook Co. Cooks and is owned and operated by Rosemary Harbrecht, a talented baker. Harbrecht specializes in customized baking, with gorgeous blackberry dacquoise or chocolate-raspberry ganache or carrot-butterscotch layer cakes. Citrus fans will love the lemon cream cake and the lemon soufflé and lemon mascarpone tarts. Brûlée has a limited quantity of daily baking available—cream cheese brownies, blueberry-orange oatmeal squares, toasted nut slice, sugar cookies, and gingersnaps, to name a few. Cookies run $10 per dozen ($11 for chocolate ones), eight-inch tarts are $15, and cakes are in the $30 range. This is fine, fine baking. Best to order ahead.

Caffè Beano

1613 – 9 Street SW, 229•1232

B EANO is the favourite coffee spot for many because they make a darned good espresso, some tasty molasses-soaked muffins, and a really decent sandwich. For others it's the tone of the place, the let's-hang-out, time-doesn't-matter feeling. And for others it's owner Rhondda Siebens—she's just so charming and enthusiastic.

Beano satisfies with all of the above, attracting a broad cross-section of Mount Royalites, youthful Beltliners, 17th Avenue strollers, and double-parkers looking for a quick cup of joe. It's a busy place, but the line usually moves quickly and service is cheerful. Just a brief coffee at Beano can buff up your entire day. In a good way.

DOWN town
That's the
Spot

Caffè Mauro

805A – 1 Street SW, 262 • 9216

A good sandwich is a joy to behold. And to consume for that matter. Salvatore Malvaso, the former chef at Da Salvatore, is whipping up some pretty tasty Italian ones in his Caffè Mauro. He roasts peppers and eggplants and slides them into house-baked focaccia with capicollo and Calabrese salami. Or he'll build you one with bread from the Rustic Sourdough Bakery and your choice from various cheeses, cold cuts, and other fillings. There are a few tables for dining in, but most people haul the sandwiches back to their offices.

Sal also makes the best traditional Italian espresso in the area. That must be consumed on-site to truly appreciate the crema.

Calgary Spiceland

1830 – 52 Street SE, 273 • 1546

FOR over twenty-eight years, the Kotadia family has brought a broad selection of Asian foodstuffs to Calgarians. Calgary Spiceland has always been the place to go for Indian spices, basmati rice, and fresh vegetables like guvar, karela, and torai. (Note on the rice: good basmati should have a harvest date on the bag; choose one that is a year or two old.)

In 2002, Spiceland moved into a much larger space and expanded their stock. It now includes everything from chapati presses and Bollywood videos to Caribbean herbs and buckets of lentils. We've even found some tasty and cheap pre-packaged meals direct from India. Even if you're not in need of anything, Spiceland makes a fascinating excursion. We never leave empty-handed.

Calgary Sweet House

5320 – 8 Avenue SE, 272 • 7234

FOR over twenty years, the Calgary Sweet House has been producing fine jalebis, burfi, and rasmalai, the sweetly addictive desserts of Indian cuisine. And it hasn't changed much in that time. It's still a high-ceilinged, rectangular room that could double as any industrial cafeteria with its red vinyl chairs and rows of tables and its cooler in the corner. The key distinction is in the room-long display counter that holds all the sweet delights. There are always a couple of dozen choices, available in single slices or by the pound.

The Sweet House also does full meals with such dishes as curried goat and tandoori chicken. It may not be a stylish room, but the Sweet House is one busy place.

Chico's Tecate Grill

3168 Sunridge Boulevard NE, 250·1112

CHICO'S TECATE GRILL is a chain out of California, and this is its only outlet in Calgary. In fact, there are only two other Chico's outside the US—one in Cairo, the other in Amsterdam.

Chico's does California-Mexican cuisine quite well for a place that looks and acts like a cafeteria. They make a selection of fresh salsas daily, roasting peppers and laying on the heat. These are no timid, wimpy sauces. Come with your tonsils ready. The tacos and burritos and such are fresh and flavourful too. Be prepared to stand in line to order and to carry your own tray, but you'll like the prices and the speedy service that come with this style of food.

Chocolaterie Bernard Callebaut

1313 – 1 Street SE, 266·4300

OVER twenty years ago, a tall, lean Belgian blew into Calgary with plans to make Cowtown the headquarters for a major chocolate business. Some thought the idea a little odd, until they tasted his creamy fillings that is.

Since then, the name Bernard Callebaut has become synonymous with the best in chocolate. The main outlet on 1st Street SE, which also houses the factory, is filled with hundreds of shapes, sizes, and flavours of filled and formed sweets. From Easter bunnies and Santas to Stampede buckles and computer disks, everything is chocolatey. You can tour the factory too, albeit from behind glass. And true to Callebaut's plan, there are thirty-five outlets across North America, including nine in the Calgary and Banff area.

www.bernardcallebaut.com

The Cookbook Co. Cooks

722 – 11 Avenue SW, 265·6066 or 1 (800) 663·8532

WITH its extensive collection of cookbooks, its coolers filled with exotic cheeses and herbs, its basement cooking school, and its knowledgeable staff, The Cookbook Co. is the epicentre of Calgary's foodie community. It's the place to go for those hard-to-find ingredients, plus instructions on how to use them. If there is a new food product on the market, it is likely to arrive here first.

The open, warehousey space is often filled with the aroma of fine cooking from the kitchen classroom below as local and international chefs ply their skills for avid food fans. Classes in France have recently been added for those who like to travel and learn about food at the same time.

www.cookbookcooks.com

Crete Souvlaki

2623 – 17 Avenue SW, 246•4777

E AT here and get gas!
Sorry, I couldn't resist the cheap joke. I love the gas station and Greek food combo that Crete Souvlaki provides. With the tiny café tucked into the OK Gas & Convenience Store just a few metres from the pumps, it's an unbeatable pit stop for fast gas and fast food.

The lamb souvlaki, the horiatiki, and the moussaka are all freshly prepared and quite good. Perhaps not as elegant or as stylish as at some of the finer Greek restaurants, but the price is right. Service is jump-to-the-pump style, and you can get your souvlaki and a side of windshield washer fluid to go.

Decadent Desserts

#103, 1019 – 17 Avenue SW, 245•5535

O NE of the finer custom bakeries in Calgary is Decadent Desserts, owned by Pam Fortier. Her repertoire includes a lemon-hazelnut cake and a strawberry-rhubarb pie as well as oatmeal-raisin cookies and biscotti. There is an abundance of chocolate, from the Chocolate Overdose cake with over a pound of Callebaut chocolate to the Fantasy Fudge cake accented with chocolate leaves. And if nuptials are in your future, ask about the elegant wedding cakes.

Decadent Desserts is not a drop-in-for-a-piece-of-cake spot. It's a place to pick up dessert orders of whole cakes or pies or cookies by the dozen. Quality and execution are exceptional and creativity is stellar.

www.decadentdesserts.ca

Domicile Organic Bistro

715 – 11 Avenue SW, 262•9780

L UNCH in an interior design shop? Well, why not?
Domicile Organic Bistro is a small one-man operation at the far end of the chic Domicile Interiors showroom. Seating is on padded benches curved around tables or on stools pulled up to a bar. They do lunch Monday to Saturday, and the menu is a tight collection of sandwiches, pizzas, curries, and such. It's good food with delicate amounts of quinoa and chickpeas, prosciutto and salmon. The crème brûlée and flourless chocolate cake are primo, and they pull a pretty decent espresso too. And you can always use the opportunity to catch up on the latest design trends.

www.domicilecreative.com

Dutch Cash & Carry

3815 – 16 Street SE, 298 • 5899 or 290 • 1838

THIS is the hardest-to-find location in the book. Just off Ogden Road and down a string of unpaved roads in Bonnybrook, DC & C shares a warehouse-type building with other tenants. There's a small sign out front, but it may take a few passes to spot, especially if someone is parked in front of that sign.

Popular with the local Dutch community, DC & C carries Dutch licorice, cheese croquettes, dark coffee, cured horse meat, and aged Gouda among their four hundred imported products. In late fall, they bring in alphabet letters made with Dutch chocolate, a popular gift for Christmas. And there's more than food – there are pots, pot scrubbers, and hardy dish towels to complete your kitchen.

Edelweiss Village

1921 – 20 Avenue NW, 282 • 6722

EDELWEISS VILLAGE is a German gift shop, grocery store, deli, bakery, and café that can fill all your Teutonic needs. The cabbage roll lunch comes with piles of sauerkraut and potato salad and your choice of wurst. It's enough to feed three people. The rouladen is a thick and tasty roll of beef, and the decadent hazelnut torte is nutty and creamy. You order these dishes, and others, at the deli counter to eat in or take home. And if you're looking for German cheeses, jams, kitchen wares, and beer steins, this is the place. Their mustard selection alone is beyond compare. They also carry goods from other countries too, places such as Holland, Switzerland, and Austria.

www.edelweissimports.com

Eiffel Tower Bakery

DOWN town
That's the Spot

1013 – 17 Avenue SW, 244 • 0103
610 – 8 Avenue SW, 232 • 1271
502 – 25 Avenue NW, 282 • 0788

WHEN the Eiffel Tower on 17th Avenue closed briefly for renovations in 2003, we were thrown into a minor tizzy. It's hard to go more than a few days without one of their chocolate croissants or a loaf of paillasse bread or a piece of Royale, my current favourite when I want an intensely chocolate dessert.

The Eiffel Tower is a superb French bakery that features uncompromising quality throughout. A new location next to the Uptown theatre has brought their baked delights, plus sandwiches on their baguettes, to downtown office workers. All the baking is done at the 17th Avenue location, and selection is best there. But parking is still best at the 25th Avenue store.

El Bombazo

2881 – 17 Avenue SE, 204•3757

E L BOMBAZO, which means "big party," specializes in Mexican and Salvadoran foods, and its strip-mall space is divided into a market, a kitchen, and a café. The short menu includes pupusas (Salvadoran stuffed tortillas), huevos rancheros, grilled chicken with pico de gallo, and beef deshebrada (a shredded meat dish with eggs and peppers). All the café fare is house-made by cooks who are constantly in motion pressing tortillas and mixing sauces. El Bombazo may be small, but they do not lack for ambition. It's also the place to pick up dolce de leche and yerba mate or to watch soccer on a television tuned to the Telemundo network. Or to just join in the party.

Evelyn's Coffee Bar

201 Banff Avenue, Banff, 762•0352
249 Bear Street, Banff, 762•0330

I T'S difficult to get good coffee in Banff. Some people say it's the hardness of the water, others say it's the high altitude that allows water to boil at too low a temperature. But two places that manage to make a decent cup are Evelyn's and her second café, Evelyn's Too.

I prefer the relaxed tone of Evelyn's Too on Bear Street. The original Evelyn's is usually packed with masses of Banff Avenue strollers. Too is in the atrium of a small mall, so the tables have more space around them. Both locations sell large cookies, scones, cakes, and such—the type of baking that is typically mass-produced and tasteless. But at Evelyn's, the food actually tastes as good as it looks.

First Mate Fish & Chips

#3, 33 Harvest Hills Drive NE, 226•3883

A VAST, ye matey! Argh! Where's a sailor to get a fine plate of fish and chips in landlocked Calgary?

Well, one place to check out is First Mate, a tiny independent shop on the shores of Harvest Hills. Perhaps that's not typical seafaring country, but First Mate manages to serve some well-crusted haddock and cod and even halibut. It's fresh, it's quick, and it's not overcooked. The french fries are decent too. Then there are the calamari, shrimp, clam, and scallop dinners, a surprising selection of seafood for such a small and understated place. Plus there's an all-you-can-eat $8 pollock meal every evening except Friday.

There's something fishy going on in them there Harvest Hills. Argh!

Friends Cappuccino Bar

45 Edenwold Drive NW (Edgepointe Village), 241·5526

I T's heartening to find a decent independent café in the burbs. It's also heartening to see one that is as strongly supported by its community as is Friends. This forty-seat Edgemont café is a gathering place for local soccer moms, home-business types, and those just looking for a good lunch.

Friends has the quality to back up the support too. Most items are made on-site, including the grilled focaccia sandwiches of turkey and mozzarella or eggplant and brie and the turtle brownies and confetti squares. Every day there are two soups, such as squash and bean or corn chowder, and a soup and sandwich special to go along with the eclectic, homey atmosphere.

Heartland Cafe

940 – 2 Avenue NW, 270·4541

T HE HEARTLAND CAFE has a granola-bar tone that smacks more of the 1970s than of any new-fangled millennium. The Sunnyside classic is as rustic as ever. It's a high-ceilinged, wood-floored brick building that creaks with every step. The regulars, mostly a crowd of natural-fibre folks, enjoy the cream of pumpkin soup and the dense muffins on the almost-healthy menu. The flavours haven't changed over the years, and the sandwiches served on thick, grainy bread remain a fine, hearty lunch.

Heartland is as much a community meeting place as it is a café. I'd venture a guess that they serve more pots of tea (decaffeinated green, that is) per capita than any other place in town.

Infuso Coffee House

1205 Bow Valley Trail (Rocky Mountain Professional Centre), Canmore, 609·2733

T HERE is no shortage of caffeine in the Bow Valley. That's good because it seems that a major activity for Canmore locals and visitors alike is hanging out at one of the numerous coffee bars in town. The favourite for many is Infuso, parked just a little out of the way on Bow Valley Trail.

Infuso makes a good cup of coffee and is known locally for their latte. And they prepare everything on their menu in-house. The Thai salad and club croissant are popular, and I am particularly fond of the carrot cake. They go through a lot of raspberry and white-chocolate scones and granola bars too.

Janice Beaton Fine Cheese

1708 – 8 Street SW, 229•0900

LOOKING for that hard to find piece of Irish Cashel Blue or Comté Fort des Russes or Venezuelan Beaver cheese? (Well, maybe not the Beaver cheese—you'd have to be a real Monty Python fan for that.) You'll likely find the first two at Janice Beaton Fine Cheese.

They pack more cheesy goodness into this tiny shop than you can shake a baguette at. They track down grand cheeses from around the world and across the province. The staff can answer virtually any *question de la fromage*—I'm always impressed at their helpful knowledge.

Aside from chunks of cheese, you will find fabulous sandwiches—with cheese of course—and other exotic deli delights too.

www.jbfinecheese.com

Jugo Juice

200 Barclay Parade SW (Eau Claire Market), 205•3300

JUGO is a full-tilt juice, smoothie, and wrap concept with thirteen Calgary locations and another sixteen across Canada. (This Eau Claire outlet is their flagship shop. See the map on page 166 for additional downtown locations.) The smoothies range from combos of strawberries, bananas, and orange juice to blends of peaches, pineapples, blueberries, mango sorbet, and cranberry juice. They even offer a coffee-based smoothie and squeeze the earthy wheat grass juice too.

Firmly rolled into twelve-inch tortillas, their wraps of smoked chicken or turkey with greens and jellies are tasty. Less heavily loaded than some, these wraps are a light complement to the smoothies.

www.jugojuice.com

Kaffa Coffee & Salsa House

2138 – 33 Avenue SW, 240•9133

KAFFA, a small brown house on 33rd Avenue, is one of the anchors of Marda Loop. It's become a community gathering place for many Loopers and for others who just like the atmosphere.

Kaffa has the tone of a seventies granola bar but with much better food. It's a coffee house with the requisite list of banana bread, Rice Krispie squares, and big chocolate chip cookies. But they also offer an eclectic list of shepherd's pie, bagels, and brioche, plus a Southwestern menu of bean burritos, tamales, and taco salads. It's nothing too elaborate, but is in keeping with the tone of the place. And if you look closely, you will see granola on the menu too.

Karma Local Arts House

2139 – 33 Avenue SW, 217 • 7955

THE name Karma is a dead giveaway. This place has the smoky aroma of a funky café, the look of a greying hippie, and a menu reminiscent of folk festivals past. The colours are dark, the furniture is indestructible, and the walls are covered in memorabilia from musicians who've performed here. Places like Karma have been around since the sixties and haven't changed much in look.

Karma is a reliable place to pop into for a soup and sandwich. But it's more about the live music, the sense of community, and just the atmosphere of the place. The food is almost an add-on that is done well enough.

www.karmapresents.com

Laggan's Mountain Bakery & Delicatessen

Samson Mall, Lake Louise, 522 • 2017

LAGGAN'S is a Lake Louise landmark. It's a bakery for all your mountain carbo-loading needs, an early morning spot for breakfast-klatching, a café for a light soup and sandwich meal, a mid-afternoon tea and scone stop for British tourists, and an all-round place to meet anyone who's not off at a spa in one of the fancy hotels.

I've never seen Laggan's without a lineup at the counter, but unless it's been inundated by a tour bus crowd, the line moves quickly. Staff are always on the go, hauling out trays of cookies and making coffee and bussing tables. It's busy, but that just means the baking is fresh.

Lazy Loaf & Kettle

8 Parkdale Crescent NW, 270 • 7810
130 – 9 Avenue SE (Glenbow Museum), 266 • 1002

IT's a toss up which is trickier to negotiate—the lineup at the Lazy Loaf's Parkdale location or the busy street-parking outside. Jockeying with caffeine-deprived Calgarians can be touchy at the best of times, but when they get within nostril-distance of the Lazy Loaf, it's best to stay out of the way.

Whichever location you visit, the coffee is revitalizing and the fresh muffins, banana loaves, and cinnamon buns are a treat. For those even hungrier, a list of sandwiches and soups is also available. And remember that holiday turkey I wrote about in The Better Butcher entry? I always stuff it with the Lazy Loaf's Kettle Bread. It makes the best stuffing.

www.lazyloafandkettle.com

Manuel Latruwe Belgian Patisserie

1333 – 1 Street SE, 261 • 1092

MANUEL and Lieve Latruwe, two skilled Belgian bakers, transform cream, butter, eggs, and flour into patisserie masterpieces here. Their multi-layered caramel cake is a combination of seven separate recipes: there's a ganache, a caramel, a vanilla cream, a glaze, some caramelized pecans, the chocolate decorations, and the cake itself. Simply stunning flavours. And gorgeous too.

They make one of the best baguettes in the city. It's lightly crusted on the outside and slightly chewy on the inside. They produce other elegant and more rustic breads too—their multi-grain is a sandwich staple in our house. And their chocolate ice cream has been declared perhaps the best in North America by Jane and Michael Stern of *Gourmet* magazine.

Montreal Bagels

8408 Elbow Drive SW, 212 • 4060

MONTREAL'S St. Viateur Bagel Shop has a couple of outlets in that city and is considered to be one of the better bagel bakeries there. Montreal Bagels here in Calgary is owned by Ramesh Sivadnanam, a former baker at St. Viateur, and the knowledge he gained there shows at his unprepossessing bakery. He sells excellent bagels that have been hand-rolled, boiled in honeyed water, and baked in a wood-fired oven.

Montreal Bagels makes the basics—the plain, poppy seed, sesame, and multi-grain bagels. They've also expanded into blueberry, whole wheat, and pumpernickel, and they build some simple sandwiches too. Basic bagels are 55¢ each or $6 for a dozen, and my ex-Montreal friends tell me they are just like the ones back home.

Nellie's

738B – 17 Avenue SW, 244 • 4616
516 – 9 Avenue SW, 265 • 5071

WHEN nothing but a huge feed of bacon, eggs, pancakes, hash browns, and toast will do, many Calgarians head for one of the six Nellie's and the Belly Buster breakfast. It'll fill any nook and cranny of your stomach and have you looking for the nearest couch in spite of all the coffee you've consumed. There is lighter fare, but hey, why bother?

Nellie's has grown from the first 17th Avenue outlet into a small breakfast and lunch empire for Roxanne Taylor-King. But it doesn't seem to matter how many she opens, there are always lineups on weekend mornings. Most folks have a favourite location, but for me, it's the downtown one with its rooftop patio.

North Sea Fish Market

10816 Macleod Trail S (Willow Park Village), 225·3460

NORTH SEA has been a seafood wholesaler for years, selling to restaurants and retail shops. But the opening of their own store in Willow Park Village has improved access to top-quality fish for those of us living in the southern reaches of Calgary. Fresh salmon (wild or farmed), scallops, swordfish, mussels, various kinds of tuna, and whatever is in season are displayed in all their oceanic glory.

Chef Brian Plunkett left his self-named restaurant in Avenida Place to join the team, and he churns out chowders and thermidors and other dishes to take home. The aroma of his hot lobster bisque rolling across the parking lot pulls in customers faster than a good fly fisherman.

Palace of Eats

1411 – 11 Street SW, 244·6602

THIS grandly named sister café to the Galaxie Diner has a look reminiscent of diners from the twenties and thirties. It's a bright room with a simple ordering counter and overhead chalkboards. There's no seating. There are a couple of stand-up areas, but it's mostly a takeout joint.

The menu features smoked meat direct from Montreal's Quebec Smoked Meat, and it's layered onto locally baked Winnipeg rye bread. The briskets are kept hot in steamers and hand cut for authenticity. There are also bagels from Montreal Bagels on Elbow Drive and real Winnipeg cream cheese. Rounding out the menu is a short list of milkshakes, Strub's dill pickles, sauerkraut, a long row of mustards, cheesecake, and Montreal-style steamed hot dogs.

www.palaceofeats.ca

Pies Plus

12445 Lake Fraser Drive SE (Avenida Place), 271·6616
Bragg Creek Shopping Centre, 949·3450

THE art of pie making has been in serious decline in recent years. Perhaps it's the challenge of the perfect pie crust, or maybe it's just that we don't have the time to dedicate to it. Regardless, it's a pleasure to see that Pies Plus has not only a serious commitment to pies, but an ongoing one as well. Jeff Cousineau and his team, including the independently operated Pies Plus in Bragg Creek, have been at it for about fifteen years now. They make a great apple pie, the popular Dream Cream, and a host of others. The summertime peach pies are tart-ilicious, and the Christmas tourtières are a Quebec classic.

Pita's Plus Donair

3132 – 26 Street NE, 735•1116

IF you're really hungry, you may be able to spend $10 at Pita's Plus. That is, if you have the $6 chicken donair (that's the big one with roasted chicken, tomatoes, lettuce, onions, and either sweet or tahini sauce, all rolled into a pita) plus a serving of tabbouleh for $2 and a rice pudding for $2. That's a big meal.

The quality is outstanding here, especially considering the price. This small, family-run café is worth the experience, not only for its value but for the welcome of its owners. And for that rice pudding.

The Planet Coffee Roasters

2212 – 4 Street SW, 541•0960
#101, 83 Bowridge Drive NW, 288•2233
150 – 9 Avenue SW (EnCana Place), 290•2200
815 – 7 Avenue SW (+15 Level, Nexen Tower), 266•1551

MORNING at our house starts quietly enough. We put the kettle on, break out the coffee container and the filters, and each make a cup. We have long since come to terms with our differing approaches to coffee. But we agree on one thing: the grounds we scoop are always The Planet's dark French, strong and black and richly scented. Life becomes just a little easier after a big mug of it.

Later in the morning, if we're working on a book like this, we'll spoon some fresh grounds into the espresso maker, stoke up some milk, and have another quick buzz. That's it for the day. We enjoy our coffee in small bursts. That's why we use The Planet.

www.planetroasters.com

Primal Grounds

3003 – 37 Street SW, 240•4185
2000 – 69 Street SW (Westside Recreation Centre), 663•0137

PRIMAL GROUNDS on 37th Street is a funky bakery, café, and coffee house, a place with lots of character and decent food. And they now have a second location too. They say that they sell happiness, that you can get food anywhere.

Primal Grounds does sandwiches, soups, wraps, hot entrees, and desserts, much of which is gluten-free. I'm particularly partial to the huge desserts. A piece of carrot cake, thick and moist with a lovely icing, is roughly the size of a brick. The sandwiches follow suit. The roast turkey and cranberry is a three-hander. What's particularly nice is the amount of fresh greens in it—you get a salad along with the bread and meat. And all that happiness too.

www.primalgrounds.com

Red Tree

2129 – 33 Avenue SW, 242 • 3246

Wᴴᴇɴ Aaron Creurer and Susan Hopkins were looking for a larger kitchen to house their growing catering company, they happened upon a space behind a store in Marda Loop. They moved in, and when the store closed, they expanded into that area too. Since then, they have used the storefront to showcase their foods and to sell ready-to-eat dishes for the burgeoning community around them.

You may find Galloway beef lasagna, pistachio fudge, pesto-stuffed chicken, or portobello tarts, just to name a few items on their lengthy list. Whatever is in the cooler will undoubtedly be way tastier than what I can do at home. They also sell condiments such as the locally produced Brassica mustards.

www.redtreecatering.com

The Roasterie

314 – 10 Street NW, 270 • 3304
227 – 10 Street NW, 283 • 8131

Mᴏsᴛ days, the sidewalks around 10th Street are filled with the aroma of roasting coffee emanating from the original Roasterie. It's a small place on the east side of 10th Street where the roaster takes up almost half the room, pushing many coffee drinkers to the small plaza outside. The coffee is fresh and robust, from the ever-popular espresso through to the Danish Breakfast Blend and the Montana Grizzly. They'll make it as strong and dark and heavy as you want.

The original location is a smoker-friendly facility. But to offer a little more room and to provide a non-smoking atmosphere, The Roasterie opened a second outlet almost across the street. Same coffee, but no smoke.

Rocky's Burgers

4645 – 12 Street SE, 243 • 0405

Sᴇᴛᴛʟᴇᴅ hip deep in prairie grasses, the former Calgary Transit bus that is Rocky's looks as if it's there to stay until it dissolves into the landscape. But owner Jim Rockwell says it's ready to roll if need be. Regulars would be devastated if it did move though. They love Rocky's hand-formed, steamed-then-grilled Alberta beef burgers layered with cheese and mustard and such. And the sides of blistering hot fries. They love the food so much, they'll stand outside in blizzard conditions to place their orders.

Two picnic tables set amongst the gopher holes out back are the dine-in option. But most regulars eat in their vehicles, which range from beat-up pickups to detailed Beamers.

Sal's Deli & Italian Market

9140 Macleod Trail S (Newport Village), 255•6011

T UCKED into an awkward strip mall on Macleod Trail, Sal's satisfies our Italian deli requirements. When we need a bottle of olive oil, a tub of marinated mushrooms, or a pile of freshly grated Parmesan, we head to Sal's. While there, we might pick up a couple of Sal's panini. Thick with cheese, Italian cold cuts, and roasted peppers and layered on a crusty roll, one of these is a meal in itself. Or if time allows, we might settle into a table for a nice pizza and some well-pulled espresso. And if we want the full taste of Sal's at home but with minimal effort, we might just pick up a lasagna to pop into the oven. *Bella!*

Serious Pizza

3406 – 3 Avenue NW, 521•4743

O UT with the pepperoni pizza! Chuck the Hawaiian and dump the salami and mushroom! It's time for a smoked salmon alfredo pizza or a chicken cordon bleu pizza or a blackened alligator Cajun pizza. We're talking Serious Pizza here.

Serious Pizza is a tiny storefront just off Parkdale Boulevard where they take pizza, well, seriously. Not in a dull and boring way, but in a creative and innovative way. They whip up pizzas from a basic vegetarian one with shredded carrots and broccoli to the house-invented "quizza," a quiche pizza.

The crust here is medium thick, breadier than the Italian style but still bringing a light tone to the pie. The toppings are high quality and the ideas are fresh.

www.seriouspizza.ca

Steeps Urban Tea House

880 – 16 Avenue SW (Mount Royal Village), 209•0076

T HE owners of Steeps have landed on the urban tea-house concept with both feet. This is no frilly, potpourri-reeking tea house. It looks like a Starbucks with a few more antiques, but smells of high-quality tea. They know how to make a decent cup of tea, whether it's a South African rooibos, a peppermint gunpowder, a masala chai, or just a good black Assam. You will also find some tasty cakes and pies from Decadent Desserts for your tea party, and on a hot day, they'll ice a brew down for you. There are cans of loose tea, bottles of chai to go, and all the pots and strainers you need for home brewing too.

www.steepstea.com

Sweet Madeira

#109, 112 Kananaskis Way, Canmore, 609·9957

AROUND Canmore, Cecilia Lortscher is known as The Cookie Lady. Around our house, she's known as That Amazing Woman Who Makes Un-Bloody-Believable Cookies. Her sweet treats are sublime.

I don't know how she does it. Her cookies don't look like anything special, but they pack more rich flavour than any others I know. The chocolate-mint ones fill the mouth with chocolate and wash the palate with mint. The Madeira Dips find a perfect balance of butter and chocolate. And the brownies (okay, I know they're not cookies; just try one) fudge-over the brain. Her banana bread and cinnamon buns are extremely decent too.

Best to call ahead though—her hours can be a bit variable.

Valbella Deli & The Griesser Spoon

104B Elk Run Boulevard, Canmore, 678·3637

MANY Calgarians escape the hassles of city life by weekending in the woody neighbourhoods around Canmore. Caught between wanting to cocoon and needing to eat, they are likely to drive the SUV over here to pick up a veggie-curry pie or a breaded, pan-ready schnitzel or some Valbella smoked meat. They often return in the morning for fresh croissants and cakes.

Separately operated from the wholesale Valbella Meats, Valbella Deli & The Griesser Spoon is run by the Austrian chefs and brothers Roland and Harry Griesser. Their selection of ready-to-eat and ready-to-cook foods is perfect for the Canmore market. If we only had more of this sort of place in Calgary.

www.griesserspoon.com

Wayne's Bagels

328 – 10 Street NW, 270·7090

WAYNE makes bagels by the traditional method. They are hand-rolled, boiled lightly, and placed two by two on a long wooden plank. They are then slipped off the plank into a sixteen-ton, wood-burning brick oven. This process produces a chewy bagel that is not too tough, has a light crust, and tastes slightly smoky.

Wayne does the typical poppy seed, sesame seed, whole wheat, garlic, and onion styles of savoury bagels. Lately he's also broadened into pumpernickel, caraway, cranberry-orange, and a few others.

In-house you can have them made into a sandwich if you're so inclined. And if you can't make it to the bakery, they are also available at the Sunterra Markets.

The Lists

These lists will guide you to various food styles and geographic areas. Entries are in alphabetical order in the "Big Eats" section of the book unless an (LE) notation follows the name of the establishment. (LE) means the entry is in alphabetical order in the "Little Eats" section. All establishments are in Calgary unless noted otherwise.

Baked Goods/Sweets

Brûlée Patisserie (LE)
Caffè Beano (LE)
Calgary Sweet House (LE)
Chocolaterie Bernard Callebaut
    (Calgary & Banff) (LE)
Decadent Desserts (LE)
Eiffel Tower Bakery (LE)
Evelyn's Coffee Bar (Banff) (LE)
Friends Cappuccino Bar (LE)
Heartland Cafe (LE)
Infuso Coffee House (Canmore) (LE)
Kaffa Coffee & Salsa House (LE)
Laggan's Mountain Bakery
    (Lake Louise) (LE)
Lazy Loaf & Kettle (LE)
Manuel Latruwe Belgian Patisserie (LE)
Montreal Bagels (LE)
Pies Plus (Calgary & Bragg Creek) (LE)
The Planet Coffee Roasters (LE)
Prairie Ink
Primal Grounds (LE)
Sweet Madeira (Canmore) (LE)
Wayne's Bagels (LE)

Banff

Banffshire Club
Barpa Bill's Souvlaki
Buffalo Mountain Lodge
Chocolaterie Bernard Callebaut (LE)
Cilantro Mountain Café
    (see Buffalo Mountain Lodge)
Coyotes

Eden
Evelyn's Coffee Bar (LE)
Grizzly House
Kootenay Park Lodge (Kootenay Park)
Le Beaujolais
Maple Leaf
St. James's Gate
Saltlik
Ticino
Typhoon
Waldhaus

Breakfast/Brunch

Avenue Diner
Belmont Diner
Buffalo Mountain Lodge (Banff)
Chez François (Canmore)
Coyotes (Banff)
Diner Deluxe
Galaxie Diner
Il Sogno
Kane's Harley Diner
Lion's Den
Nellie's (LE)
Priddis Greens (Priddis)
Quarry (Canmore)
Sage Bistro (Canmore)
Silver Dragon
Thomsons

Canadian

Buffalo Mountain Lodge (Banff)
Café Metro

Deer Lodge (Lake Louise)
Maple Leaf (Banff)
Oh! Canada
Panorama
The Ranche
The Rimrock
River Café
Rouge
Sage Bistro
Thomsons
Wildwood

Canmore

Chez François
Copper Door
Crazyweed Kitchen
Des Alpes
The Griesser Spoon
   (see Valbella Deli & The Griesser
   Spoon) (LE)
Infuso Coffee House (LE)
Mélange
Murrieta's
Quarry
Sage Bistro
Valbella Deli & The Griesser Spoon (LE)

Caribbean

Dutchie's
Stranger's

Chinese

Buddha's Veggie
Dragon Pearl
Golden Inn
Harbour City
Leo Fu's
Silver Dragon
Silver Inn

Coffee Bars

Caffè Beano (LE)
Caffè Mauro (LE)
Evelyn's Coffee Bar (Banff) (LE)
Friends Cappuccino Bar (LE)
Heartland Cafe (LE)
Infuso Coffee House (Canmore) (LE)
Kaffa Coffee & Salsa House (LE)
The Planet Coffee Roasters (LE)
Primal Grounds (LE)
The Roasterie (LE)

Contemporary

Banffshire Club (Banff)
The Belvedere
Brava Bistro
Buffalo Mountain Lodge (Banff)
Cafe Divine (Okotoks)
Catch
Cilantro
Copper Door (Canmore)
Coyotes (Banff)
Crazyweed Kitchen (Canmore)
Deer Lodge (Lake Louise)
Divino
The Gypsy
Indochine
The Living Room
Mango Shiva
Mélange
Mescalero
Murrieta's (Calgary & Canmore)
Muse
Quarry (Canmore)
The Ranche
River Café
Rouge
Sino
Sugo
Teatro
Thomsons
Wildwood

Diners

Avenue Diner
Belmont Diner
Boogie's Burgers (LE)
Diner Deluxe
Galaxie Diner
Kane's Harley Diner
Lion's Den
Palace of Eats (LE)
Spolumbo's

Drinks

Big Rock Grill
Buzzards
The Conga Room
James Joyce
The Joyce on 4th (*see* James Joyce)
Jugo Juice (LE)
Karma Local Arts House (LE)
St. James's Gate (Banff)
Vintage
Wildwood

French/Continental

Chez François (Canmore)
Des Alpes (Canmore)
Eden (Banff)
Eiffel Tower Bakery (LE)
Fleur de Sel
JoJo Bistro
La Chaumière
La P'tite Table (Okotoks)
Le Beaujolais (Banff)
Le Bistro Béni
Manuel Latruwe Belgian Patisserie (LE)
Owl's Nest
Piq Niq
Post Hotel (Lake Louise)
Priddis Greens (Priddis)
Rouge

German/Austrian

The Bavarian Inn (Bragg Creek)
Edelweiss Village (LE)
New Berliner
Waldhaus (Banff)

Greek

Barpa Bill's Souvlaki (Banff)
Crete Souvlaki (LE)
Parthenon
Santorini Taverna

High Tone

Banffshire Club (Banff)
The Belvedere
Carver's
Catch
Da Paolo
Eden (Banff)
La Chaumière
Le Beaujolais (Banff)
Owl's Nest
Panorama
Post Hotel (Lake Louise)
The Rimrock
Teatro

Historic Setting

Annie's (LE)
Avenue Diner
Banffshire Club (Banff)
Belmont Diner
The Belvedere
Ben Venuto
Bonterra
Buzzards
Catch
Cilantro
The Conga Room
Deer Lodge (Lake Louise)

Diner Deluxe
Divino
Galaxie Diner
The Gypsy
Heartland Cafe
Il Sogno
Jacqueline Suzanne's
James Joyce
Kootenay Park Lodge (Kootenay Park)
Murrieta's (Calgary location)
Piq Niq
Post Hotel (Lake Louise)
The Ranche
The Rimrock
Rouge
Teatro
Thomsons

Lion's Den
The Living Room
Mescalero
Moroccan Castle
Muse
Prairie Ink
River Café
Sakana Grill
Santorini Taverna
Sultan's Tent
Sumo
Sushi Ginza
Thai Boat
Thai Place
Thai Sa-On
Waldhaus (Banff)

Indian

Anpurna
Baba Ka Dhaba (LE)
Calgary Spiceland (LE)
Calgary Sweet House (LE)
Clay Oven
Glory of India
Kashmir
Mango Shiva
Puspa
Rajdoot

Interesting Ambience

Bodega
Café Metro
Centini
Copper Door (Canmore)
Domicile Organic Bistro (LE)
Dragon Pearl
Fleur de Sel
Grizzly House (Banff)
The Highwood
Kane's Harley Diner
La Brezza

Italian

Ben Venuto
Bonterra
Caffè Mauro (LE)
Centini
Da Paolo
Divine Ambrosia
Il Sogno
La Brezza
La Tavola
Lina's Italian Market
Sal's Deli & Italian Market (LE)
Sandro
Spolumbo's
Sugo
Teatro

Japanese

Daikichi
Sakana Grill
Shikiji
Sobaten
Sumo
Sushi Ginza
Towa Sushi
Yuzuki

Lake Louise

Deer Lodge
Laggan's Mountain Bakery (LE)
Post Hotel

Latin American

Boca Loca (LE)
Chico's Tecate Grill (LE)
The Conga Room
El Bombazo (LE)
Juan's
Latin Corner

Middle Eastern

A & A Foods & Deli (Lebanese) (LE)
Aida's (Lebanese)
Atlas Specialty Supermarket &
    Restaurant (Persian) (LE)
Istanbul (Turkish)
Pita's Plus Donair (Lebanese) (LE)
Red Saffron (Persian)

Most Obscure

A & A Foods & Deli (LE)
Anpurna
Atlas Specialty Supermarket &
    Restaurant (LE)
Baba Ka Dhaba (LE)
Clay Oven
Divine Ambrosia
Dutch Cash & Carry (LE)
Dutchie's
Jonas'
Marathon
Mimo
Parthenon
Stranger's

Okotoks

Cafe Divine
La P'tite Table

One of a Kind (Almost)

Bow Bulgogi House (Korean)
The Cookbook Co. Cooks
    (Cookbooks & Ingredients) (LE)
Dutch Cash & Carry (Dutch) (LE)
Grizzly House (Banff)
    (Fondue & Exotic Game)
The Highwood (Culinary School)
Janice Beaton Fine Cheese (Cheese) (LE)
Jonas' (Hungarian)
Little Chef (Family)
Marathon (Ethiopian)
Mt. Everest's Kitchen (Nepalese)
Pfanntastic Pannenkoek Haus (Dutch)
Red Tree (Catering) (LE)
Restaurant Indonesia (Indonesian)
Steeps Urban Tea House (Tea) (LE)
Ticino (Banff) (Swiss-Italian)
Tropika (Malaysian)
Typhoon (Banff) (Eclectic Asian)

Pizza

Sandro
Serious Pizza (LE)

Red Meat

The Bavarian Inn (Bragg Creek)
The Belvedere
The Better Butcher (LE)
Buchanan's
Buzzards
Café Metro
Carver's
Grizzly House (Banff)
James Joyce
The Joyce on 4th (see James Joyce)

Little Chef
New Berliner
Palace of Eats
Red Saffron
The Rimrock
Rocky's Burgers (LE)
Saltlik (Calgary & Banff)
Silver Inn
Spolumbo's
Vintage
Waldhaus (Banff)
Wildwood

Romantic

Brava Bistro
JoJo Bistro
The Living Room
Muse
Owl's Nest
Panorama
Rouge
Teatro

Seafood

Boyd's
Catch
Daikichi
First Mate Fish & Chips (LE)
Murrieta's (Calgary & Canmore)
North Sea Fish Market (LE)
Pelican Pier
River Café
Sakana Grill
Sumo
Sushi Ginza
Towa Sushi
Yuzuki

Thai

Bamboo Palace (Laotian cuisine also)
Chili Club

The King & I
Rose Garden
Thai Boat
Thai Place
Thai Sa-On

Vegetarian

A & A Foods & Deli (LE)
Aida's
Anpurna
Bodega
Buddha's Veggie
Clay Oven
Glory of India
Jugo Juice (LE)
Kashmir
The King & I
Marathon
Moroccan Castle
Prairie Ink
Puspa
Rajdoot
Restaurant Indonesia
Sultan's Tent

Vietnamese

Bow Bulgogi House
    (Korean cuisine also)
Indochine (French-Vietnamese
    Fusion)
Mekong
Saigon
Sino (Vietnamese Fusion)
Trong-Khanh

Western Mediterranean

Bodega (Tapas & Spanish)
Mimo (Portuguese)
Moroccan Castle (Moroccan)
Sultan's Tent (Moroccan)

The Best of the Best

The following will guide you to the best of the best. Entries are in alphabetical order in the "Big Eats" section of the book unless an (LE) notation follows the name of the establishment. (LE) means the entry is in alphabetical order in the "Little Eats" section. All establishments are in Calgary unless noted otherwise.

Best Bang for the Buck

A & A Foods & Deli (LE)
Aida's
Anpurna
Avenue Diner
Barpa Bill's Souvlaki (Banff)
Boogie's Burgers (LE)
Bow Bulgogi House
Boyd's
Cafe Divine (Okotoks)
Coyotes (Banff)
Daikichi
Diner Deluxe
Harbour City
The Highwood
Jacqueline Suzanne's
Kane's Harley Diner
Lion's Den
Little Chef
Mekong
Nellie's (LE)
Pelican Pier
Pita's Plus Donair (LE)
Prairie Ink
Restaurant Indonesia
Saigon
Sobaten
Trong-Khanh
Tropika
Yuzuki

Best Business Lunch

If someone else is paying:
The Belvedere
Buchanan's
Carver's
Catch
Centini
Da Paolo
Il Sogno
La Tavola
Murrieta's (Calgary & Canmore)
Teatro
Wildwood

If you are paying:
Avenue Diner
Boyd's
Café Metro
Caffè Mauro (LE)
Indochine
Indulge
Lazy Loaf & Kettle (LE)
Piq Niq
Prairie Ink
Rose Garden
Saigon
Spolumbo's
Yuzuki

Best Patios/Decks

The Bavarian Inn (Bragg Creek)
Big Rock Grill
Bonterra

Buchanan's
Buzzards
Cilantro
Cilantro Mountain Café (Banff)
   (*see* Buffalo Mountain Lodge)
Deer Lodge (Lake Louise)
La Chaumière
La P'tite Table (Okotoks)
Latin Corner
The Living Room
Mescalero
Oh! Canada
Prairie Ink
Priddis Greens (Priddis)
The Ranche
River Café
Rouge
Sage Bistro (Canmore)
Teatro
Wildwood

Best People Watching

The Belvedere
Bodega
Brava Bistro
Cilantro
Divino
James Joyce
Kane's Harley Diner
Laggan's Mountain Bakery
   (Lake Louise) (LE)
Latin Corner
Lina's Italian Market
Mescalero
Quarry (Canmore)
River Café
Teatro

Best Service

Banffshire Club (Banff)
Da Paolo
Des Alpes (Canmore)

Eden (Banff)
Fleur de Sel
The Highwood
JoJo Bistro
Jonas'
La Chaumière
La P'tite Table (Okotoks)
Le Bistro Béni
Leo Fu's
Little Chef
Mescalero
Mt. Everest's Kitchen
Owl's Nest
Pfanntastic Pannenkoek Haus
Priddis Greens (Priddis)
Restaurant Indonesia
Rouge
Santorini Taverna
Sultan's Tent
Teatro
Thai Boat
Thai Place
Thai Sa-On
Ticino (Banff)
Vintage
Waldhaus (Banff)

Best View

Annie's (LE)
Buffalo Mountain Lodge (Banff)
Cilantro Mountain Café (Banff)
   (*see* Buffalo Mountain Lodge)
Eden (Banff)
Kootenay Park Lodge (Kootenay Park)
Murrieta's (Canmore location)
Panorama
Post Hotel (Lake Louise)
Priddis Greens (Priddis)
Quarry (Canmore)
The Ranche
River Café
Sage Bistro (Canmore)
Waldhaus (Banff)

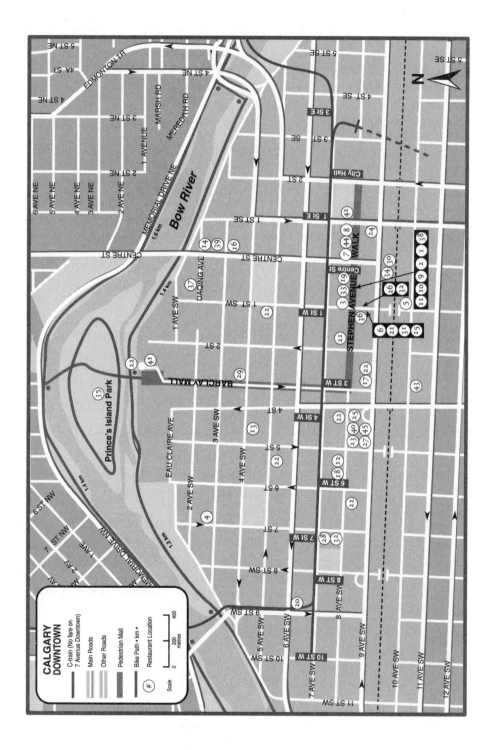